To
Todd and Jan Moser

"*Ministers* are the *Messengers of Christ* unto his People, and therefore *Angels of the Churches*. . . . And have not *You* had *your Messengers*, my *Brethren*? . . . And let a *People so favoured of God* see how they ought to *receive* and entertain the *Messages* bro't them from God by their *Ministers*."

—Benjamin Colman

Table of Contents

Figures vi

Tables vii

Forewords x
    By Richard F. Lovelace x
    By Mark A. Noll xi

Preface xiii

Introduction xv

Chapter 1: Manuductio ad Ministerium 1
    Introduction 1
    Cotton Mather, Pastor 3
    Epilogue: To the Great Awakening 24

Chapter 2: The Flourishing of the Kingdom of Christ 26

Chapter 3: Tending God's Vineyard 44
    Introduction 44
    First ("Old Brick") Church 47
    Second ("Old North") Church 56
    Third ("Old South") Church 63
    Fourth ("Brattle Street") Church 79

Chapter 4: Nurturing New Vines 90
    Introduction 90
    Fifth ("New North") Church 91
    Sixth ("New South") Church 99
    Seventh ("New Brick") Church 102
    Eighth ("Hollis Street") Church 112
    Ninth ("West" or "Lynde Street") Church 116
    Tenth ("Bennet Street") Church 124
    Eleventh Church 125

Conclusion: A People So Favored of God 138

Appendix: Church Statistics and Community Demographics 153

Bibliography 161
    Primary Sources 161
    Secondary Sources 169

Index 181

Figures

Map 1: Captain John Bonner's map of Boston, 1722; revised by William Price, 1769 viii

Map 2: Bonner/Price map with locations of meetinghouses highlighted ix

Chart 1: First Church, first-time admissions to membership and baptisms 55

Chart 2: First Church, admissions to membership by gender 55

Chart 3: Second Church, first-time admissions to membership and baptisms 62

Chart 4: Second Church, covenant renewals 62

Chart 5: Third Church, first-time admissions to membership and baptisms 76

Chart 6: Third Church, admissions to membership by gender 76

Chart 7: Third Church, covenant renewals by gender, 1669–1709 78

Chart 8: Third Church, covenant renewals by gender, 1710–1760 78

Chart 9: Fourth Church, first-time admissions to membership and baptisms 88

Chart 10: Fifth Church, first-time admissions to membership and baptisms 98

Chart 11: Fifth Church, covenant renewals 98

Chart 12: Sixth Church, first-time admissions to membership and baptisms ... 100

Chart 13: Sixth Church, covenant renewals 100

Chart 14: Seventh Church, first-time admissions to membership and baptisms 111

Chart 15: Seventh Church, covenant renewals 111

Chart 16: Eighth Church, first-time admissions to membership and baptisms . 114

Chart 17: Ninth Church, first-time admissions to membership and baptisms ... 123

Chart 18: Ninth Church, covenant renewals 123

Chart 19: Aggregate first-time admissions to membership and baptisms 139

Chart 20: Boston population and death rate 142

Chart 21: Massachusetts population 142

Tables

Table 1: First-time admissions to membership 153
Table 2: Admissions to membership by gender, selected churches 155
Table 3: Covenant renewals, selected churches 156
Table 4: Covenant renewals by gender, Third Church, 1669–1760 157
Table 5: Baptisms 158
Table 6: Population and death rate 160

Map 1: Captain John Bonner's map of Boston, 1722;
revised by William Price, 1769

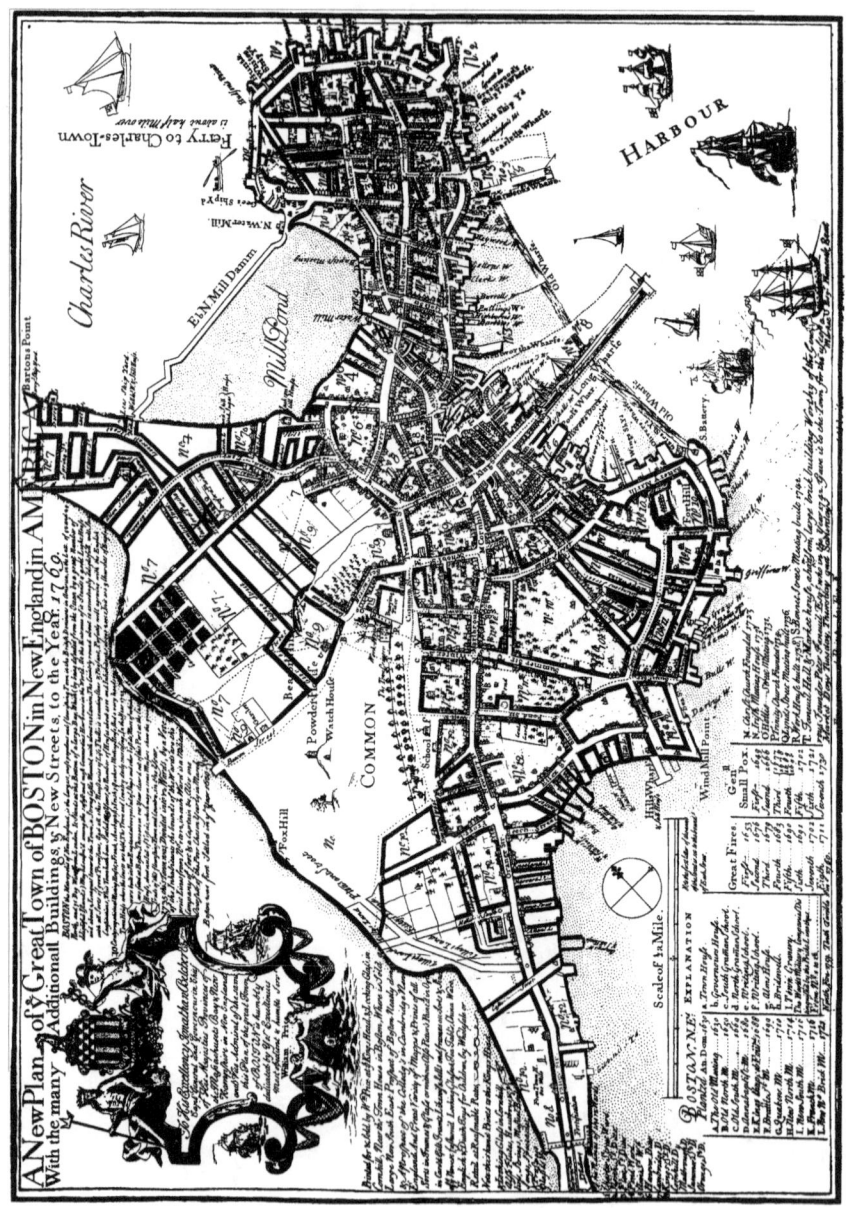

Map 2: Bonner/Price map with locations of meetinghouses highlighted

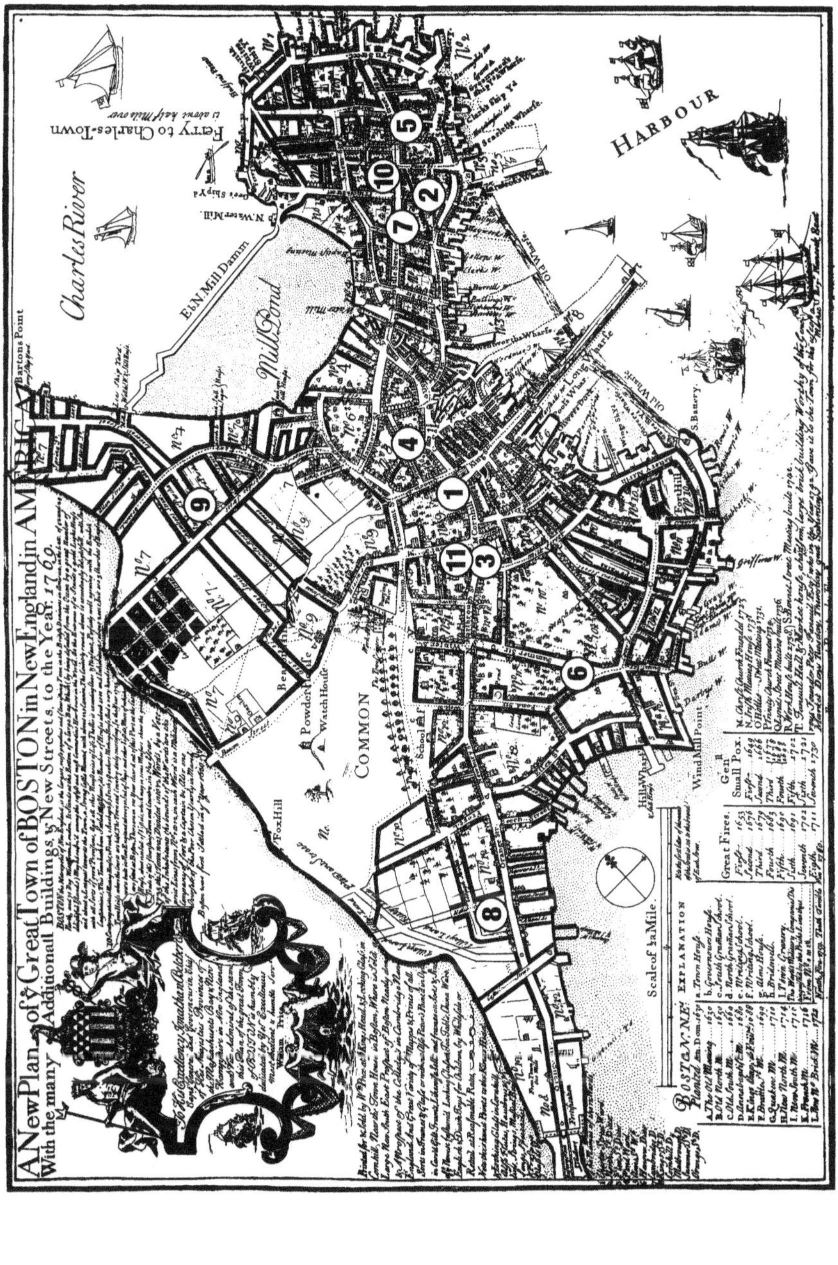

Forewords

By Richard F. Lovelace
Emeritus Professor of Church History
Gordon-Conwell Theological Seminary

George Harper's *A People So Favored of God* is a cogent and illuminating consideration of Boston's Congregational churches during the half-century bracketing the Great Awakening. Harper demonstrates with hard data that the Awakening was neither invented by contemporary itinerants nor concocted by later chroniclers, as several scholars have recently alleged. Instead, it was an earthshaking event, enlarging many churches friendly to the revived Puritanism of Jonathan Edwards and George Whitefield.

Harper shows that those Boston ministers who were most responsive to the Awakening had already been predisposed to the notion of revival by the ministry of Cotton Mather, as I myself have argued in *The American Pietism of Cotton Mather: Origins of American Evangelicalism*. Mather's premillennial concerns had predicted both significant spiritual decline and also outpourings of the Spirit on the eighteenth-century church, finding positive evidence of the latter in Francke's Pietism at Halle. Mather's local disciples were thus made susceptible to the currents of postmillennial optimism which were to develop out of Edwards's theology.

Harper also shows that many Boston ministers were moving from the pastor/scholar ministry model of Edwards and the earlier Puritans to an activist pattern of pastoral engagement with parishioners and potential converts. In this they were building on the innovations of Richard Baxter at Kidderminster, echoing the activism of the Middle Colony revivalists of the Log College, and anticipating the nineteenth-century pastoral strategies of Lyman Beecher and Charles Finney. In other words, far from an isolated event, the Great Awakening was a hinge on which America's spiritual history turned.

Harper's exhaustive research brings to life in our imaginations the spiritual ferment in Boston's Congregational churches during this important era as no previous secondary study has done. His is a groundbreaking book.

Forewords

By Mark A. Noll
Francis A. McAnaney Professor of History
University of Notre Dame

Solid books concerning the history of Christianity in colonial New England abound for the early Puritan generations in the seventeenth century and for the era of the Great Awakening in the mid-eighteenth century. By contrast, the period in between—from roughly the Salem Witch Trials in the early 1690s to the outbreak of revival in the mid-1730s—has been neglected by historians. The result is that, as Edmund S. Morgan once quipped, there are now almost as many books about the American Puritans as there were Puritans themselves, and the labors of historians have produced an almost equally prodigious quantity of scholarship concerning Jonathan Edwards, George Whitefield, and the other luminaries of the Great Awakening. But because attention to what happened between the flourishing of Puritan New England and the outbreak of revival has been considerably less, students of the period still stumble in trying to account for the way in which the highly structured world of Puritan religious life gave way to the free-form entrepreneurialism of evangelical revival.

It is one of the signal merits of George Harper's close-grained history of Boston's Congregational churches in roughly the first two-thirds of the eighteenth century that he shows why neglect of this intervening period is a mistake. Harper's account of Boston's churches before, during, and after the well-publicized revivals of the early 1740s features questions of continuity over instances of disruption. With his gaze fixed especially on patterns of pastoral authority and ministerial practice as they evolved over several generations, he not only provides convincing explanations for why certain things did change in the 1740s, but also opens up a number of neglected subjects for the best kind of critical scrutiny.

In Harper's account, for instance, understanding the long-term Christian history of Boston's influential churches depends upon grasping the significance of the great earthquake of 1727 as well as the impact of Whitefield's famous visit in the fall of 1740. Likewise, to gain a clearer sense of the churches' general influence in the city, Harper shows why charting birth-rates and death-rates is just as important as paying attention to quarrels over the new revival practices. Similarly, to fathom the variable fate of individual churches—why some of the city's eleven Congregational churches flourished and others declined—depends upon insights from pastoral practice (who was out and about engaging the lay populace) as well as from theology (who was preaching what from the pulpits). By broadening the canvas of his investigation—by treating questions of church history in broad instead of narrow historical settings—Harper actually makes it possible to understand better the narrower questions of theology and individual pastoral practice.

This work follows in a path blazed by Richard Lovelace, one of Harper's mentors at Gordon-Conwell Theological Seminary. When Lovelace published his pioneering book on the pastoral labors of Cotton Mather (*The American Pietism of Cotton Mather: Origins of American Evangelicalism*, 1979), he provided a clear advertisement for why it was important to study carefully the development of late-Puritan New England. Regrettably, too few historians have followed the path that Lovelace blazed. George Harper, by contrast, caught the vision of what could be accomplished by serious attention to that period, and the result is a monograph expanding fruitfully upon Lovelace's seminal insights. In addition, it is worth noting that Harper's study of pastoral practices in Boston during the first half of the eighteenth century parallels the emphases recently highlighted by W. R. Ward in what have become the most convincing general studies of Western European and North Atlantic religious renewal in the seventeenth and eighteenth centuries (*The Protestant Evangelical Awakening*, 1992; *Christianity under the Ancien Régime, 1648–1789*, 1999).

George Harper's attention to structural change over time, as well as his careful dealing with standard themes of theology and revival, allows this book to open up the lives of an unusually wide range of Boston's ministers—an interesting group whether studied individually or together. So in these pages we learn still more about well-known pastors like Cotton Mather and Charles Chauncy. But we are also introduced to many others who, at least in their local circumstances, were also individuals of character (sometimes eccentric character), gravity, and consequence. Joseph Sewall, William Cooper, Ebenezer Pemberton, senior and junior—these are not familiar names, even to veteran students of the period. Yet Harper's account of the ways in which they negotiated the shifting circumstances of a half-century and more makes for interesting biographical reading, even as it contributes to the book's main arguments.

In a word, readers of *A People So Favored of God* have much in store as they work through the chapters of this book. In a quiet, unassuming way the volume illuminates a number of important matters during an important period in an important place. Even more, its success at demonstrating how critical the long view can be, even for events that are usually studied as isolated and dramatic particulars, offers a model for other historians who would expend the patient effort for other subjects that has yielded such good results here.

Preface

It is a truism that scholars stand on the shoulders of scholars who have gone before them. Still, underlying this truism is a fundamental truth. I owe a great debt to many historians, living and dead. Most I know only from their writings, but a few I have had the chance to meet, and several have become mentors.

The very first historian I ever knew was MacDonald Fleming, who taught me history and served as my advisor during my years at Indian Springs School in Alabama. I doubt that Mac realizes what an impact he had on me, not only in the classroom but even more in his manner of life. I count it a privilege to call him my friend.

I first came to the question of pastoral ministry in colonial New England as I was seeking a topic for my undergraduate thesis at the Massachusetts Institute of Technology. Arthur D. Kaledin, my advisor, guided me in preparing a study of Cotton Mather's approach to the pastorate. Abridged and greatly revised, with helpful comments from Richard F. Lovelace, of Gordon-Conwell Theological Seminary, and the late David Levin, of the University of Virginia, this was eventually published in the *Westminster Theological Journal*; it forms the basis of the first chapter.

Several years later, as a student at Gordon-Conwell, I prepared a research paper for Garth M. Rosell on the question of pastoral ministry in Boston's Congregational churches during the Great Awakening. This project gave me my first chance to familiarize myself with the church records stored in the City Clerk's Archives at Boston City Hall. Later, two courses on American Christianity taught by C. Conrad Wright at the Harvard Divinity School spurred my further exploration of the documentary sources as well as the secondary literature.

After I began doctoral studies at Boston University, I shaped some of my material into a research paper for James A. Henretta. With valuable suggestions from Michael McGiffert, then the editor of the *William and Mary Quarterly*, this was published in the *New England Quarterly*; it forms the basis of the second chapter. As I began to consider erecting my dissertation on its foundation, David D. Hall, then my advisor, and Norman Pettit offered several helpful suggestions. After Dr. Hall left Boston University for the Harvard Divinity School, Carter Lindberg became my advisor and first reader. Also pitching in were Stephen A. Marini, of Wellesley College, and Dr. Lovelace, my second and third readers, respectively, and Harry S. Stout, of Yale University and Yale Divinity School. Their insights and encouragement were essential to my dissertation's successful completion.

After graduation I shelved the material for several years. Eventually, though, I began to consider revising my dissertation for publication. Among those encouraging me in this, both verbally and by their example, were my friends Randall Gleason, of the International School of Theology–Asia, and Rod Leupp, then of the Asia Pacific Nazarene Theological Seminary. After many months of labor, that first edition was published in 2004 by the University Press of America. More recently, kind words from Kenneth P. Minkema, of Yale University's Jonathan Edwards Center, and from James Stock, of Wipf & Stock Publishers, have emboldened me to prepare this second edition in order to take account of important recent publications.

I owe a great debt to friends who have aided me in one way or another. Most notably, Stephen H. Owades provided crucial assistance with typesetting. I have received sage counsel from other friends—from Ernest Manges, of the Cebu Graduate School of Theology, Mark A. Noll, now of the University of Notre Dame, Glen Shellrude, now of Alliance Theological Seminary's extension campus in New York City, Junias Venugopal, now of Columbia Biblical Seminary, and Charles E. White, of Spring Arbor College, to name just a few.

I owe an even greater debt to my wife Anne, whose advice has always been indispensable and whose constant encouragement has been vital, and to our daughters, Ruth and Meg, whose tolerance for my prolonged preoccupation with this material has been impressive.

Librarians occupy a prominent place in any scholar's pantheon. Without the assistance of many librarians and the bibliographic resources of a number of schools and archives, my original research would have been impossible. I am grateful for the assistance I received at Boston University's Mugar Memorial Library and School of Theology Library, Harvard's Andover-Harvard Theological Library, Gordon-Conwell's Burton L. Goddard Library, Gordon College's Jenks Learning Resource Center, the Congregational Library, the Massachusetts Historical Society, and the City Clerk's Archives in Boston City Hall.

As the above should make clear, the credit for whatever is of value in the text that follows belongs to a multitude. To me alone belongs the blame for whatever is not.

Introduction

> Historians of early American thought no longer write out of a sense of gratitude for the past, especially when they come to the Puritans. They do not believe that American Puritanism has anything special or compelling to tell us about what we should value or how we should live. . . . For them, the Puritan tradition is little more than a darkened cave, an illegitimate constraint, the origin of our many afflictions.[1]

If modern historians have erred in their conception of New England Puritanism, this is in large measure because they have insisted on viewing the movement in flattened perspective, neglecting and even denying dimensions that would give its image much-needed depth. Too many scholars have given absolute primacy to literary and intellectual considerations, seeing social and cultural factors as mere epiphenomena. One result has been that in grappling with the Great Awakening, the mid-eighteenth-century revival associated with the ministries of itinerant evangelists like George Whitefield and Gilbert Tennent as well as parish ministers like Jonathan Edwards and John Cleaveland, these historians have set theological factors in the driver's seat, describing the Awakening's propagation as based on the New Lights' promulgation of the concept of the "new birth," and taking the Old Lights' hostility to reflect the early influence of the sort of rationalism that would subsequently issue in moralistic Arminianism, Arianism, and finally full-blown Unitarianism.

This account is at best incomplete and at worst misleading. The Great Awakening was as much a challenge to traditional patterns of ecclesiology as to soteriological and christological novelties. Embrace of revival often carried with it rejection of the broad consensus on the nature of the pastoral office that had prevailed across New England since soon after settlement of the Bay Colony, while repudiation of revival almost invariably connoted a last-ditch defense of that same pastoral paradigm. Indeed, such considerations—the perceived inadequacies of the old clericalism, or the perceived threat to clericalism of the new itinerancy—generally preceded and even precipitated theological wrangling. The Old Lights' stress was on the minister as *preacher*, while many New Lights instead focused their attention on the minister as *pastor*; where Old Lights emphasized above all the painstaking preparation and delivery of erudite sermons, these New Lights were at least as interested in systematic visitation, catechesis, religious societies, and other tools of hands-on ministry. The thesis of

---

1. David Harlan, "A People Blinded from Birth: American History According to Sacvan Bercovitch," *Journal of American History*, vol. 78, no. 3 (December 1991): 951.

this study is that the pastoral dimension must therefore be given a place of primacy in analyses of the era.

This thesis can be tested. If the Great Awakening did indeed reflect and even issue from a crisis in pastoral care, with many exponents consequently looking to new approaches while their adversaries hewed to the old ways, then almost by definition the opponents of revival would have been less effective as pastors, with their congregations showing stasis and even decline, while those served by progressive revivalists would have been more likely to have seen vitality and growth. Moreover, those New Light clergy—and there were many such—whose approach to the ministry nevertheless differed little from that of their Old Light antagonists ought to have been no more successful than the latter as pastors, with their own churches wasting away as well. The religious community defined by Boston's eleven Congregational churches and their associated parishes organized between 1630 and the Revolutionary War forms a sort of laboratory for the testing of these assertions.

Accordingly, this study will begin with an examination of an important local precedent for the pastoral activism embraced by many New Lights, then it will proceed to a tightly focused consideration of the Great Awakening in Boston as a pastoral phenomenon, building on this with an extended inquiry into local pastors' words and deeds and the demographic health of individual congregations as well as that of the aggregate Congregational community. In conclusion, some reflections will be offered on the Awakening's prolonged aftershocks in Federalist Boston. It is hoped that by thus admitting a measure of light into the "darkened cave" of American Puritanism, by scrutinizing an unfamiliar aspect of this most familiar of colonial religious cultures, we may indeed come to a deeper understanding of "what we should value [and] how we should live."

Chapter 1:
Manuductio ad Ministerium

O how happy have been the *Pastors of this town* in having Him at our Head.[1]

Introduction

Cotton Mather has long fascinated historians of colonial America. This is not difficult to understand; with his idiosyncratic blend of vanity and insecurity, scholarship and credulity, conservatism and innovation, Mather could almost be said to offer something for everyone. Progressive scholars of an earlier generation saw him as nothing more than the last, dullest defender of New England's dying orthodoxy—and there is at least an element of truth to their claim.[2] On the other hand, Richard Hofstadter described him as nothing less than an unwitting herald of secular, post-theocratic New England—and even this exercise in scholarly hyperbole is not without its point.[3] Recently he has been portrayed in a more flattering light, as a transitional figure who drew on the example of English Puritans like Richard Baxter as well as Continental Pietists like August Hermann Francke in laying the foundations for what emerged in the next century as

---

Most of the material in this chapter appeared in an earlier draft as "*Manuductio ad Ministerium*: Cotton Mather as Pastoral Innovator," *Westminster Theological Journal*, vol. 54, no. 1 (Spring 1992): 79–97. An abbreviated version was presented at the 1991 annual meeting of the American Society of Church History.

1. Thomas Prince, *The Departure of Elijah Lamented* (Boston: D. Henchman, 1728), 22.
2. Among those taking this perspective were Barrett Wendell, in *Cotton Mather: The Puritan Priest* (New York: Dodd, Mead and Co., 1891; reprint, New York: Harcourt, Brace and World, 1963); Charles Francis Adams, in *Massachusetts: Its Historians and Its History* (Boston: Houghton Mifflin, 1893), 65–66, 81; Worthington Chauncey Ford, in his Preface to *The Diary of Cotton Mather*, 2 vols. (New York: Frederick Ungar, 1911), 1: vii-xvii; Brooks Adams, in *The Emancipation of Massachusetts: The Dream and the Reality*, rev. ed. (Boston: Houghton Mifflin, 1919), passim; and Vernon L. Parrington, in *Main Currents in American Thought*, vol. 1, *The Colonial Mind, 1620–1800* (New York: Harcourt, Brace, 1927), 106–117. An early rebuttal was offered by Clifford K. Shipton in "The New England Clergy of the 'Glacial Age,'" *Publications of the Colonial Society of Massachusetts*, vol. 32 (1933–1937): 24–54.
3. Richard Hofstadter, *Anti-Intellectualism in American Life* (New York: Alfred A. Knopf, 1963), 62–63.

American evangelicalism.[4] There have been treatments of Mather as historian and hagiographer, as social conservator and cultural apologist, as ecclesiastical power-broker and political meddler, even as amateur scientist.[5]

Surprisingly, what is still lacking is a study of Mather as pastor—indeed, as pastoral innovator.[6] Patricia Tracy's trenchant assessment of most historians' analyses of Jonathan Edwards might be applied just as well to present-day Mather scholarship: "Jonathan Edwards has been extensively studied as a philosopher-theologian; but, strangely, his career as a *pastor*—preacher, counselor, disciplinarian—has received only minimal attention. . . . Part of [our misunderstanding] of Edwards's thought has derived from our forgetting that Edwards was not a thinker by profession. . . . Edwards was a *pastor*."[7] As with Edwards, so with Mather.

---

4. For the fullest development of this position, see Richard F. Lovelace, *The American Pietism of Cotton Mather: Origins of American Evangelicalism* (Grand Rapids, Mich.: Christian University Press and William B. Eerdmans, 1979).

5. On Mather as historian, compare Peter Gay's caustic comments in *A Loss of Mastery: Puritan Historians in Colonial America* (Berkeley, Calif.: University of California Press, 1966; reprint, New York: Random House, Vintage Books, 1968), 53–87, with Kenneth B. Murdock's more affirmative assessment in his Introduction to *Magnalia Christi Americana: Books I and II*, by Cotton Mather, ed. Kenneth B. Murdock and Elizabeth W. Miller (Cambridge: Harvard University Press, Belknap Press, 1977), 27–48. Ralph Boas and Louise Boas, in their slender volume, *Cotton Mather: Keeper of the Puritan Conscience* (Hamden, Conn.: Archon Books, 1964), present Mather primarily as "conservator" (ibid., 258). Otho T. Beall, Jr., and Richard H. Shryock, in *Cotton Mather: First Significant Figure in American Medicine* (Baltimore, Md.: Johns Hopkins University Press, 1954), have written glowingly of Mather's forays into medical science; but contrast Ola Elizabeth Winslow's less sanguine assessment of Mather's activities during Boston's smallpox epidemic of 1721–1722 in *A Destroying Angel: The Conquest of Smallpox in Colonial Boston* (Boston: Houghton Mifflin, 1974), 32–58.

6. Although recent biographies by David Levin and Kenneth Silverman portray Mather in a far more constructive light than did Perry Miller or, in an earlier era, Wendell and Parrington, they devote relatively little space to the day-by-day specifics of his work as pastor. For example, the index to Levin's volume lists only four passages touching on Mather's pastoral activities, against five on his fasts and seven on his experience of angelic visitations; see *Cotton Mather: The Young Life of the Lord's Remembrancer, 1663–1703* (Cambridge: Harvard University Press, 1978), 352–353. Similarly, Silverman's index includes just four such entries, these being mainly concerned with matters such as sermons delivered and ministerial councils attended; see *The Life and Times of Cotton Mather* (New York: Harper and Row, 1984), 473. Although Lovelace's volume sheds more light on Mather's discharge of his pastoral responsibilities, its narrower focus precludes a full exploration of these matters.

7. Patricia J. Tracy, *Jonathan Edwards, Pastor: Religion and Society in Eighteenth-Century Northampton*, American Century Series (New York: Hill and Wang, 1979), 4, 7.

Cotton Mather, Pastor

As the grandson of Richard Mather and John Cotton and the oldest son of Increase Mather, from his birth the young Cotton bore on his shoulders the weight of hopes and expectations signified by his imposing appellation. President Urian Oakes's remarks on the occasion of his graduation from Harvard are well known: "What a name! . . . [W]hat names! . . . I despair not that in this youth Cotton and Mather shall in fact as in name coalesce and revive!"[8] Spending much of his life in the shadow of his demanding father, Cotton learned to expect of himself labors of piety, scholarship, and charity that would have felled one of lesser abilities.[9] His genius, though, lay not so much in any *de novo* creative impulse as in the flair for innovative synthesis evident even in his baroque literary style.[10] This synthetic bent has misled many historians. After all, he paid profound tribute to New England's received orthodoxy, proclaiming in time-hallowed language the terms of God's covenants, urging the importance of the sinner's preparation for conversion, and wrestling with the doctrine of assurance.[11] Still, he was well aware of the stresses already rending New England's ecclesiastical order, and of the underlying problems to which those stresses pointed. Like his father, he saw around him a church in spiritual decline; by way of response, like his father, he became a master of the jeremiad, with even his magnum opus, the *Magnalia Christi Americana*, in one sense merely an extended exercise in that form.[12]

Significantly, Mather laid the blame for New England's declension at the feet of an *"Unsuccessful Ministry"* who must "rowse up Themselves, and do all that is in Them" if the church's decline were to be reversed—"A thing how often, how often urged for! but how *Unsuccessfully*."[13] Admittedly, his own efforts along those lines seem less impressive than those of the little band of reformers who in 1698 organized Fourth ("Brattle Street") Church, the so-called "Manifesto Church" that called Benjamin Colman as its first pastor. It was Colman's flock, not Mather's Second ("Old North") Church, that took the apparently radi-

---

8. Quoted in Samuel Eliot Morison, *Harvard College in the Seventeenth Century*, 2 vols. (Cambridge: Harvard University Press, 1936), 2: 467. Mather, Morison suggests, "never did recover from that" (ibid.).

9. On Increase's suffocating influence over Cotton, see Silverman, *Life and Times*, 25–26. "Puritan culture," Silverman notes, "stressed entire dependence on one's father for a model of behavior" (ibid., 25).

10. For a discussion of various critical assessments of this, see Murdock, Introduction to *Magnalia*, 37–43.

11. Robert Middlekauff, *The Mathers: Three Generations of Puritan Intellectuals, 1596–1728* (New York: Oxford University Press, 1971), 248–251.

12. For an extensive discussion of the *Magnalia*, see Sacvan Bercovitch, *The Puritan Origins of the American Self* (New Haven, Conn.: Yale University Press, 1975).

13. Cotton Mather, *The Ambassadors Tears* (Boston: T. Fleet, 1721), 24.

cal step of breaking with traditional New England Congregationalism on a wide range of topics, including the nature of the church covenant, the manner of admission to church membership, the method of congregational government, and the grounds for access to the sacraments.[14] But Fourth Church's leadership left untouched the underlying pattern of Puritan clericalism; indeed, the manner of Colman's ordination, together with his role as the sole examiner of applicants for membership in the new church, only served to reinforce the tendency.[15] It was this clericalism itself that Mather came to see as the fundamental problem.

Primeval New England Congregationalism had been, if anything, anticlerical in temperament. Pastors of the first generation, men such as Richard Mather of Dorchester and John Wilson of Boston, were driven by their understanding of the ministry's covenantal basis to see themselves primarily in relation to their congregations rather than to one another.[16] Over the years, though, this idealistic perspective was tested to the limit by a series of major crises, beginning with the "Antinomian" controversy of 1637, as well as a host of petty squabbles in countless parishes over such annoyances as late wages and inadequate supplies of firewood. Perhaps inevitably, pastors began to look to their fellow-pastors for support and then identity. The ministry became a profession, and ministers learned to think of themselves as clergy, i.e., as members of a class of professionals bound together by their common calling, training, struggles, and aspirations as they stood near the apex of New England's increasingly stratified social order.[17]

---

14. On Fourth Church's innovations, see Perry Miller, *The New England Mind: From Colony to Province* (Cambridge: Harvard University Press, 1953; reprint, Boston: Beacon Press, 1961), 241–242. For more on this congregation, see chapter 3 below.

15. Colman held Presbyterian ordination to the Christian ministry generally, rather than Congregational ordination to Fourth Church's pastorate specifically; the traditional requirement that applicants for membership give a relation of their religious experience before those already members was dispensed with at Fourth Church, in favor of a private examination by the minister alone; and any questions concerning baptism, which was to be available indiscriminately to all infants who might be presented, were to be left to the minister alone, not the members, for resolution. See Miller, *From Colony to Province*, 242; and E. Brooks Holifield, *The Covenant Sealed: The Development of Puritan Sacramental Theology in Old and New England, 1570–1720* (New Haven, Conn.: Yale University Press, 1974), 192.

16. See Samuel Eliot Morison, *Builders of the Bay Colony*, rev. ed. (Boston: Houghton Mifflin, 1964), 105–134; and Williston Walker, *Ten New England Leaders* (New York: Silver Burdett, 1901), 49ff. For a recent discussion of the first generation's stress on ecclesiastical consensus, see James F. Cooper, Jr., *Tenacious of Their Liberties: The Congregationalists in Colonial Massachusetts* (New York: Oxford University Press, 1999), esp. 14–18.

17. This process of professionalization has been described by David D. Hall in *The Faithful Shepherd: A History of the New England Ministry in the Seventeenth Century* (Chapel Hill, N.C.: University of North Carolina Press, 1972); see also, for the late

In too many communities, this nascent clericalism triggered a predictably hostile response from parishioners, their hostility in turn triggering a further clericalist entrenchment. The sad cycle often ended with a church waging open war against its settled minister while the minister embraced all the more ardently a pastoral paradigm that stressed personal piety, long hours of study, powerful preaching—and, implicitly, isolation from his congregation.[18] Increase Mather

---

eighteenth and early nineteenth centuries, Donald Scott, *From Office to Profession: The New England Ministry, 1750–1850* (Philadelphia: University of Pennsylvania Press, 1978). For a detailed description of patterns of ministerial education, training, election, and installation prevailing across the region, see J. William T. Youngs, Jr., *God's Messengers: Religious Leadership in Colonial New England* (Baltimore, Md.: Johns Hopkins University Press, 1976), 11–39. For accounts of Puritan New England's stratified social hierarchy and the clergy's place within it, see E. Brooks Holifield, *A History of Pastoral Care in America: From Salvation to Self-Realization* (Nashville, Tenn.: Abingdon Press, 1983), 48–56; and Harry S. Stout, *The New England Soul: Preaching and Religious Culture in Colonial New England* (New York: Oxford University Press, 1986), 106–108. For a description of the process by which this stratification grew from one community's egalitarian roots, see Kenneth A. Lockridge, *A New England Town: The First Hundred Years; Dedham, Massachusetts, 1636–1736* (New York: W. W. Norton, 1970). For a recent reconsideration of early religious conflict in the Bay Colony, see Michael P. Winship, "'The Most Glorious Church in the World': The Unity of the Godly in Boston, Massachusetts, in the 1630s," *Journal of British Studies*, vol. 39, no. 1 (January 2000): 71–98; and idem, *Making Heretics: Militant Protestantism and Free Grace in Massachusetts, 1636–1641* (Princeton, N.J.: Princeton University Press, 2002).

18. See the painful descriptions in Ola Elizabeth Winslow, *Meetinghouse Hill: 1630–1783* (New York: Macmillan, 1952; reprint, New York: W. W. Norton, 1972), 211–212, 214–218, and passim; and Stephen Foster, *The Long Argument: English Puritanism and the Shaping of New England Culture, 1570–1700* (Chapel Hill, N.C.: University of North Carolina Press, 1991), 191–193. For an account of the relatively tranquil prelude, see Timothy H. Breen and Stephen Foster, "The Puritans' Greatest Achievement: A Study of Social Cohesion in Seventeenth-Century Massachusetts," *Journal of American History*, vol. 60, no. 1 (June 1973): 5–22. James W. Schmotter, in "Ministerial Careers in Eighteenth-Century New England: The Social Context, 1700–1760," *Journal of Social History*, vol. 9, no. 2 (Winter 1975): 249–267, explores the subsequent decline in clerical status reflected in the rising frequency of ministers' disputes with their congregations. J. William T. Youngs, Jr., in "Congregational Clericalism: New England Ordinations before the Great Awakening," *William and Mary Quarterly*, 3d series, vol. 31, no. 3 (July 1974): 481–492, notes the reflexive rise across the region of "an obsession with the importance of the ministry which can be described as Congregational clericalism" (ibid., 481–482) and observes: "It is evident . . . that the early Protestant ideal . . . of a 'priesthood of all believers' had all but vanished for the New England of the 1720s and 1730s" (ibid., 489). For more on this point, see Youngs, *God's Messengers*, 64–91; on the hostile lay response, see ibid., 97–102. On the further clericalist impulse this response elicited from many clergy, see David Harlan, *The Clergy and the Great Awakening in New England* (Ann Arbor, Mich.: UMI Research Press, 1980), 31–47. For a helpful overview of the

made the latter explicit: "Let Ministers of the Gospel spend as little time as may be in fruitless and Complemental Visits: but let them keep close to their Studies. Blessed Mr. Mitchel [Jonathan Mitchell, pastor of the church in Cambridge from 1649 to 1668] ... gave me a *Word of Advice* ... [:] *'keep out of all Company whatsoever as far as the rules of Christianity and Civility will allow, for you will surely find that for the most part, the time spent in your Study, will be profitably spent.'* I have found his advice good and true."[19]

Although the elder Mather's perspective was doubtless colored by his personal preference for solitude, the ministerial priorities he articulated here and elsewhere were in fact scarcely different from those of his more gregarious peers.[20] For example, the approach taken by Samuel Willard, pastor of Boston's Third ("Old South") Church from 1678 until his death in 1707, was practically identical. In *A Compleat Body of Divinity*, the posthumously published compilation of two hundred and fifty of Willard's lectures traversing the entire span of New England orthodoxy, he dealt with the question of a minister's relationship to his flock almost exclusively in terms of the congregation's duty to honor, respect, and obey its faithful pastor.[21] His *Brief Directions to a Young Scholar Designing the Ministry* is as eloquent in what it does not say as in what it actually says, subsuming the minister's responsibilities under such headings as the cultivation of a life of prayer, the assiduous study of scripture, the development of theological acumen, and consultation with fellow clergy on persistent difficulties, but passing over without mention such obvious practical concerns as catechesis and pastoral visitation.[22] This scholarly, sacerdotal approach to the ministry,

---

entire process, see Erik R. Seeman, *Pious Persuasions: Laity and Clergy in Eighteenth-Century New England* (Baltimore, Md.: Johns Hopkins University Press, 1999), 3–14. Schmotter, in "The Irony of Clerical Professionalism: New England's Congregational Ministers and the Great Awakening," *American Quarterly*, vol. 31, no. 2 (Summer 1979): 148–168, notes the irony that "a concern for professional stability . . . produced conditions that led to the very instability most pastors sought to avoid" (ibid., 149).

19. Increase Mather, *The Work of the Ministry Described*, in *Practical Truths, Plainly Delivered* (Boston: B. Green, 1718), 136–137. Increase's approach to the ministry, which focused on top-down mechanisms such as the sermonic jeremiad and the ceremony of covenant renewal, has been well described by Foster in *Long Argument*, 213–230. Michael P. Winship takes apples for oranges when he characterizes this approach as "the equivalent of a parish-based evangelism" ("Were There Any Puritans in New England?," *New England Quarterly*, vol. 74, no. 1 [March 2001]: 129).

20. On Increase's "love of privacy," see Silverman, *Life and Times*, 7–8.

21. Samuel Willard, *A Compleat Body of Divinity in Two Hundred and Fifty Expository Lectures on the Assembly's Shorter Catechism* (Boston: B. Green and S. Kneeland, 1726). Perry Miller hails this treatise as "New England's *summa*" (*From Colony to Province*, 213).

22. Samuel Willard, *Brief Directions to a Young Scholar Designing the Ministry* (Boston: J. Draper, 1735). The contrast between Willard's treatise and Cotton Mather's

Chapter 1: Manuductio ad Ministerium 7

preached and practiced by Willard, the elder Mather, and a host of others, exercised enormous influence among New England's clergy over the ninety years bracketed by the Cambridge Platform of 1648 and the Great Awakening of the early 1740s.

Inevitably, there was more to ministry in New England than could be accommodated by such a one-dimensional paradigm. Catechesis remained a concern of many ministers, and pastoral visitation was a specialty of some who had neither the gifts nor the temperament for the scholarly pursuits that kept others so late in their studies.[23] Moreover, the deep concern for evangelism in the wider community that was voiced and acted on by numerous seventeenth- and eighteenth-century clergy puts the lie to common claims of Puritan "tribalism."[24] The typi-

---

Manuductio ad Ministerium, also intended as a volume of advice to those embarked on training for the pastorate, is striking. For more on this, see below.

23. The best account of this neglected aspect of ministry in Puritan New England is George Selement's monograph, *Keepers of the Vineyard: The Puritan Ministry and Collective Culture in Colonial New England* (Lanham, Md.: University Press of America, 1984), esp. 13–42. Selement sets himself against intellectual and social historians alike, rejecting the former's assumption that clerical and collective cultures were one and the same, so that ministers in their writings could be said to have spoken for society at large, but rebuffing as well the latter's insistence on a gulf between clergy and society so great that ministers could be said to have spoken for no one but themselves. He argues that although clerical and collective cultures were not synonymous, it was precisely in the strenuous pastoral activities of catechesis and visitation that ministers worked to minimize and bridge whatever gap might separate them from their parishioners. See also idem, "Publication and the Puritan Minister," *William and Mary Quarterly*, 3d series, vol. 37, no. 2 (April 1980): 219–241, in which he rejects the common stereotype that has the New England pastor subordinating everything else to his preparation of volume after volume for the printing press. Still, even he is forced to admit (ibid., 231–232) that the closer one comes to Boston, the closer such an image comes to reality—a crucial point for this study. His works are best seen, not as freestanding essays on pastoral ministry in New England, but as a sort of "reality check," offering a warning against other essays' oversimplification. For a consideration of colonial ministers' practice in regard to catechesis, and a grudging concession as to just how infrequently this was often carried out, see Youngs, *God's Messengers*, 47–49; for a discussion of various approaches to pastoral visitation, see ibid., 49–53.

24. The classic statement of the case for Puritan "tribalism" is by Edmund S. Morgan in *The Puritan Family: Religion and Domestic Relations in Seventeenth-Century New England*, rev. ed. (New York: Harper and Row, Harper Torchbooks, 1966), 161–186. Morgan charges that the Puritans became so obsessed with the salvation of their own children that they turned a blind eye to the needs of the wider community; the result was that "theology became the handmaid of genealogy, [and] Puritanism no longer deserved its name" (ibid., 186). Against this, Selement points to the concern for evangelism evident from New England's founding in the ministries of men like Samuel Cheever of Marblehead and William Williams of Hatfield, not to mention more familiar figures like the

cal Puritan minister's conception of his calling surely involved action as well as reflection, time among parishioners in their homes and places of employment as well as long hours alone with his books. Nevertheless, it was for good reason that these pastors were often called "teaching elders." Though public proclamation and private visitation coexisted within a single pastoral paradigm, the former had clear primacy.[25] Whether or not every Puritan minister merited the designation of "*So Big Study Man*" with which Native Americans at New Haven supposedly hailed John Davenport, most of them certainly aspired to the title, or at least cast their eyes longingly in its direction.[26]

In a day when so many New England clergy had thus come to identify the essence of the ministry with the laborious preparation and delivery of powerful sermons in the "plain style," Cotton Mather's priorities were strikingly different. Seizing on long-neglected facets of traditional Puritanism, and meshing these with the latest proposals of Richard Baxter and other British Dissenters as well as Continental Pietists such as August Hermann Francke, the younger Mather located the heart of the pastorate neither in the study nor in the pulpit but in the office more broadly defined, in the minister's calling as "shepherd of the sheep." In taking this step, for all his undoubted filiopietism, he was embracing an activist approach to the pastorate far removed from that of his father.

For example, it is striking that while Increase devoted most of the week to preparation for his time in the pulpit, Cotton, by his own estimate, spent no more than seven hours preparing a typical sermon.[27] Yet it might be argued that in thus lending special prominence to time-hallowed but too-often ignored dimensions of Puritan pastoral practice, Cotton honored his elders in a fashion all the more striking for its subtlety. In short, he reminded his fellow clergy that they had always been better pastors than their own theories would have allowed and recalled them to a vision of the ministry more fully consonant with their own rich heritage.

Mathers (*Keepers of the Vineyard*, 43–59). Further, he notes that about six percent of the Puritan preachers in his sample, 32 of 531, engaged in missionary outreach, hardly what one would expect of a culture consumed by "tribalism" (ibid., 52).

25. Stout comments: "Like the founders, second-generation ministers spent as much time in their studies as possible and defined their vocation primarily in terms of the regular sermon" (*New England Soul*, 91). On the "time-consuming" process of sermon preparation, see Youngs, *God's Messengers*, 56.

26. Quoted in Selement, *Keepers of the Vineyard*, 14.

27. On Increase, see Michael G. Hall, *The Last American Puritan: The Life of Increase Mather* (Middletown, Conn.: Wesleyan University Press, 1988), 71–72; on Cotton, see Silverman, *Life and Times*, 195. Stout, in *New England Soul*, 152–153, discusses another pastor of Cotton's generation, John Barnard, Jr., of Marblehead, who was closer to Increase in his habits of preparation, taking only four hours to write out a given sermon, but investing, he estimated, "perhaps a week or a fortnight" (ibid., 153) in exegetical preliminaries.

Chapter 1: Manuductio ad Ministerium 9

Mather's activist perspective on the pastorate is reflected in his writings' unusual stress on the importance of a systematic program of visitation and catechesis.[28] His concern that pastors leave the comfort of their book-lined studies and involve themselves in the daily struggles of their parishioners is evident, for example, in a volume published in 1705 titled *The Rules of a Visit*: "A most exemplary minister of God, could say to his people, 'I have taught you publickly, and from house to house [Acts 20:20].'"[29] Pastoral visitation's importance, he urged, lay in its ability to engage individuals who might pay little heed to the pastor's sermons.[30] Great though the demands of such an enterprise would undoubtedly be, its potential rewards were greater still:

> It is indeed a very Difficult undertaking, and it requires much Wisdom, and all the Arts of a winning Address, and a flaming Zeal for God, and Faith in Christ, and Love to Souls, to manage the undertaking. But certainly, it would be of admirable Importance, for the *Winners of Souls*, to go about *from House to House*, every where spreading the *Nets of Salvation*, for all that come in our way. *Up and be Doing*, O Ambassadors of God! Visit your Neighbors; Inform your Selves from them, what may be their special *Necessities*; their special *Temptations. Adapt* your discourses unto them; Discourse with them, till *their hearts burn* within them. Find out, whether they *know the Things of their Peace*. Obtain from them their *Consent* unto the Covenant of Grace proposed in the Gospel; obtain from them Resolutions, with the Help of Grace, to do what the Gospel does demand of them. Give not over, till you may hope, that you have *Espoused* the Souls of the *Young People* unto the Lord JESUS CHRIST. *Catechise* the Children, and Inoculate on them the *Admonitions* which may be fetched out of the *Catechism*. Leave them in a *Flood of Tears*: yea, sometimes leave them not, without *Praying* to the glorious GOD, that each person in the *Family*, may have special and suited Favours of Heaven, poured out upon them. *God speed the Plough*, that shall be thus at work for him![31]

Mather's sermon for William Waldron's ordination in 1722 as the pastor of Boston's newly organized Seventh Church expressed the same sense of priorities: "IS the *Pastor* a Man whose *Labours* for the Instruction, the Conversion, the Salvation of his People are *unwearied*? . . . DOES he *Watch* and watchfully take all *Opportunities*, privately as well as publickly, to let fall the most *suitable Truths* upon them? . . . HAS he a tender sense of the *Temptations* and *Afflictions*,

---

28. John T. McNeill notes: "Visiting, catechizing, distributing books of piety, and faithfulness in reproof and consolation are recommended by Mather; but his treatment of these commonplaces is often far from commonplace" (*A History of the Cure of Souls* [New York: Harper and Row, 1951; Harper's Ministers Paperback Library, 1977], 277).

29. Cotton Mather, *The Rules of a Visit: An Essay upon That Case, How the Visits of Christians to One Another, May Be So Managed, As to Answer the Noble Designs of Christianity* (Boston: T. Green, 1705), 15.

30. Ibid.

31. Ibid., 16–17.

in which any of the People are Languishing? . . . Is he as ready to visit the *Poor* as the *Rich*? Will he hazard his own *Health* to visit the *Sick*? . . . Of such a *Pastor*, it must be said, *He loves his People*. He may want many Qualifications, that would brighten a Man of GOD; but certainly he will deserve this Testimony; *He loves his People*."[32] Five years later, mourning Waldron's death, Mather reminded his "Younger Brethren in the Evangelical MINISTRY" of their responsibilities: "A glorious CHRIST has committed His Flocks into your Hands. . . . In your *Pastoral Visits* you will *Exhort, and Comfort, and Charge every one of them, as a Father doth his Children*. You will enquire into their *state*, and will tender your *Best Advice* unto them, and will disperse the savoury *Books*, which may leave the *Salt* of *Truth* among them."[33]

Mather's point concerning a pastor's use of books as part of a program of visitation, so characteristic of his own ministry, will be examined further below. But equally characteristic, as these passages demonstrate, was his passion for pastoral visitation itself. In *The Minister*, another ordination sermon from 1722, he even responded indirectly to his father's invocation of "blessed Mr. Mitchel": "Tho' our *Time* is to be by far the most of it, *spent Alone*[,] . . . Yet we should have our *visiting Time*; And our Visits, how, how *many* we make, and how *much*, to be gainers, by what we shall communicate better than the *choicest Silver* in them! . . . [T]here are the *pastoral Visits*, which are to be made on the pure Designs of *knowing the state of the Flock*, and suiting it with Admonitions, *Exhorting* and *Comforting* and *Charging* EVERY ONE, as *a Father does his Children, That they should walk worthy of God.*"[34]

Mather's fullest description of New England's church order, his *Ratio Disciplinae Fratrum Nov-Anglorum*, published in 1726, included a detailed consideration of the Puritan minister's responsibilities: "A Pastor being one that is to *watch for the Souls* of his Flock, *as one that is to give an Account*, there are *Private* as well as *Publick* Services expected of him."[35] These "Services" included not only the visitation of the sick and bereaved and the solemnization of marriages and funerals (he commented on the latter's novelty) but especially catechesis.[36] "Some of the *Pastors*," he noted with approval, "chuse to do this Part of their Office after the *Pauline* way, To teach from *House to House*. And

---

32. Cotton Mather, *Love Triumphant* (Boston: S. Kneeland, 1722), 8–10. For a discussion of Waldron's ministry, see chapter 4 below.

33. Cotton Mather, *Hor-Hagidgad* (Boston: S. Gerrish, S. Kneeland, N. Belknap, and B. Love, 1727), 4.

34. Cotton Mather, *The Minister* (Boston: S. Kneeland, 1722), 37.

35. Cotton Mather, *Ratio Disciplinae Fratrum Nov-Anglorum: A Faithful Account of the Discipline Professed and Practised in the Churches of New England* (Boston: S. Gerrish, 1726), 103.

36. Ibid., 103–117.

Chapter 1: Manuductio ad Ministerium

perhaps *no way more significant!*"[37] In one of his best-known works, *Bonifacius: An Essay upon the Good*, he commended this enterprise to the fledgling minister: "*My son*, I advise you, to set a special value upon that part of your ministry, which is to be discharged in PASTORAL VISITS. . . . [Y]ou will never more *walk in the spirit*, than when you thus *walk* about your flock, to do what good you can among them."[38]

Mather being Mather, he did more than merely urge on his fellow clergy the importance of such a program of visitation. In *A Brief Memorial, of Matters and Methods for Pastoral Visits*, he produced a manual that a minister might actually use for guidance in house-to-house calling, doing his best in this three-page pamphlet to provide for every contingency, from the initial knock on the door to the parting benediction. When the pastor entered a home, he was to inquire after the family members' spiritual condition. What had they done "*to settle Good Terms with Heaven?*" What special temptations "*discourage and encumber their Essays for Living unto God?*" If they had met with adversity, the minister should help them to hear "the Voice of GOD" in their plight; if they had experienced singular prosperity, he must remind them of the "*Precious Fruits*" that God expected.[39]

The pastor should encourage family members to industry and honesty with "*Lessons of Piety*" that would return to them in the course of their day's work. Did the family have its regular times for Bible reading and prayer?[40] Was the children's education provided for? The head of the household must be reminded that he himself was responsible for their religious education. If the children were present, the minister might ask them a few well-chosen catechetical questions. Had the householder made provision for the religious education of his servants as well?[41] Those family members within the church covenant were to be reminded of the "Bonds of God" upon them. Those qualified to receive the Lord's Supper were to be encouraged to partake and shown how to prepare for this. The pastor might then read from an appropriate Biblical text—Mather suggested Mark 10:13–16, the story of Jesus and the little children—and give a short talk.

---

37. Ibid., 105.

38. Cotton Mather, *Bonifacius: An Essay upon the Good* (Boston: S. Gerrish, 1710; reprint, Cambridge: Harvard University Press, Belknap Press, 1966), 77.

39. Cotton Mather, *A Brief Memorial, of Matters and Methods for Pastoral Visits* (Boston: n.p., 1723), 1.

40. Ibid., 2. Mather's *Small Offers towards the Service of the Tabernacle in the Wilderness* (Boston: R. Pierce, 1689) offered householders lavish advice on the why and how of family devotions: "Each man pretends to be a *King in his own house*; he should there be a *Priest*, and a *Prophet* too" (ibid., 28–29). See also his *A Family Well-Ordered* (Boston: B. Green and J. Allen, 1699); *A Family-Sacrifice* (Boston: B. Green and J. Allen, 1703); and *Family Religion Excited and Assisted* (Boston: n.p., 1705).

41. Mather, *Brief Memorial*, 2.

In parting, he should leave them with an appropriate verse, such as Matthew 16:26: "For what is a man profited, if he shall gain the whole world, and lose his own soul?"[42]

Such a program of pastoral visitation provided a natural opening for catechesis, another activity in which Mather distinguished himself from most of his Puritan contemporaries.[43] His son Samuel, in a published sermon on Cotton's death, took note of this, observing: "How much Good he did by his *private Instruction* is inconceivable."[44] In *The Man of God Furnished*, published in 1708, Cotton laid out more fully his views on the significance of this ministry of training in basic Christian doctrine, invoking the dictum of Clement of Alexandria: "Without catechising, we shall soon be without Christianity."[45] He stressed the responsibility, not only of parent for child, but of master for servant, and even of teacher for pupil. "A Sanctifying *Transformation* of their Souls," he reminded schoolmasters, "were a Nobler Thing, than meerly to construe Ovid's *Metamorphoses*."[46] He advised pastors that catechesis ought to precede sermonizing, noting that "your *Unattentive Hearers* (if they may sometimes be called *Hearers!*) take not near so much notice of what you speak in the *Pulpit*, as they would of what you might Speak unto them, in the more *Approaching* and *Familiar* way of Catechising."[47]

As with pastoral visitation, Mather coupled his insistence on the importance of catechesis with a number of practical suggestions. For the young, he offered a simplified version of *Milk for Babes*, a children's catechism already in wide use across the region.[48] For those adults "of the Dullest and Lowest Capacity," he suggested a catechism of only three questions.[49] For householders, he compiled an abridgement of the Westminster Shorter Catechism in thirty-two questions, suggesting that family members might cover one question per day before their

---

42. Ibid., 3.

43. For Reformed antecedents, see McNeill, *Cure of Souls*, 192–217, 247–269, and 275–278.

44. Samuel Mather, *The Departure and Character of Elijah Considered and Improved* (Boston: G. Rogers, 1728), 21.

45. Cotton Mather, *The Man of God Furnished: The Way of Truth Laid Out* (Boston: S. Phillips, 1708), 2.

46. Ibid., 10.

47. Ibid., 15.

48. Ibid., 20–30. Mather published similar catechetical material for children in *Cares about the Nurseries* (Boston: T. Green, 1702); *Much in a Little* (Boston: Benjamin Eliot, 1702); *The Summ of the Matter* (Boston: n.p., 1709); and *The A, B, C. of Religion* (Boston: T. Green, 1713). See Thomas James Holmes, *Cotton Mather: A Bibliography of His Works*, 3 vols. (Newton, Mass.: Crofton Publishing Corp., 1974), 1: 4–5, 113–115; 2: 605–610, 714–715; and 3: 1040.

49. Mather, *Man of God Furnished*, 32.

Chapter 1: Manuductio ad Ministerium 13

evening prayers, traversing its entirety in a month.⁵⁰ For those with greater ability, he offered a much longer catechism, with special sections devoted to refuting Quakers, Pelagians, Antinomians, and Anabaptists.⁵¹ In all of this, his concern was that souls be directed "to the Good GOD, and His Glorious CHRIST."⁵²

Eager that the minister's influence in a household linger long after his visit had ended, Mather urged that clergy bring with them *"Books of Piety"* to be left with their parishioners.⁵³ Always a believer in the power of the printed page, he counseled that "by the *Expense* of a few Pence, it may be so, that we shall *save a soul from Death!*"⁵⁴ In 1712 Mather himself went so far as to produce a volume, *Pastoral Desires*, intended for that very purpose. An imposing 116-page omnibus, the book opened with catechetical concerns, urging on the reader the desirability of the knowledge of "the Truths of our Holy Religion."⁵⁵ First came summaries of the faith that might be suitable for even the youngest children—scripture portions such as Micah 6:8 and John 3:16;⁵⁶ the Apostles' Creed;⁵⁷ and a simple catechism of three questions:

The First Question

Who made you and all the World?

The Answer

The Great God made me to Serve Him.

The Second Question

Who saves the Children of Men from all their miseries?

---

50. Ibid., 33–43.
51. Ibid., 47–127.
52. Ibid., 132.
53. Mather, *Minister*, 39. For a discussion of one parishioner's diligent devotional use of Mather's book, *A Midnight Cry* (Boston: S. Phillips, 1692), see Seeman, *Pious Persuasions*, 34–37. George Whitefield's even more systematic use of the printed word to further his ministry as an itinerant is explored by Frank Lambert in "'Pedlar in Divinity': George Whitefield and the Great Awakening, 1737–1745," *Journal of American History*, vol. 77, no. 3 (December 1990): 812–837; and *"Pedlar in Divinity": George Whitefield and the Transatlantic Revivals, 1737–1770* (Princeton, N.J.: Princeton University Press, 1994).
54. Mather, *Minister*, 39.
55. Cotton Mather, *Pastoral Desires: A Short Catalogue of Excellent Things Which a Pastor Will Desire to See Approved and Practised and Abounding among His People; A Book Design'd to Be Lodg'd and Left in Their Hands by One Desirous to Be Such an One in His Pastoral Visits to the Houses of All His People* (Boston: T. Green, 1712), 4.
56. Ibid., 7–8.
57. Ibid., 8–9.

The Answer

> JESUS CHRIST, who is both God and man, Saves them that Look unto Him.

The Third Question

What will become of you when you die?

The Answer

> If I obey JESUS CHRIST, my Soul will go to the Heavenly Paradise; and He will afterwards raise me from the Dead. If I be wicked, I shall be cast among the Devils.[58]

Then came a longer doctrinal summary in seven articles, covering such tenets of orthodoxy as the existence and attributes of God, the fallen state of humanity, God's provision for redemption in the person of Christ, the nature of conversion, the place of good works, the function of the sacraments, and the coming judgment.[59] From dogma, Mather turned to experiential religion, stressing that his readers must have not only a knowledge of its truth but a taste of its power; they must become "*Converts of Zion*, . . . by the experience of a Real and Thorough CONVERSION to God."[60] Sinners "must come to an *Immediate Resolution* for *Conversion*, and a life of Religion. . . . The *Resolution* of *Conversion* and *Religion*, . . . admits no Delay."[61]

Next Mather addressed specific members of the household. The baptized he reminded of the significance of their entry into the external covenant. Those in full communion he urged to examine their hearts continually, that they might be "*fruitful Christian*[*s*]"—"One[s] who with Diligence and with Discretion [pull] together at both the *Oars* of [their] *Two Callings*: [their] *General* [i.e., their shared calling as believers] and [their] *Personal* [i.e., their particular vocations]."[62] Whatever their estate, he encouraged them to nurture their private devotional lives, the "Religion of the Closet"; he suggested prayer "*Twice a Day* at least," with whole days regularly set aside for extended meditation.[63] Families must also cultivate the "*Religion of the Household*," centering on daily prayer and Bible-reading in corporate devotions.[64]

Beyond this, Mather urged that individuals involve themselves in one of the religious societies so dear to his heart: "It is most certain, wisely to uphold *Religious Societies*, is to befriend all true *Religion*. The *Private Meetings of Religious People, for the Exercises of Religion*, Experience tells us, That where they have been kept alive, and under a Prudent Conduct, the Christians that have

---

58. Ibid., 9–10.
59. Ibid., 10–14.
60. Ibid., 14.
61. Ibid., 24–26.
62. Ibid., 30–44, 64, 66.
63. Ibid., 73, 74, 76–78.
64. Ibid., 78–79.

composed them, have like so many *Living Coals* kept one another alive, and kept up the Life of Christianity in the Vicinity."[65] He closed the volume with specific exhortations for the poor, the rich, the young, and the old; in whatever state they might be, they must cast themselves on "the Glorious JESUS."[66]

In addition to writing extensively on the question of pastoral visitation, Mather committed a substantial portion of his time to this work in his own parish. For example, in a diary entry from March of 1683, early in his ministerial tenure at Second Church, he set himself to "as soon, as is convenient, sett apart one Afternoon, every Week, to visit all the Families, in our Neighbourhood; and therein essay, as handsomely as I can, to bring Persons of all Ages and Sexes, unto an Acquaintance with God."[67] Several years later he recalled what had followed:

> I sett upon Visiting all the Families of our Church, taking sometimes one and sometimes two, Afternoons in a week for that purpose.
>
> I still sent aforehand unto the Families, that I intended at such a Time to visit them, and when I came unto them, I essay'd . . . to treat every Person particularly about their everlasting Interests; and the young People I still asked some Questions of the Catechism, from the Answers whereof I made as lively Applications unto them as I could, for the engaging of them unto the Service of God.

---

65. Ibid., 88. For more on such societies, see below.

66. Ibid., 90–94, 114.

67. Mather, *Diary*, 1: 55, entry for March 26, 1683. A few comments on the reliability of such passages from Mather's diary are in order at this point. Virginia Bernhard, in "Cotton Mather's 'Most Unhappy Wife': Reflections on the Uses of Historical Evidence," *New England Quarterly*, vol. 60, no. 3 (September 1987): 341–362, poses but does not resolve the central question: "Just how much of Mather's diary is to be taken at face value?" (ibid., 361). Any adequate response must begin by taking account of David Levin's observation that "the two fat volumes first published in 1912 as *The Diary of Cotton Mather* are for [the earliest years after 1681] not a diary at all" but Mather's "Reserved Memorials," intended as "a spiritual guide for his 'little folks'—his sisters and brothers and perhaps some of the other pupils whom he tutored during these years," dealing mainly with "prayers, resolutions, meditations, or other pious expressions." Instead of recording "his daily experience, secular or devotional," they "abstract his periodic exercises of solitary devotion and record some of his extraordinary religious experiences" (*Young Life*, 63). Lovelace notes a subsequent shift: "After 1709 [Mather's] *Diary* ceases to record the details of his soul struggles and becomes an account of his weekly cycle of 'Good Devices'" (*American Pietism*, 162). Although Mather's *Diary*, with its extensive distillations from original records that he then apparently destroyed (see Levin, *Young Life*, 63), is thus anything but a *cinéma vérité* transcript of events, there seems to be no good reason not to accept its account of specific actions it presents him as having taken. Certainly all recent biographers have done so. Its interpretive remarks regarding those actions are, of course, open to question.

> I enjoy'd a most wonderful Presence of God with mee, in this Undertaking; and seldome left a Family, without many Tears of Devotion dropt by all sorts of Persons in it.
>
> I could seldome dispatch more than three or four Families in an Afternoon; and the work was as laborious as any in all my Ministry. But I dispatch'd more than fifty Families, in two or three months; promising to the Lord, that when hee had carried mee thro' my Undertaking, I would keep a Day of Thanksgiving to Him, on that Occasion.[68]

Mather evidently found such work both rewarding and demanding, "a Service wherein I enjoy a strange Presence and Conduct of Heaven, but go thro' very spending Labour."[69] His diary is studded with confessions of neglect and resolutions of reform that strike a chord in the heart of any pastor: "I grow too slack, in *pastoral Visits* of my Neighbours. Lord, help mee!"[70] "I purposed ... that I would quicken my *pastoral Visits*, to the Families of my Neighbours; and scatter among the Families, my little Book, of a *Family well-ordered*."[71] "To Renew my *pastoral Visits*, with more stated Exactness and prudent Fervency, is one special Purpose, which I am now putt upon, and accordingly the Divine Help therein, I make one special Article of my Supplications."[72] "My pastoral Visits to the Flock must be revived; enquiries into the State of every one must be proposed; one Afternoon in a fortnight must be sett apart for this Purpose. I must not be weary of this Work for the Lord."[73] "I am reviving my Cares to visit the Flock, and I would as soon as I can, gett furnished with my *Echo's of Devotion*, (which is not yet published,) that I may lodge the Book in all the Families where I come."[74] "Visit, visit, visit,—more frequently, more fruitfully. Redeem Thursday's Afternoons, for my own Part of the Town."[75]

The high regard in which Mather held this ministry, and the frustration he felt at the perceived inadequacy of his own efforts, are readily apparent. It is surely no coincidence that Second Church grew steadily through most of his pastorate, with fully half of those receiving baptism there during his forty-three-year ministry ultimately giving a satisfactory relation of their religious experience and entering into full communion.[76]

---

68. Ibid., 1: 114–115, entry for February 6, 1686.
69. Ibid., 1: 367–368, entry for October 16, 1700.
70. Ibid., 1: 201, entry for July 23, 1696.
71. Ibid., 1: 304, entry for June 7, 1699.
72. Ibid., 1: 319, entry for October 18, 1699.
73. Ibid., 2: 230, entry for August 16, 1713.
74. Ibid., 2: 334, entry for February 13, 1716.
75. Ibid., 2: 352, entry for May 21, 1716.
76. This is demonstrated by a tabulation of the entries in Mather's own log; see Second Church, Records, Vol. 2: "Cotton Mather's Book," Massachusetts Historical Society, Boston. For a further discussion of Second Church and its pastors, see chapter 3 below.

Something further should be said about Mather's reliance on religious societies as a means of facilitating church renewal.[77] In his *Ratio Disciplinae*, he described these private meetings as one of the "special customs" of the churches of New England whose perpetuation in a particular community had much to do with determining the "*Power of Godliness*" in that place.[78] Moreover, he practiced what he preached; almost his first effort on behalf of the gospel in Boston was his establishment of just such a society in 1679, at the tender age of sixteen.[79]

In connection with this event, Mather composed a little volume, *Religious Societies*, finally published in 1724, that described such groups' nurture. In his account, a dozen or so individuals might come together without benefit of clergy in a private home once or twice a month. The meeting's agenda would include prayers led by each of the men in turn, the singing of psalms, the reading or rehearsal of sermons or devotional works, and the sharing of spiritual concerns and personal needs.[80] He saw such groups as vital to the health of church and community alike: "Such a Meeting should look upon themselves as bound up in one *Bundle of Love*, and count themselves obliged, in very close, and strong *Bonds*, to be serviceable unto one another. . . . If any One in the Society shall fall into *Affliction*, all the Rest should study presently to Relieve and Support the Afflicted Person in all the ways imaginable. If any should fall into *Temptation*, the Rest should watch over him, and with the *Spirit of Meekness*, with the *meekness of Wisdom*, endeavour to recover him."[81]

In Mather's *Manuductio ad Ministerium*, a handbook for pastors-to-be much like Willard's volume noted above, he urged that spiritually-minded students organize themselves into support groups along the same lines: "Form a SODALITY. What I mean, is, Prevail with a Fit Number, (*Six* or *Seven* may be a Competency, or Fewer, if you can't find so many,) of Sober, Ingenious, and

---

77. See Thomas S. Kidd, "'The Very Vital Breath of Christianity': Prayer and Revival in Provincial New England," *Fides et Historia*, vol. 36, no. 2 (Summer-Fall 2004): 23.

78. Mather, *Ratio Disciplinae*, 191.

79. See the discussion in Levin, *Young Life*, 74–76. "It would be hard," Levin observes, "to overemphasize the significance of this first public work by Cotton Mather" (ibid., 74). Note the parallel to Count Nikolaus Ludwig von Zinzendorf's organization of a religious fellowship while a teenager studying at the University of Halle; see A. J. Lewis, *Zinzendorf the Ecumenical Pioneer: A Study in the Moravian Contribution to Christian Mission and Unity* (London: SCM Press, 1962), 26.

80. Cotton Mather, *Religious Societies: Proposals for the Revival of Dying Religion by Well Ordered Societies for That Purpose* (Boston: J. Phillips, 1724), 2. See also idem, *Private Meetings Animated and Regulated* (Boston: T. Green, 1706). Mather's *Rules for the Society of Negroes* (Boston: B. Green, 1693) and *Early Religion* (Boston: Benjamin Harris, 1694), 115–117, set forth guidelines by which specific kinds of groups were to be governed.

81. Ibid., 3.

Industrious Young Men, to Associate with you, and meet *One Evening* in a *Week*, for the spending of Two or Three Hours, in a *Profitable Conversation*. At this Interview, let there always be a sort of *Director*."[82] As will be seen below, several students at Harvard College who would later be numbered among his protégés did exactly this.

Again, Mather's stress on religious societies is apparent not only in his writings on that subject but in his own pastoral practice. From the outset of his ministry, he devoted a substantial portion of his time to the organization and support of several types of societies. In 1683, four years after his earliest such effort, already noted, and in his first year as pastor of Second Church, he attempted to found a "Young Men's Association" in Boston's South End.[83] When he had difficulty recruiting enough youths from that neighborhood, he encouraged some of them to join a similar society he had already helped to found in the North End.[84] In time, "when there were such Numbers of Young Men from the *South* End of the Town, joined unto the Meeting at the *North*, as that I could make of them enough to constitute a distinct Meeting[,] . . . [t]hey did so, and at their first Setting up, I preach'd unto them."[85] In 1685 he took steps to initiate a fellowship group along similar lines for local ministers and their families.[86] As late as the mid-1730s, almost a decade after his death, clergy who had been associated with him were still holding such meetings approximately once a month for spiritual fellowship as well as consultation about pastoral concerns.[87]

---

82. Cotton Mather, *Manuductio ad Ministerium: Directions for a Candidate of the Ministry* (Boston: T. Hancock, 1726; reprint, New York: Columbia University Press, 1938), 72–73. Samuel Mather described the *Manuductio* as *"full of Learning"* (*Departure and Character of Elijah*, 20). Youngs, in *God's Messengers*, 19–20, discusses both the *Manuductio* and Willard's similar volume, *Brief Directions to a Young Scholar Designing the Ministry*, but fails to note their striking differences.

83. Note that responsibility for such an undertaking in that neighborhood ought to have fallen first to the ministers of Third Church; Mather was evidently stepping into what he saw as something of a pastoral vacuum. See the discussion in Levin, *Young Life*, 98. See also Patricia U. Bonomi's reflections on similar groups of young men and women organized by other pastors in *Under the Cope of Heaven: Religion, Society, and Politics in Colonial America* (New York: Oxford University Press, 1986), 117.

84. Mather, *Diary*, 1: 67–68, entry for July 9, 1683. He dedicated his treatise, *The Young Man's Glory* (Boston: R. Pierce, 1690), to "the Praying and Private Meetings of YOUNG PEOPLE in BOSTON, More especially to two or three such Assemblies, in the North-part of the TOWN."

85. Mather, *Diary*, 1: 68, entry for July 9, 1683.

86. Ibid., 1: 106, entry for October 24, 1685; 1: 125, entry for March 20, 1686.

87. Thomas Prince, "Diary of the Rev. Thomas Prince, 1737," ed. Albert Matthews, in *Publications of the Colonial Society of Massachusetts*, vol. 19, *Transactions, 1916–1917* (Boston: Colonial Society of Massachusetts, 1918), 340, entry for January 28, 1737; 342, entry for February 28, 1737; 344, entry for April 25, 1737; 350, entry for June 20,

Chapter 1: Manuductio ad Ministerium

In January of 1687, Mather recorded in his diary a further resolution: "I will perswade several Gentlemen belonging unto our Congregation, to combine into a private Meeting, Wherein they shall, once a Fortnight, seek the Face and hear the Word of God, in their several Families together."[88] Some time later, he noted, this group "had their first Meeting at my House."[89] Moreover, he observed, "[s]everal religious Families there are among us, not yett joined unto any of the private Meetings in our Neighbourhood; I would therefore address them, to gett into this way of their Edification."[90] He put such emphasis on these societies precisely because they elicited the direct involvement of the laity in aspects of Christian ministry often considered by his contemporaries to be the prerogative of the clergy.[91]

Mather's religious societies are often mistaken for the "Reforming Societies" or "Societies for the Suppression of Disorders" that he championed later in his career as a means of buttressing community morals and civic order.[92] Perry Miller, for one, uses these latter efforts in order to caricature all of Mather's attempts at encouraging such lay associations as nothing more than "a mechanism . . . to organize social pressures. . . . Here is a prophecy of Protestant, small-town, Middle Western culture of the nineteenth century; [Mather's efforts point to] the advent of Main Street."[93]

Richard Lovelace, stressing the distinction between the reforming societies and their religious counterparts, rejects Miller's characterization: "[These] societies were employed as socio-religious associations for the spiritual and corporal care of whole neighborhoods. Thus they not only predicted some of the features of the nineteenth-century voluntary societies that were their lineal descendants,

---

1737; 351, entry for July 4, 1737; 355, entry for August 15, 1737; 358, entry for September 26, 1737; 361, entry for November 7, 1737; and 363, entry for December 5, 1737. This "Diary" consists of Prince's notes interleaved through an almanac, the original of which is now held in the Massachusetts Historical Society Archives, Boston.

88. Mather, *Diary*, 1: 135, entry for January 8, 1687.

89. Ibid.

90. Ibid.

91. Participation in one such group by John Barnard, Sr., a deacon in Mather's church, is discussed by Seeman in *Pious Persuasions*, 27–28; Seeman notes that the elder Barnard's involvement enabled him to "take an active role in formulating his own piety" (ibid., 28).

92. See ibid., 2: 27, entry for February 3, 1710; see also Mather's *Methods and Motives for Societies to Suppress Disorders* (Boston: B. Green and J. Allen, 1703). Levin notes that Mather "had thirteen or fourteen of [the reforming societies] going strong by the end of 1701" (*Young Life*, 273).

93. Miller, *From Colony to Province*, 411. For another example of this mistaken approach, see J. M. Bumsted and John E. Van de Wetering, *What Must I Do to Be Saved? The Great Awakening in Colonial America*, Berkshire Studies in History (Hinsdale, Ill.: Dryden Press, 1976), 32, 43.

but in some measure surpassed those as expressions of local spiritual and moral concern.... Mather's equal concern for the spiritual well-being of his community and for its material, social, and political needs makes him uniquely fascinating to modern Christians weary of the ... unnatural separation between these realms, or the reduction of one into the other."[94]

In Mather's encouragement of religious societies as in so much else, he was more the creative synthesist than the bold trail-blazer. Robert Middlekauff, following Miller's lead in blurring the distinctions between the religious societies and their reforming counterparts, and moreover ignoring Mather's lifelong interest in these matters already noted above, suggests that Mather derived his ideas in large measure from English developments of the 1690s.[95] More reasonably, Lovelace notes precedents in German Pietism as well as English and American Puritanism.[96] Puritans like Richard Baxter in turn drew heavily on the precedent set by Continental Reformers like Martin Bucer.[97]

---

94. Lovelace, *American Pietism*, 224.

95. Middlekauff, *Mathers*, 269–270. Middlekauff is correct in finding a precedent for at least the reforming societies in these English innovations, though his neglect of fundamental distinctions between religious and secular societies causes him to draw misleading conclusions; see Lovelace, *American Pietism*, 218–224.

96. Lovelace, *American Pietism*, 215–218. See also Michael J. Crawford, *Seasons of Grace: Colonial New England's Revival Tradition in Its British Context* (New York: Oxford University Press, 1991), 45. For brief comments on the use of religious societies by Johann Arndt and Philip Jakob Spener, see Mark A. Noll, *The Rise of Evangelicalism: The Age of Edwards, Whitefield, and the Wesleys*, A History of Evangelicalism: People, Movements, and Ideas in the English-Speaking World, ed. David W. Bebbington and Mark A. Noll (Downers Grove, Ill.: InterVarsity Press, 2003), 61, 62; and W. R. Ward, *Early Evangelicalism: A Global Intellectual History, 1670–1789* (Cambridge: Cambridge University Press, 2006), 27–31. The English Puritan precedent is exemplified in the experience of John Wilson, founding pastor of Boston's First Church, during his student days at Cambridge University: "[H]e saw that they who were nicknamed Puritans, were likely to be the desirablest companions for one that intended his own everlasting happiness: and pursuant to the advice he had from doctor [William] Ames, he associated himself with a pious company in the University, who kept their meetings in Mr. Wilson's chamber, for prayer, fasting, holy conference, and the exercises of true devotion" (Thomas Prince, *A Chronological History of New-England, in the Form of Annals* [Boston: Kneeland and Green, 1736], 371).

97. On Bucer's use of "Christlichen gemeinschaften"—Christian fellowships or communities—as a disciplinary tool in Strasbourg, see Amy Nelson Burnett, *The Yoke of Christ: Martin Bucer and Christian Discipline*, Sixteenth Century Essays and Studies, vol. 26 (Kirksville, Mo.: Sixteenth Century Journal Publishers, 1994), 180–207; idem, "Confirmation and Christian Fellowship: Martin Bucer on Commitment to the Church," *Church History*, vol. 64, no. 2 (June 1995): 202–217; James Kittelson, "Martin Bucer and the Ministry of the Church," in *Martin Bucer: Reforming Church and Community*, ed. D. F. Wright (Cambridge: Cambridge University Press, 1994), 89–94; Gottfried Hammann,

Mather himself certainly felt that the religious societies he championed were nothing new, arguing in his *Magnalia Christi Americana* that they were as American as apple pie: "In the beginning of the country, the ministers had their frequent meetings.... The private Christians also had their private meetings, wherein they would seek the face, and sing the praise of God; and confer upon some questions of practical religion, for their mutual edification."[98] The English Congregationalist minister and historian Daniel Neal, Mather's near-contemporary, described the functioning of such "private meetings" in early Plymouth: "Mr. *Brewster* . . . preached and performed all other Offices of a Minister among them, except administering the Sacraments: Besides this, they had Meetings on the Week Days, wherein some of the Elder Brethren prayed and expounded some Portion of Scripture to the rest."[99]

As commonplace as these meetings may have been in the early seventeenth century, though, by the early eighteenth century they had become quite rare.[100] This slide into disuse was initiated by their association with Anne Hutchinson's "Antinomian" conventicles. Marilyn J. Westerkamp observes: "During [Hutchinson's] trial, particular emphasis was placed upon her house meetings, not merely as the means by which she disseminated her opinions but as acts in themselves disruptive due to the female, lay leadership."[101] As Westerkamp suggests,

---

"Ecclesiological Motifs behind the Creation of the 'Christlichen Gemeinschaften,'" trans. D. F. Wright, in *Martin Bucer*, 129–143; and David Wright, "Sixteenth-Century Reformed Perspectives on the Minority Church," *Scottish Journal of Theology*, vol. 48, no. 4 (1995): 473–476. On the link between Bucer and Baxter, see J. William Black, "From Martin Bucer to Richard Baxter: 'Discipline' and Reformation in Sixteenth- and Seventeenth-Century England," *Church History*, vol. 70, no. 4 (December 2001): 644–673.

98. Cotton Mather, *Magnalia Christi Americana*, 2 vols. (Hartford, Conn.: Silas Andrus and Son, 1853; reprint, Carlisle, Penn.: Banner of Truth Trust, 1979), 1: 241–242.

99. Daniel Neal, *The History of New-England, Containing an Impartial Account of the Civil and Ecclesiastical Affairs of the Country, to the Year of Our Lord, 1700*, 2d ed., 2 vols. (London: J. Clarke, R. Ford, and R. Cruttenden, 1747), 1: 129.

100. See the extensive discussion in Charles E. Hambrick-Stowe, *The Practice of Piety: Puritan Devotional Disciplines in Seventeenth-Century New England* (Chapel Hill, N.C.: University of North Carolina Press, 1982), 137–143.

101. Marilyn J. Westerkamp, "Anne Hutchinson, Sectarian Mysticism, and the Puritan Order," *Church History*, vol. 59, no. 4 (December 1990): 493. Thomas Shepard, one of Hutchinson's leading clerical opponents, argued for a close connection between the proliferation of her private meetings and the spread of her unorthodox tenets; see Mark A. Peterson, *The Price of Redemption: The Spiritual Economy of Puritan New England* (Stanford, Calif.: Stanford University Press, 1997), 10. For more on these meetings, see Emery Battis, *Saints and Sectaries: Anne Hutchinson and the Antinomian Controversy in the Massachusetts Bay Colony* (Chapel Hill, N.C.: University of North Carolina Press, 1962), 89–92 and passim; Stephen Foster, "New England and the Challenge of Heresy, 1630 to 1660: The Puritan Crisis in Transatlantic Perspective," *William and Mary*

the process of pastoral retrenchment was accelerated by these meetings' fundamental incompatibility with full-blown Puritan clericalism.[102] Their refurbishment by Mather, which at first glance seems such a radical departure, was in fact simply a return to the region's pastoral roots.

What were the sources on which Mather drew in developing his broader pastoral paradigm? Surely one of the most important, as already noted, was the example of Richard Baxter, the great English Puritan pastor and autodidact theologian whose labors in his parish at Kidderminster had come to serve as a model for so many other Dissenting ministers.[103] Mather's library, at that time one of New England's largest, included several of Baxter's books. Significantly, Mather's diary includes half a dozen references to Baxter; a typical entry notes that he had "read Mr. *Baxter's Gildas Salvianus* again, to animate a dire care for the Souls of the Flock."[104] The latter volume, familiar to generations of readers as *The Reformed Pastor*, is perhaps Baxter's best-known treatise, distilling lessons derived from his fourteen years' ministry in Kidderminster. He addressed it to his fellow pastors, hoping to persuade them to adopt in their own parishes his systematic approach to pastoral care and stressing the importance of their private

---

Quarterly, 3d series, vol. 38, no. 4 (October 1981): 624–660; and Winship, *Making Heretics*, 55–56, 141, and 171–172.

102. The authorities' ongoing efforts at expunging such meetings included a confrontation with one recalcitrant member of Boston's First Church: "Our sister Sarah Keayne was in the name of the Lord Jesus, with the Consent of the Church in Open Assembly Admonished of hir Irregular prophesying in mixt Assemblies and for Refusing ordinarily to hear in the Churches of Christ" (Richard D. Pierce, ed., *The Records of the First Church in Boston, 1630–1868*, 2 vols. [Boston: Colonial Society of Massachusetts, 1961], 1: 46, entry for November 22, 1646). A subsequent entry in First Church's records (ibid., 1: 49) notes that on October 24, 1647, Keayne was excommunicated. See also Kidd, "'Vital Breath of Christianity,'" 23; David D. Hall, *Worlds of Wonder, Days of Judgment: Popular Religious Belief in Early New England* (New York: Alfred A. Knopf, 1989), 64; and David S. Lovejoy, *Religious Enthusiasm in the New World: Heresy to Revolution* (Cambridge: Harvard University Press, 1985), 62–86. Somewhat later, English societies championed by the likes of Samuel Wesley drew similar expressions of concern from a few Anglican bishops; see Noll, *Rise of Evangelicalism*, 67, and the sources cited in his n. 27. Finally, note the hostile reaction of Old Light ministers such as Charles Chauncy to New Light ministers' aggressive use of religious societies as an important pastoral tool during the era of the Great Awakening; for example, see Chauncy's *Letter from a Gentleman in Boston, to Mr. George Wishart, One of the Ministers of Edinburgh, Concerning the State of Religion in New-England* (Edinburgh: n.p., 1742). For more on this last point, see chapter 2 below.

103. Note Mather's reference to "the great *Baxter*" (*Bonifacius*, 146).

104. Mather, *Diary*, 2: 498, entry for January 6, 1718.

instruction, encouragement, and exhortation of their flocks.[105] In light of Mather's agenda, many of Baxter's suggestions have the ring of familiarity: "See that in every family there are some useful moving books, beside the Bible. If they have none, persuade them to buy some: if they be not able to buy them, give them some if you can."[106] He went so far as to insist that catechesis and house-to-house visitation ought to be "the chief business of the [pastor's] day."[107] Even a cursory examination of *The Reformed Pastor* will show the similarity of Baxter's and Mather's pastoral priorities.

Another source on which Mather drew was the German Pietism emanating from the University of Halle and typified by Halle's guiding light, August Hermann Francke.[108] Mather and Francke corresponded regularly for nearly two decades, and in Mather's later years his avowed goal of fashioning an American "PIETY" clearly reflected Halle's influence.[109] Moreover, as has often been remarked, his religious societies bear a striking resemblance to the Pietist *collegia pietatis*.[110] On the other hand, too much should not be made of Francke's influence on him. As has already been shown, his religious societies were homegrown rather than imported.[111] Moreover, his first correspondence with Francke dates from 1710 or 1711, long after his own understanding of the ministry had

---

105. J. I. Packer observes: "To upgrade the practice of personal catechizing from a preliminary discipline for children to a permanent ingredient in pastoral care for all ages was Baxter's main contribution to the development of Puritan ideals for the ministry; and it was his concern for catechizing that brought *The Reformed Pastor* to birth" (Introduction to *The Reformed Pastor*, by Richard Baxter, ed. William Brown [Glasgow: William Collins, 1829; reprint, Carlisle, Penn.: Banner of Truth Trust, 1974], 13).

106. Baxter, *Reformed Pastor*, 101.

107. Ibid., 211.

108. See the discussion in Lowell H. Zuck, "Cotton Mather and German Pietism," *Historical Intelligencer*, vol. 2, no. 1 (Fall 1982): 11–16. See also Lovelace, *American Pietism*, 32–40 and passim; and F. Ernest Stoeffler, ed., *Continental Pietism and Early American Christianity* (Grand Rapids, Mich.: William B. Eerdmans, 1976).

109. Zuck, "German Pietism," 11, 13. "PIETY" became a stock phrase with Mather; see *Manuductio*, 104, 105, 106, 107, and passim. In the preface to his book, *The Heavenly Conversation* (Boston: B. Green, 1710), he offered lavish praise to Francke and his "*mighty men of* PIETY"; he even dared to appropriate the title of Lutheran Pietism's most influential treatise for his own *Pia Desideria* (Boston: S. Kneeland, 1722). See also Bumsted and Van de Wetering, *What Must I Do to Be Saved?*, 42–43.

110. Zuck, "German Pietism," 12.

111. Lovelace notes: "Although the concept of the *collegia pietatis* has been mainly attached to German Pietism in the past, . . . the strongest roots of the conventicle approach seem to be in the Reformed tradition, in its English Puritan and Dutch Precisianist extensions" (*American Pietism*, 218).

matured.[112] The example of Halle seems to have functioned in his thought more as validation of paths already taken than as stimulus to new terrain.[113]

Epilogue:
To the Great Awakening

As Mather's life neared its close, the stability of New England's standing order was more appearance than reality. Internal pressures had continued to mount over the course of his years at Second Church, so that now clergy and their congregations were too often separated by a yawning chasm of class-consciousness reflected in painful incidents such as the controversy over smallpox inoculation that traumatized Boston during the epidemic of 1721–1722.[114] The result was that in this new age of commercialism and secularization, at the very moment when the churches of New England stood most in need of renewal, their pastors were often least able—indeed, least inclined—to take the steps necessary to minister more effectively. Mather and his great rival, Solomon Stoddard, for all their decades-long sniping at one another in pulpit and print alike, nevertheless shared a willingness to undertake any labor, to rework even the most timeworn traditions, in order that they might speak more effectively to the spiritual needs of their respective communities.[115] For Mather as for Stoddard, the exten-

---

112. Zuck, "German Pietism," 11.

113. Lovelace observes: "There is clear evidence . . . that Mather's already established direction was only reinforced by his contact with Halle" (*American Pietism*, 33). Mather himself, in a letter to Anthony William Boehm dated August 6, 1716, described American Puritanism not as derivative of but rather "of a piece with . . . Frederician Pietism" (*Selected Letters of Cotton Mather*, ed. Kenneth Silverman [Baton Rouge: Louisiana State University Press, 1971], 215).

114. Stout cites "a complex web of internal tensions and anxieties in church and state" which "[t]he formal continuities of their office and the old habits of superiority that linked ministers to their venerable predecessors could not conceal. . . . Traditional social categories were about to explode and splinter in many directions" (*New England Soul*, 185). Concerning the smallpox epidemic of 1721–1722, Perry Miller notes that Boston's ministers based their advocacy of inoculation on nothing more substantial than an appeal to authority; such authority their opponents simply—and violently—rejected (*From Colony to Province*, 348). See also Maxine Van de Wetering, "A Reconsideration of the Inoculation Controversy," *New England Quarterly*, vol. 58, no. 1 (March 1985): 46–67; and Winslow, *Destroying Angel*, 32–58. For a discussion of the increasingly fractious, fractured nature of provincial society itself, see Youngs, *God's Messengers*, 5–10.

115. Stout comments: "[A]ll of Stoddard's innovations were designed to bring people into the church and under his powerful ministry" (*New England Soul*, 99). See also Holifield, *Covenant Sealed*, 208–210; Crawford, *Seasons of Grace*, 47–49; Paul R. Lucas, "'An Appeal to the Learned': The Mind of Solomon Stoddard," *William and Mary Quarterly*, 3d series, vol. 30, no. 2 (April 1973): 257–292; idem, *Valley of Discord: Church*

sion of Christ's kingdom was the essence of the gospel ministry. But these men stood apart from many of their peers.

In Boston, most of Mather's fellow clergy were unswayed by his arguments and example. The social forces making for sacerdotalism and pastoral isolation meant that he and his disciples, men like Thomas Prince and John Webb, were swimming against the stream of long-established and constantly reinforced tradition.[116] Still, their day was to come. In the 1740s, when the Great Awakening shook the churches of New England like a colossal earthquake, the course of events in Boston was largely determined by the clericalist fault line running through the community's heart.[117] Ministers who were sensitive to this could make good use of Mather's pastoral tools, so that the upheaval might become a constructive experience for their congregations. Others were less fortunate. Old Light ministers, in fact, made support for the creaking clerical status quo the indispensable badge of orthodoxy. The consequence was that in Boston, as will be argued below, the initial phase of controversy over the Awakening revolved around the clash of opposed conceptions of church and ministry embodied in the radically divergent pastoral styles embraced by Old Light and many New Light clergy. If the Old Lights saw themselves as embattled defenders of the ways of their fathers, these New Lights found their own pastoral exemplar in Cotton Mather.

---

and Society along the Connecticut River, 1636–1725 (Hanover, N.H.: University Press of New England, 1976), 105–202; Ralph J. Coffman, *Solomon Stoddard*, Twayne's United States Authors (Boston: G. K. Hall and Co., Twayne Publishers, 1978), 141–175; Keith J. Hardman, *The Spiritual Awakeners: American Revivalists from Solomon Stoddard to D. L. Moody* (Chicago: Moody Press, 1983), 27–45; and John B. Carpenter, "New England's Puritan Century: Three Generations of Continuity in the City upon a Hill," *Fides et Historia*, vol. 35, no. 1 (Winter-Spring 2003): 53–54.

116. On Mather's disciples, see Miller, *From Colony to Province*, 451; and Emory Elliott, *Power and the Pulpit in Puritan New England* (Princeton, N.J.: Princeton University Press, 1975), 201. For more on individual disciples, see below.

117. Regarding Connecticut, Richard L. Bushman observes: "The conflict between order and piety defined a fissure along which the religious quakes accompanying the Great Awakening split [local] society wide open" (*From Puritan to Yankee: Character and the Social Order in Connecticut, 1690–1765* [Cambridge: Harvard University Press, 1967; reprint, New York: W. W. Norton, Norton Library, 1970], 182).

Chapter 2:
The Flourishing of the Kingdom of Christ

> The Great Awakening was a reaction against the formalism of an accepted orthodoxy.... But it was much more than a theological controversy. It was a complex episode, involving not only religion, but ... the whole social structure of the colonies. A society was in upheaval.[1]

In all of American history, few events have had quite so cataclysmic an impact on their times as the Great Awakening. It should not be surprising, then, that there are almost as many perspectives on this traumatic episode as historians examining the record. Some authors have eulogized the Awakening as an assertion of democratic ideals, a prologue to revolution, while others have written it off as an early example of the anti-intellectualism they see threaded through the nation's historical narrative.[2] William G. McLoughlin has argued that the Awakening merely manifested colonial society's shift of philosophical paradigms, an "ideological transformation [that was] necessary to the dynamic growth of the nation in adapting to basic social, ecological, psychological, and economic changes."[3] Resisting this reductionism, many evangelical historians have pre-

---

Some of the material from this chapter appeared in an earlier draft as "Clericalism and Revival: The Great Awakening in Boston as a Pastoral Phenomenon," *New England Quarterly*, vol. 57, no. 4 (December 1984): 554–566.

1. Conrad Wright, *The Beginnings of Unitarianism in America* (Boston: Starr King Press, 1955; reprint, Hamden, Conn.: Archon Books, 1976), 30.

2. For the former approach, see, for example, Winslow, *Meetinghouse Hill*, 230, 238–239, 250; Alan Heimert, *Religion and the American Mind: From the Great Awakening to the Revolution* (Cambridge: Harvard University Press, 1966), 94 and passim; Harry S. Stout, "Religion, Communication, and the Ideological Origins of the American Revolution," *William and Mary Quarterly*, 3d series, vol. 34, no. 4 (October 1977): 519–541; Nathan O. Hatch, *The Sacred Cause of Liberty: Republican Thought and the Millennium in Revolutionary New England* (New Haven, Conn.: Yale University Press, 1977), passim; and Robert Middlekauff, *The Glorious Cause: The American Revolution, 1763–1789*, Oxford History of the United States, vol. 2 (New York: Oxford University Press, 1982), in which the Revolutionaries are presented as "children of the twice-born" (ibid., 26). For the latter approach, see, for example, Hofstadter, *Anti-Intellectualism*, 64 and passim; and idem, *America at 1750: A Social Portrait* (New York: Alfred A. Knopf, 1971; reprint, New York: Random House, Vintage Books, 1973), 291 and passim.

3. William G. McLoughlin, *Revivals, Awakenings, and Reform: An Essay on Religion and Social Change in America, 1607–1977*, Chicago History of American Religion (Chicago: University of Chicago Press, 1978), 8. For other examples of this approach, see

ferred to perpetuate the legacy of Joseph Tracy, describing the Awakening as a pietist phenomenon that had much in common with the awakenings of the nineteenth century.[4] Such scholarly stances might be multiplied almost without end.[5]

Larzer Ziff, *Puritanism in America: New Culture in a New World* (New York: Viking Press, 1973), 300–305; and Benjamin W. Labaree, *Colonial Massachusetts: A History* (Millwood, N.Y.: KTO Press, 1979).

4. See, for example, John D. Woodbridge, Mark A. Noll, and Nathan O. Hatch, *The Gospel in America: Themes in the Story of America's Evangelicals* (Grand Rapids, Mich.: Zondervan, 1979), 140–141; and Thomas A. Askew and Peter W. Spellman, *The Churches and the American Experience: Ideals and Institutions* (Grand Rapids, Mich.: Baker Book House, 1984), 42–51. See also Joseph Tracy, *The Great Awakening: A History of the Revival of Religion in the Time of Edwards and Whitefield* (Boston: Tappan and Dennet, 1842; reprint, Carlisle, Penn.: Banner of Truth Trust, 1976); and Edwin Paxton Hood, *The Great Revival of the Eighteenth Century* (Philadelphia: American Sunday School Union, 1882), 281–302. Eugene E. White puts a pejorative spin on this point: "The pattern of revival hysteria established during Jonathan Edwards' Northampton revival of 1734, and given definite form by the Great Awakening, still remains a part of our American culture" ("Decline of the Great Awakening in New England: 1741 to 1746," *New England Quarterly*, vol. 24, no. 1 [March 1951]: 51).

5. See, for example, Perry Miller, "Jonathan Edwards and the Great Awakening," in *Errand into the Wilderness* (Cambridge: Harvard University Press, 1956; reprint, New York: Harper and Row, Harper Torchbooks, 1964), 153–166; idem, "The Great Awakening from 1740 to 1750," in *Nature's Nation* (Cambridge: Harvard University Press, Belknap Press, 1967), 78–89; Rhys Isaac, "Evangelical Revolt: The Nature of the Baptists' Challenge to the Traditional Order in Virginia, 1765–1775," *William and Mary Quarterly*, 3d series, vol. 31, no. 3 (July 1974): 345–368; Gary B. Nash, *The Urban Crucible: Social Change, Political Consciousness, and the Origins of the American Revolution* (Cambridge: Harvard University Press, 1979), 204–227; and the survey of various approaches in Martin E. Marty, *Faith of Our Fathers*, vol. 4, *Religion, Awakening, and Revolution* (Wilmington, N.C.: McGrath Publishing Co., 1977), 67–81. For an extreme reductionist perspective that sees the Awakening as resulting in large measure from the conflux of a diphtheria epidemic and an economic recession, superimposed on "an already critical social and economic situation," see James A. Henretta, *The Evolution of American Society, 1700–1815: An Interdisciplinary Approach* (Lexington, Mass.: D. C. Heath, 1973), 131–132. Equally reductionist, albeit from a slightly different angle, is John C. Miller, who in "Religion, Finance, and Democracy in Massachusetts," *New England Quarterly*, vol. 6, no. 1 (March 1933): 29–58, attributes the Awakening solely to the region's economic crisis and identifies it mainly with the countryside and the lower classes, asserting that the revival "cut a swath between rich and poor, stimulating the hostility that already divided them" (ibid., 30). The definitive refutation of Miller's analysis remains Edwin Scott Gaustad's "Society and the Great Awakening in New England," *William and Mary Quarterly*, 3d series, vol. 11, no. 4 (October 1954): 566–577; Gaustad argues that the Awakening "knew no boundaries, social or geographical, that it was both urban and rural, [and] that it reached both lower and upper class" (ibid., 567). Still, this is not to say that the Awakening did not exacerbate or even initiate divisions; indeed, factors such as age, gen-

Fortunately, these need not be taken as mutually exclusive; rather, most of them offer insights that must be accommodated by any comprehensive account of the events of that era.[6] Still, their shared tendency to exalt the life of the mind over

---

der, class, family ties, and even geography were subtly manifested in many communities' experience of the revival. For further exploration of this point, see J. M. Bumsted, "Revivalism and Separatism in New England: The First Society of Norwich, Connecticut, as a Case Study," *William and Mary Quarterly*, 3d series, vol. 24, no. 4 (October 1967): 588–612; idem, "Religion, Finance, and Democracy in Massachusetts: The Town of Norton as a Case Study," *Journal of American History*, vol. 57, no. 4 (March 1971): 817–831; Cedric B. Cowing, "Sex and Preaching in the Great Awakening," *American Quarterly*, vol. 20, no. 3 (Fall 1968): 624–644; James Walsh, "The Great Awakening in the First Congregational Church of Woodbury, Connecticut," *William and Mary Quarterly*, 3d series, vol. 28, no. 4 (October 1971): 543–562; Harry S. Stout, "The Great Awakening in New England Reconsidered: The New England Clergy," *Journal of Social History*, vol. 8, no. 1 (Fall 1974): 21–47; John W. Jeffries, "The Separation in the Canterbury Congregational Church: Religion, Family, and Politics in a Connecticut Town," *New England Quarterly*, vol. 52, no. 4 (December 1979): 522–549; and Rosalind Remer, "Old Lights and New Money: A Note on Religion, Economics, and the Social Order in 1740 Boston," *William and Mary Quarterly*, 3d series, vol. 47, no. 4 (October 1990): 566–573.

6. One exception is the argument advanced by Jon Butler in "Enthusiasm Described and Decried: The Great Awakening as Interpretative Fiction," *Journal of American History*, vol. 69, no. 2 (September 1982): 305–325, that "prerevolutionary revivals should be understood primarily as regional events" (ibid., 322), and that these localized outbreaks were essentially conservative rather than radical in their impact, "reinforc[ing] ministerial rather than lay authority even as they altered some clergymen's perception of their tasks and methods" (ibid., 323)—in other words, that what is commonly referred to as the Great Awakening was neither truly great nor an authentic awakening. To some extent anticipating Butler is J. M. Bumsted: "[T]he revival itself was in large measure an attempt by the standing clergy of New England to resolve ecclesiastical problems without altering the basic structure of such institutions as the halfway covenant and the parish system" ("Revivalism and Separatism," 588). For rejoinders targeted especially at Butler, see Susan O'Brien, "A Transatlantic Community of Saints: The Great Awakening and the First Evangelical Network, 1735–1755," *American Historical Review*, vol. 91, no. 4 (October 1986): 811–832; Frank Lambert, "The Great Awakening as Artifact: George Whitefield and the Construction of Intercolonial Revival, 1739–1745," *Church History*, vol. 60, no. 2 (June 1991): 223–246; and my own article, noted above, from which this chapter is derived. For further discussion of the Awakening's international scope, see Noll, *Rise of Evangelicalism*, 76–135; Crawford, *Seasons of Grace*; idem, "New England and the Scottish Religious Revivals of 1742," *American Presbyterians: Journal of Presbyterian History*, vol. 69, no. 1 (Spring 1991): 23–32; W. R. Ward, *The Protestant Evangelical Awakening* (Cambridge: Cambridge University Press, 1992); and idem, *Christianity under the Ancien Régime, 1648–1789*, New Approaches to European History (Cambridge: Cambridge University Press, 1999). For further discussion of Butler's argument, see the Conclusion below.

the humdrum details of daily existence has predisposed them to an outlook on colonial American revivalism that is in certain respects fundamentally mistaken.

Too often the Great Awakening has been described as an intellectual (or, for many, anti-intellectual) movement first and a social and pastoral phenomenon only secondarily, if at all. Advocacy of the Awakening in the northern colonies is seen as a natural corollary to the Calvinistic worldview defended by Jonathan Edwards and George Whitefield, while the opposition of Old Lights like Charles Chauncy is claimed to spring from the same Enlightenment presuppositions that would ultimately issue in Arianism and full-blown New England Unitarianism.[7] But such an argument is at best anachronistic. After all, it has been conclusively demonstrated that during the early 1740s most New Lights and Old Lights still worked within a common theological framework of moderate Calvinism.[8]

---

7. Joseph Tracy offers a particularly spectacular example of this line of reasoning, arguing that "[t]he history of the 'Great Awakening' is the history of [an] idea" (*Great Awakening*, xiii), what he describes elsewhere as "the idea of the 'new birth'" (ibid., ix). For a more balanced account of the rise of "conversionism" fostered by the Awakening, see Marty, *Religion, Awakening, and Revolution*, 94–99. Other treatments giving primacy to the realm of ideas include Leonard Woolsey Bacon, *A History of American Christianity*, American Church History Series, vol. 12 (New York: Christian Literature Co., 1897; reprint, New York: Charles Scribner's Sons, 1921), 155–180; Willard L. Sperry, *Religion in America*, American Life and Institutions (New York: Macmillan, 1946), 143–145; William Warren Sweet, *The Story of Religion in America*, 2d ed. (New York: Harper and Brothers, 1950), 127–137; Max Savelle and Robert Middlekauff, *A History of Colonial America*, rev. ed. (New York: Holt, Rinehart and Winston, 1964), 304–305; Winthrop S. Hudson, *Religion in America* (New York: Charles Scribner's Sons, 1965), 59–82; and Cedric B. Cowing, *The Great Awakening and the American Revolution: Colonial Thought in the Eighteenth Century* (Chicago: Rand McNally, 1971), 40–74. Heimert baldly asserts: "The parties into which American Protestantism was divided by the Awakening are best understood, and most accurately described, in intellectual terms" (*American Mind*, 3). Teasing out the implications of this dictum for the New Lights, he declares: "What was accomplished in the Awakening was the translation of a single precept [justification by grace] into the quintessence of doctrine" (ibid., 38). Coupling the intellectualist approach with an unusually pejorative treatment of the revivalists are Lovejoy, *Religious Enthusiasm in the New World*, 178–214; idem, *Religious Enthusiasm and the Great Awakening* (Englewood Cliffs, N.J.: Prentice-Hall, 1969), 6; and idem, "Shun Thy Father and All That: The Enthusiasts' Threat to the Family," *New England Quarterly*, vol. 60, no. 1 (March 1987): 71–85. For a similar viewpoint, see John Corrigan, *The Hidden Balance: Religion and the Social Theories of Charles Chauncy and Jonathan Mayhew* (Cambridge: Cambridge University Press, 1987), esp. 20–58.

8. See Wright, *Beginnings of Unitarianism*, 9–27. Edwin Scott Gaustad observes that "[i]n the early phases of the upheaval, . . . the sentiments of [Edwards and Chauncy] are at times almost indistinguishable" (*The Great Awakening in New England* [New York: Harper and Row, 1957; reprint, Gloucester, Mass.: Peter Smith, 1965], 84). Bushman notes the consequences: "The New Lights were frustrated because the theological distinc-

Further, contrary to present-day popular opinion, the necessity of conversion was not initially debated.[9] At least in the Awakening's first phase, even Chauncy himself continued to assert the centrality of regeneration in language remarkably similar to that of Edwards and Whitefield: "There is nothing betwixt you and the place of blackness of darkness, but a poor frail, uncertain life. You hang, as it were, over the bottomless pit, by the slender thread of life, and the moment that snaps asunder, you sink down into perdition. . . . Who has bewitched you, O sinners, that you are thus lost to all sense of your own safety and interest! . . . Awake thou that sleepest, and call on thy God!"[10]

Given modern misconceptions on this point, it perhaps comes as a surprise to learn that the young Chauncy was quite capable of extending a warmhearted evangelistic appeal: "Are there not multitudes *at ease in Zion*, who have upon their minds no concern about their sins, no fear of the Divine wrath; but are going on calmly and quietly in the broad way to death and hell? If there are any here present, whose consciences tell them, they are the men, let me beseech you, as you love your souls, and would not be the destroyer of them, to bethink your selves. . . . You are certainly in circumstances of amazing hazard: O realize it to be so! . . . Your help is only in GOD, through JESUS CHRIST. O cry mightily to him! He may hear from heaven, and convert and save you."[11]

Nor was Chauncy alone in this regard among those opposed to the Awakening. For example, Mather Byles joined him in stressing the importance of regeneration: "The main Subject which our Lord JESUS CHRIST insisted on in the constant Course of his Ministry, was the Necessity of Conversion and the New Birth. . . . One Reason that Men fall Short of this saving Change, is the not acknowledging [the Holy Spirit] as they ought. Did men regard the Operation of the

---

tions between the Old Lights and themselves were not always clear. Most conservatives held to the same orthodoxy as the friends of the revival and made no objection to the Calvinist conceptions of depravity and salvation by grace alone. . . . The issue . . . was one of emphasis and balance" (*From Puritan to Yankee*, 213).

9. On the extensive soteriological common ground shared by Old Light and New Light Congregationalists, see Stout, *New England Soul*, 222.

10. Charles Chauncy, *The New Creature Describ'd* (Boston: G. Rogers, 1741), 20–21. Compare Edwards's own language in his well-known sermon, "Sinners in the Hands of an Angry God": "The God that holds you over the pit of hell, much as one holds a spider, or some loathsome insect, over the fire, abhors you, and is dreadfully provoked. . . . O sinner! Consider the fearful danger you are in: 'tis a great furnace of wrath, a wide and bottomless pit, full of the fire of wrath, that you are held over in the hand of that God, whose wrath is provoked and incensed as much against you as against many of the damned in hell" (*The Sermons of Jonathan Edwards: A Reader*, ed. Wilson H. Kimnach, Kenneth P. Minkema, and Douglas A. Sweeney [New Haven, Conn.: Yale University Press, 1999], 57–58).

11. Charles Chauncy, *The Out-Pouring of the Holy Ghost* (Boston: T. Fleet, 1742), 35.

Chapter 2: The Flourishing of the Kingdom of Christ

Holy SPIRIT more, there would be more frequent Converts. Men are apt to trust to their own Strength when they set about the Work of Conversion. They rob the Spirit of GOD of his Glory, and so it all comes to nothing. He it is who makes this great Change in men."[12]

Since many of the Old Lights were eventually to lapse into tepid moralism, the young Byles's evangelical fervor is quite striking: "Some think that to be converted is only to profess the Christian Religion. They fancy that to turn from Heathenism to Christianity is all that is implied in it. To talk of a Baptised Person's being afterward converted they think is Cant and Superstition.... If we speak of our being *Converted*, they ask, why what were you before? *Jews*, or *Turks*, or *Heathen*? Alas, the fatal Mistake!"[13]

Like Chauncy, Byles could put an existential edge on his message: "From what we have heard, *O let us labour instantly after saving Conversion. Turn ye, Turn ye, why will ye die*.... Now be convinced that you cannot give this Turn to your selves. Learn to feel and be sensible how attached to Self and Creatures you are. Mourn it and confess it before GOD: and tell him how undone you are without his Almighty Grace.... This divine and saving Turn of Soul, may be given to you, as you are in the Use of these appointed Means labouring to obtain it."[14]

As this suggests, Byles was under no illusions in regard to the spiritual ability of the unconverted: "[A]ll Mankind ... are dead in Trespasses and Sins. They are cold and lifeless Corpses, unable to help themselves, and can do nothing spiritually Good. They are not able as of themselves, to think so much as a good Thought: And they have only a Power of chusing which Sin to commit. They may if they please talk of a *Free-Will*, and amuse themselves with the idle Notion. But alas, they are *free amongst the dead*."[15]

The bottom line is that, as already noted, at first Chauncy, Byles, and most of their Old Light comrades shared with the nascent New Lights the basic theological tenets of moderate Calvinism. In the Awakening's initial phase, the Old Lights' concern was mainly to urge moderation and to argue for a variety of experiences of regeneration, not all of which need climax in a spiritual crisis. For example, while Chauncy granted that many might feel real anguish prior to their conversion, he observed that this was "*various* in its degree.... None have reason to call in question the truth of their *renovation*, MEERLY because they han't so *great* or *so long* terrors as others have felt."[16]

---

12. Mather Byles, *The Nature and Necessity of Conversion* (Boston: S. Kneeland and T. Green, 1732), 1, 4–5.

13. Ibid., 5.

14. Ibid., 8.

15. Mather Byles, *The Flourish of the Annual Spring* (Boston: Rogers and Fowle, 1741), 11; Byles first preached this sermon in mid-1739.

16. Chauncy, *New Creature*, 28.

Chauncy insisted that a person might know that he was reborn without necessarily knowing when or how this happened: "Don't trouble yourselves . . . with fears and doubts about your conversion, meerly because you can't relate the time and circumstances of it, with that . . . exactness which some others may be able to do. Search your heart thorowly, to see whether you are indeed partakers of a *new nature*; that's the main thing."[17] Similar passages abound in sermons by Chauncy's contemporaries, Old Light and New Light alike.[18] Five years later, Jonathan Edwards himself was to make the very same distinction.[19]

This means that in the beginning the Old Lights' disagreement with the New Lights was not over soteriology at all, but rather over ecclesiology. The Old Lights' initial hostility to the Awakening was merely a response to the means by which itinerant evangelists—Whitefield, the Tennents, James Davenport, and their myriad imitators—pursued ends that in themselves Chauncy and his allies were originally willing to affirm. Early opposition to the revivalists centered on the understanding of the ministry, and thus of the church, that conservative critics felt was implicit in New Light practice. For example, the Old Lights strongly rejected the validity of itinerant preaching and lay "exhorting" and repudiated the censoriousness of "enthusiasts" as the cause of countless church controversies and schisms.

Allegations by Chauncy and others of widespread doctrinal error on the part of untrained zealots, which figure so prominently in some present-day scholars'

---

17. Ibid., 30.

18. For example, Joseph Sewall, a New Light minister serving Boston's Third Church, argued: "[W]e must not presume to limit and restrain the infinite Spirit of God in this manner. . . . No doubt there may be great Variety as to Degrees of Terror, as to the Time Persons are kept under it, and the like. And we must take heed that in this respect we do not make our particular Experiences general Rules to judge of the State of Men. . . . Therefore such as find upon strict and impartial Examination, that they abhor themselves for Sin . . . , and so turn from all Sin unto God, . . . that they are willing to submit to Christ as their Prince and Saviour, trusting only to his Righteousness . . . and taking his Yoke upon them: I say, these Persons ought not to distress themselves, because they can't give such a distinct Account of the Time and Manner of this Work of Conviction, as some others can" (*The Holy Spirit Convincing the World of Sin, of Righteousness, and of Judgment* [Boston: J. Draper, 1741], 22–24).

19. In 1746 Edwards warned: "'Tis to be feared that some have gone too far towards directing the Spirit of the Lord, and marking out his footsteps for him, and limiting him to certain steps and methods. Experience plainly shows, that God's Spirit is unsearchable and untraceable, in some of the best of Christians, in the method of his operations, in their conversion. Nor does the Spirit of God proceed discernibly in the steps of a particular established scheme, one half so often as is imagined" (*Treatise Concerning Religious Affections*, in *The Works of Jonathan Edwards*, ed. Perry Miller et al., vol. 2: *Religious Affections*, ed. John E. Smith [New Haven, Conn.: Yale University Press, 1959], 161–162).

analyses, were in fact of secondary importance.[20] They seem to have functioned mainly as a rhetorical device to underscore the Old Lights' insistence that responsibility for the exposition of the Word could only be entrusted to those who had had sufficient schooling—in other words, to established clergy like themselves.[21]

Chauncy and his associates saw the Awakening first and foremost as a frontal assault on New England's standing order[22]—and, not incidentally, as an attempt to topple the clergy from their position at its pinnacle: "What prejudices are there in the minds of too many people against the standing ministry, tho' perhaps as faithful a one as any part of the world is favour'd with? And how general is the disposition they discover to flock after every *weak* and *illiterate* EXHORTER, to the contempt of their *pastors*, who have spent, it may be, the most of their days, in faithful services for their souls?"[23]

Chauncy went so far as to argue that New Light pastors were traitors to their own class: "[T]he *Body of the Ministers* were never treated with more Insult and Contempt than by Multitudes, and of those too, who once esteemed them the Glory of *New England*: Nor were they ever more hardly censured than by some of their *own Order*, from whom they might have expected better Things."[24] He urged that, rather than sanctioning a movement that could only end in ecclesiastical anarchy, his fellow ministers ought to "do what they can to keep one another from being despised."[25] Above all, he counseled the maintenance of the

---

20. For corroboration of this point, see below. Hofstadter takes several of Chauncy's statements out of context and too much at face value in order to make it appear that the lack of education of many New Light partisans was "one of the central issues of the Great Awakening" (*Anti-Intellectualism*, 70).

21. Gaustad observes: "Besides creating jealousies and threatening prerogatives, itinerancy flaunted [*sic*] the Congregational theory of the ministerial office" (*Great Awakening*, 70).

22. Bushman comments: "[C]onservatives opposed the Awakening [initially because] they saw the growth of [a] critical spirit which assaulted more violently than ever the already weakened foundations of ecclesiastical authority" (*From Puritan to Yankee*, 203). See also Lovejoy, *Religious Enthusiasm and the Great Awakening*, 15. For a provocative discussion of New Light hostility toward the religious establishment, see Philip J. Greven, Jr., *The Protestant Temperament: Patterns of Child-Rearing, Religious Experience, and the Self in Early America* (New York: Alfred A. Knopf, 1977), 120–121. On the elitism of Chauncy and other Old Light representatives of Boston's religious establishment, see chapters 3 and 4 below.

23. Chauncy, *Holy Ghost*, 43. Schmotter notes that "for most New England ministers the Great Awakening represented above all a professional crisis" ("Clerical Professionalism," 148).

24. Charles Chauncy, *Ministers Cautioned against the Occasions of Contempt* (Boston: Rogers and Fowle, 1744), 12.

25. Ibid., 46.

clerical status quo ante bellum: "See to it, that you *know your own station*, and *act within your own sphere*. ... Let *ministers* then act in *their place*, and do all the good they can *as ministers*; and let *private men* keep within *their line*, and do what good they can *in that*; and let them not step into *another's station*, and do the work that is proper to him."[26]

The Old Lights' infatuation with clericalism blinded them even to the traditional paradigm's most obvious deficiencies. One clear example of this is to be found in the ministry of Samuel Mather, Cotton's son, whose opposition to the Awakening eventually led to his dismissal from his position at Second Church.[27] Samuel embraced a view of pastoral priorities which was practically a throwback to that of his grandfather Increase: "[W]e are, for Jesus' sake, *to take the best Care we can for our People.—We are to shew this Care by constantly and conscientiously preaching the Gospel* of Christ unto them.—In order to our doing This, we should be *diligent and faithful in studying our Discourses* for them. Instead of employing so much of our precious Time in *fruitless Conversation* ... and *prodigally wasting our Hours* ... , we should employ our *close Cares and industrious Labours to provide the Food of Life* for our People."[28]

Samuel granted a place to less closeted forms of ministry only by way of grudging concession: "[A]ltho' I am abundantly satisfied, from the Observation of those, that have gone before me, and by my own Experience also, that if we spend by far *the greater part of our Time* at Home and in our Studies, *the Time will be most profitably spent* by us; yet ... we should sometimes *visit among our People*."[29] He even praised one recently deceased minister's pastoral detachment as the key to his powerful sermonizing: "Towards the Close of his *short Life* ... He appeared ... to be growing more abstracted from the World, more weaned from the People and Things of it, more dead to the low Enjoyments of the present Life, more risen with CHRIST and living above with HIM; and hence more vehement and pathetic in Preaching."[30]

In short, Old Lights like Chauncy and Samuel Mather were staunch ecclesiological traditionalists from the very first, stoutly defending the clericalist paradigm that had long prevailed across New England.[31] Eventually, of course, their rigidity concerning the church came to be coupled with enormous pliability

---

26. Chauncy, *New Creature*, 42.

27. For more on Mather's dismissal, see chapters 3 and 4 below.

28. Samuel Mather, *Of the Pastoral Care* (Boston: Thomas Fleet and John Fleet, 1762), 19–20; Mather delivered this sermon to the annual assembly of Massachusetts Congregational clergy.

29. Ibid., 21.

30. Samuel Mather, *The Walk of the Upright, with Its Comfort* (Boston: Michael Dennis, 1753), 23. The minister in question was Ellis Gray, one of Seventh Church's pastors.

31. For a discussion of this paradigm, see chapter 1 above.

concerning the atonement, election, and even the Trinity.³² For example, a decade after the Awakening, the younger Mather offered lavish praise for another recently deceased minister. Regarding controverted doctrinal questions, he claimed, this pastor "was careful not to insist on those Points, about which wise and good Protestants have different Sentiments and various Ways of explaining themselves," but regarding polity, "it was a trouble to Him, when any of the Children of the Land went off from the *Congregational Way*: For he thought, that *They* changed for the worse."³³ In the early 1740s, though, such latitudinarianism still lay in the future, even for Chauncy. The immediate challenge, from the Old Lights' point of view, was the Awakening's threat to the clericalist standing order. They saw their fears borne out as the Awakeners proceeded to shatter the prevailing pastoral synthesis, ushering in an era of debate, bickering, and finally open warfare. Where consensus had once held sway, now religious parties began to emerge.³⁴

Local opponents of the Awakening first spoke with one voice in *The Testimony of the Pastors of the Churches in the Province of the Massachusetts-Bay in New-England*.³⁵ This document began with an examination of alleged "*Errors in Doctrine*" whose cursory nature corroborates the above contention that these were of secondary importance. It then offered an extensive treatment of "*Disorders in Practice*" under six headings, the first five of which directly addressed

---

32. Joseph Haroutunian describes the Old Lights' drift into heterodoxy: "The Awakening had been the fruit of Calvinistic preaching. The idea of the awful majesty of the sovereign God . . . had been the dominant [note] of the preaching of the revivalists. Therefore, it was natural that people of sobriety and learning, especially the clergy, should have leaned towards views which negated such ideas. Heresy crept in unawares, and the movement away from Calvinism began its tortuous course" (*Piety versus Moralism: The Passing of the New England Theology* [New York: Henry Holt, 1932], 9). Corrigan claims that the Old Lights' doctrinal schizophrenia—ecclesiological conservatism joined to soteriological liberalism—in fact represented a subtle dialectical equipoise; see *Hidden Balance*, 30 and passim.

33. Mather, *Walk of the Upright*, 28–29. The minister in question was William Welsteed, Ellis Gray's colleague at Seventh Church. Mather eulogized Welsteed as well as Gray in this sermon because both had recently died.

34. Conrad Wright describes this disruption and realignment in the theological sphere in *Beginnings of Unitarianism*, esp. 28ff. See also James W. Jones, *The Shattered Synthesis: New England Puritanism before the Great Awakening* (New Haven, Conn.: Yale University Press, 1973).

35. Gaustad, *Great Awakening*, 63; Thomas S. Kidd, *The Great Awakening: The Roots of Evangelical Christianity in Colonial America* (New Haven, Conn.: Yale University Press, 2007), 159–160; Joseph S. Clark, *A Historical Sketch of the Congregational Churches in Massachusetts from 1620 to 1858* (Boston: Congregational Board of Publication, 1858), 169–170.

the itinerants' perceived assault on New England's standing order, and more specifically their threat to the clergy's place at the head of society:

1. The *Itinerancy*, as it is called, by which either *ordained Ministers*, or *young Candidates*, go from Place to Place, and without the Knowledge, or contrary to the Leave of the *stated* Pastors in such Places, assemble their People to hear *themselves* preach, arising, we fear, from too great an Opinion of *themselves*, and an uncharitable Opinion of *those Pastors*, and a Want of Faith in the great *Head* of the Churches, is a Breach of *Order*, and contrary to the *Scriptures*. . . .
2. *Private* Persons of *no Education*, and but *low Attainments* in Knowledge, in the great Doctrines of the Gospel, without any *regular Call*, under a Pretence of *exhorting*, taking upon themselves to be *Preachers* of the Word of GOD, we judge to be an heinous Invasion of the *ministerial Office*, offensive to GOD, and destructive of these Churches, contrary to *Scripture*. . . .
3. The *ordaining* and *separating* of any Persons to the Work of the *evangelical Ministry*, at *large*, and without any *special Relation* to a *particular Charge*, which some of late have unhappily gone into, we look upon as contrary to the *Scriptures*, and directly opposite to our *Platform*. . . .
4. The Spirit and Practice of *Separation* from the *particular Flocks* to which Persons belong, to join themselves with and support, *lay Exhorters*, or *Itinerants* is very subversive to the Churches of CHRIST, opposite to the Rule of the Gospel. . . .
5. Persons assuming to themselves the Prerogative of GOD, to *look* into and *judge* the *Hearts* of their Neighbours, *censure* and *condemn* their *Brethren*, especially their *Ministers*, as *Pharisees*, *Arminians*, *blind*, and *unconverted*, etc., where their Doctrines are agreeable to the Gospel, and their Lives to their Christian Profession, is, we think, most contrary to the Spirit and Precepts of the Gospel.[36]

Established clergy long accustomed to a regulated market for their services might easily resent this new ecclesiastical environment in which they were forced to endure not just occasional competition but steady rivalry and even their adversaries' sneers and insults. It should come as no surprise that the Old Lights took this perspective; less expected is the observation that many establishment New Lights shared their sentiments. Although Congregational defenders of the Awakening may not have made the standing order quite so much of a sacred cow, most of them were just as disturbed at the thought of losing their place of privilege. The New Lights' reply to *The Testimony of the Pastors of the Churches* was *The Testimony and Advice of an Assembly of Pastors of Churches*

---

36. *The Testimony of the Pastors of the Churches in the Province of the Massachusetts-Bay in New-England, at Their Annual Convention in Boston, May 25, 1743* (Boston: Rogers and Fowle, 1743), 6–11. For a similar expression of hostility to the Awakening on the part of one element of the laity, see *The Testimony and Advice of a Number of Laymen Respecting Religion, and the Teachers of It, Address'd to the Pastors of New-England* (Boston: n.p., 1743).

Chapter 2: The Flourishing of the Kingdom of Christ 37

in New-England.[37] In this document they took the position that while the revival's excesses were not of its essence, there was indeed much to be lamented in what had happened, especially in regard to the encroachments of itinerants and lay exhorters:

> Indeed it is not to be denied that in some Places many Irregularities and Extravagancies have been permitted to accompany it, which we would deeply lament and bewail before GOD.... We would therefore, in the *Bowels of Jesus*, beseech such as have been Partakers of this Work, or are zealous to promote it, that they *be not ignorant of* Satan's *Devices*; that they *watch* and *pray* against Errors and Misconduct of every Kind, lest they blemish and hinder that which they desire to honour and advance. Particularly, ... That *Laymen* do not invade the Ministerial Office, and under a Pretence of *Exhorting* set up *Preaching*; which is very contrary to Gospel Order, and tends to introduce Errors and Confusion into the Church. That *Ministers* do not invade the Province of others, and in *ordinary Cases* preach in another's Parish without his Knowledge, and against his Consent: Nor encourage *raw* and *indiscreet* young *Candidates*, in rushing into particular Places, and preaching publickly or privately, as some have done to the no small Disrepute and Damage of the Work in Places where it once promis'd to flourish.... That People beware of entertaining Prejudices against their *own Pastors*, and don't run into *unscriptural* Separations. That they don't indulge a *disputatious Spirit*, which has been attended with mischievous Effects.[38]

Benjamin Colman, the New Lights' leading voice in Boston and a prominent patron of Edwards and Whitefield, sounded the same warning: "[S]*ending forth Ministers* unto the Church of the living GOD is a Thing that should not be done but on *mature Deliberation*.... I *wish* before GOD and in his *Fear*, that these among *our selves* who have of *late Years* taken upon them *to go about exhorting* and preaching, grossly *unfurnished* with ministerial *Gifts* and Knowledge, would suffer *those* Words of the LORD to sink *deep* into their Hearts; to check them in their bold Career, and blind *Censures* of many faithful *Pastors*, into whose *Folds* they are daily breaking.... And it were to be *wished* that People would beware of such straggling *illiterate Teachers* and avoid them."[39] Indeed, Edwards himself had already issued a similar admonition in his *Thoughts Concerning the Present Revival of Religion in New England*: "The common people in exhorting one another ought not to clothe themselves with the like authority with that which is proper for ministers.... When private Christians, that are no more than

---

37. Gaustad, *Great Awakening*, 65–66; Kidd, *Great Awakening*, 160–161; Clark, *Historical Sketch*, 169–170.

38. *The Testimony and Advice of an Assembly of Pastors of Churches in New-England, at a Meeting in Boston July 7, 1743* (Boston: S. Kneeland and T. Green, 1743), 10–11.

39. Benjamin Colman, *One Chosen of God and Called to the Work of the Ministry, Willingly Offering Himself* (Boston: Rogers and Fowle, 1746), 10, 17.

mere brethren, exhort and admonish one another, it ought to be in an humble manner, rather by way of entreaty, than with authority; and the more, according as the station of persons is lower.... It will be a very dangerous thing for laymen, in either of these respects, to invade the office of a minister; if this be common among us we shall be in danger of having a stop put to the work of God."[40]

The point is that clerical elitism was surprisingly pervasive. By the time of the Awakening, even Colman, who had come to occupy his pulpit in a highly irregular manner, nevertheless viewed the local religious establishment through rose-colored glasses: "[W]e have seen with *Joy* and great Thankfulness to GOD (to WHOM is all the Glory) the rich *Provision* made for our Churches, through the *New-English Provinces* from the Days of *our Fathers*."[41] Nor was he reticent in staking the Congregational clergy's claim on society's gratitude: "*Ministers* are the *Messengers of Christ* unto his People, and therefore *Angels of the Churches*.... And have not *You* had *your Messengers*, my *Brethren*? ... And let a *People so favoured of God* see how they ought to *receive* and entertain the *Messages* bro't them from God by their *Ministers*."[42]

Still, in spite of their clericalist reflexes, Boston's New Light clergy were generally far more open to change and innovation in pastoral practice than were their Old Light counterparts.[43] For example, William Cooper, Colman's longtime colleague at Fourth Church, took the opportunity afforded by a teenager's funeral to speak in praise of the religious societies once championed by Cotton Mather: "[The deceased] now [after his conversion] chose for his Companions those that fear'd the Lord; and associated with some such who meet every Lord's day Evening for the Exercises of Religion, and found it of Advantage to him."[44]

Cooper had an enviable reputation as a spiritual counselor.[45] After his sudden death in 1743, a glowing, albeit anonymous, encomium was recorded in Thomas

---

40. Jonathan Edwards, *Some Thoughts Concerning the Present Revival of Religion in New England*, in *The Works of Jonathan Edwards*, ed. John E. Smith et al., vol. 4: *The Great Awakening*, ed. C. C. Goen (New Haven, Conn.: Yale University Press, 1972), 484, 486–488.

41. Colman, *One Chosen of God*, 11.

42. Benjamin Colman, *Faithful Pastors Angels of the Churches* (Boston: J. Draper, 1739), 6–7, 23; Colman delivered this sermon on the Sunday following the funeral of the Rev. Peter Thacher, one of the pastors of Fifth Church.

43. Note that the contrast on this point was a matter of degrees; as noted in the previous chapter, even the most elitist of Old Lights occasionally called on parishioners, and even the most progressive of New Lights spent a great deal of time in sermon preparation. But the latter made a priority as well of matters such as visitation and catechesis, while the former subordinated and marginalized these concerns.

44. William Cooper, *The Service of God Recommended to the Choice of Young People* (Boston: T. Fleet, 1726), 28.

45. For further comments on Cooper's ability in this regard, see chapter 3 below.

Prince's *Christian History*: "As a Pastor, [Cooper] was faithful, laborious, vigilant and compassionate. In his private Applications to Souls (and Multitudes resorted to him *in the late remarkable Day of divine Visitation*) *he was an Interpreter, a Messenger one among a Thousand*."[46] Prince himself commented: "[*W*]*e would observe, that as the Rev. Mr.* COOPER *greatly rejoyced in the late remarkable* Revival of Religion *among us, declaring that since the Year* 1740, *more People had sometimes come to him in Concern about their Souls in* one Week's *Time than in the whole* twenty[-]four Years *of his preceeding Ministry.*"[47]

Colman was much more of a traditionalist, persisting in his view of the pulpit as the near-exclusive focus of the pastor's ministry.[48] Still, even he unbent enough after Cooper's death to praise his associate's ministry in the most striking of terms: "And *such* were the Manner of your more worthy *Pastor deceased*, whose *Praise was in all the Churches*, for his *faithful* Ministry among you in private, and in publick, through the *Prime* of Life, for near *thirty Years*."[49]

The service in which this sermon was delivered saw the ordination of Samuel Cooper to the ministry as his father's successor at Fourth Church. Although Colman, as preacher, stuck to familiar clericalist motifs, Joseph Sewall offered a charge to the ordinand that sounded other themes: "*Use your best Endeavours to know the State of the Flock*, that you may give to every one his Portion in due Season. Feed CHRIST'S Sheep, feed his Lambs. Be ready to Counsel and pray with the Sick, and to speak a Word in Season to them that are weary. Say to the Righteous, that it shall be well with him; unto the Wicked, that it shall be ill with him."[50]

Thomas Foxcroft, Chauncy's colleague at First Church and a stalwart New Light, had argued for such an activist approach to the pastorate from the very outset of his own ministry: "A Minister's work does not *all* lie in the *Study* and

---

46. Thomas Prince, *The Christian History, Containing Accounts of the Revival and Propagation of Religion in Great-Britain and America for the Year 1743* (Boston: S. Kneeland and T. Green, 1744), 339.

47. Ibid.

48. Colman's sermon on the death of Peter Thacher, quoted above, features many references to Thacher's exercise of his public office in sermon, prayer, singing, and other aspects of corporate worship, but it has nothing at all to say about private pastoral activities such as catechesis and visitation. Suggestively, Clayton Harding Chapman's "Life and Influence of Rev. Benjamin Colman, D.D." (Th.D. dissertation, Boston University, 1947), the only recent biography of Colman, devotes many pages to his ecclesiastical politicking but practically none to his work as a pastor. Chapman's proposal that Colman's "character found expression . . . above all else in the promotion of peace between the [ministerial] brethren" (ibid., 184) puts a positive spin on this essentially negative conclusion.

49. Colman, *One Chosen of God*, 9.

50. Ibid., 29. For a comment on the significance of Sewall's charge to Cooper, see Youngs, *God's Messengers*, 136.

Pulpit. 'Tis not a *bare* preparing for, and circulating thro' the common *Set* of public exercises, that is a *fulfilling the Ministry*; but proper occasions are to be wisely *chosen*, and faithfully *improved* for more *retir'd* endeavours."[51] Like Cotton Mather, Foxcroft invoked New England's history on behalf of renewal-oriented institutions such as the religious society. In stirring language he cited the founders: "They united *in using the best* Methods, *with the greatest Diligence and wisest Application, for the promoting of Religion*.... Then might be seen Elders, both ruling well and labouring in the Word and Doctrine, watching for Souls, as they that must give an account.... Then might be seen Christians meeting frequently in Private for Acts of social Religion, and serious Conference.... Well might the Consequence of all this be the flourishing of the Kingdom of Christ."[52]

When the Great Awakening brought Boston's churches a further season of "flourishing," one of the first consequences was a heightened demand for religious meetings, both public and private. The regular public lectures, on Thursday afternoons at First Church and Tuesday evenings at Fourth Church, were soon so overcrowded that additional lectures were begun, on Friday evenings at Third Church and on Tuesday and Friday evenings at Fifth Church. Thomas Prince noted a further ramification: "Nor were the people satisfied with all these lectures: But as private societies for religious exercises, both of younger and elder persons, both of males and females by themselves, in several parts of the town, now increased to a much greater number than ever, viz., to near the number of thirty, meeting on Lord's day, Monday, Wednesday and Thursday evenings; so the people were constantly employing the ministers to pray and preach at these societies, as also at many private houses where no formed society met: and such numbers flocked to hear us as greatly crowded them."[53]

New Light clergy in other Massachusetts communities soon joined those of Boston in focusing renewed attention on such societies. Benjamin Bradstreet, pastor of the parish church in Gloucester, expressed his excitement in the pages of Prince's *Christian History*: "I am sure that *in my little Parish* there is of late a very considerable Reformation and Revival of Religion.... Tho' I had labour'd hard for it, yet I could never persuade *young Person*[s], to form themselves into a *Society*.... And now we have *two Societies* of *young Persons* who meet

---

51. Thomas Foxcroft, *A Practical Discourse Relating to the Gospel-Ministry* (Boston: Nicholas Buttolph, 1718), 30–31; Foxcroft delivered this sermon on the occasion of his ordination and installation at First Church.

52. Thomas Foxcroft, *Observations Historical and Practical on the Rise and Primitive State of New-England. With a Special Reference to the Old or First Gather'd Church in Boston* (Boston: S. Kneeland and T. Green, 1730), 34–36; Foxcroft delivered this sermon to mark the centennial of the founding of First Church.

53. Quoted in Tracy, *Great Awakening*, 118. See Seeman, *Pious Persuasions*, 163; and Peterson, *Price of Redemption*, 227.

Chapter 2: The Flourishing of the Kingdom of Christ 41

together *twice in the Week* to read, sing, and pray; *to each* of which *I preach once a Quarter*."⁵⁴ The numerical consequences for Bradstreet's congregation were readily apparent: "Our *Lectures* . . . are *fuller* and *better* attended. . . . [W]e have had in *about twelve Months* past . . . *about forty* added to the *Church*."⁵⁵

Henry Messinger and Elias Haven, pastors of the two parish churches in Wrentham, reported similar developments: "[T]he *religious Societies* of *young People* that were *before* found in the Town, grew *much more numerous*; and *other Societies* were set up, and continue in various Parts of the Town, both among *young People* and *Heads of Families*. And both *Family-Meetings* and *young Men's* religious Meetings are much frequented."⁵⁶ Erik Seeman notes that such lay-led meetings "generated much of the momentum for conversion" in the Awakening, as they had in other colonial revivals.⁵⁷ The fact that they were lay-led, grating as it did on ingrained Old Light clericalism, led to skeptics' suspicion both of the meetings themselves and of the various spiritual benefits attributed to them by New Light enthusiasts.⁵⁸

The conclusion is clear. All of Boston's Congregational ministers, New Lights as well as Old Lights, had imbibed to a greater or lesser extent at the fountain of ecclesiastical elitism. Still, most New Light ministers at least tempered their clericalism, willingly and even eagerly re-implementing time-hallowed but long-neglected patterns of pastoral care that seemed better suited to support what they perceived as a work of God in their midst. Old Light ministers saw this openness to change, this deeper traditionalism, as a betrayal of

---

54. Prince, *Christian History . . . for the Year 1743*, 188.

55. Ibid.

56. Ibid., 241. A number of other New England communities saw a similar proliferation of religious societies during the Awakening, e.g., Bridgewater (Tracy, *Great Awakening*, 129), Sutton (ibid., 163–164), and Gloucester (ibid., 184), all in Massachusetts, and Lyme, Connecticut (ibid., 138, 140, 144, 151). For a comment on the role of such lay-led meetings in the first stage of the revival in another Connecticut town, see Jeffries, "Canterbury Congregational Church," 525, 527. For a transatlantic parallel, see the discussion of Scottish "praying Societies" in Prince, *Christian History . . . for the Year 1743*, 86, 271–274.

57. Seeman, *Pious Persuasions*, 148. See also Stephen J. Stein, "Editor's Introduction," in *The Works of Jonathan Edwards*, ed. Perry Miller et al., vol. 5: *Apocalyptic Writings*, ed. Stephen J. Stein (New Haven, Conn.: Yale University Press, 1977), 37.

58. Chauncy, *Letter to George Wishart*. In Northampton, Massachusetts, though Jonathan Edwards also made use of religious societies, he presided over their meetings himself; see Kenneth P. Minkema, "Old Age and Religion in the Writings and Life of Jonathan Edwards," *Church History*, vol. 70, no. 4 (December 2001): 697.

fellow clergy and a dangerous concession to the false premise they perceived at the Awakening's heart.[59]

On the one hand, it is much too simple to say that the Great Awakening, even in Boston, can be described entirely in terms of the clash of opposing conceptions of the ministry. Especially after 1742, Old Lights began to articulate and elaborate a theological agenda in support of what had originally been nothing more than a reflexive aversion to New Light practices. On the other hand, at least in its initial phase, the controversy surrounding the Awakening centered on the perceived rejection of the traditional clerical model as this had come to be embodied in the ministry of pastors such as Charles Chauncy, and the corresponding embrace by pastors such as William Cooper of an activist paradigm derived, via Cotton Mather, from primal New England precedent.[60] The Awakening's pastoral dimension, so often passed over or misunderstood, is in fact fundamental.

In its negative aspect, the Awakening represented a major crisis in pastoral care; more positively, it offered pastors an opportunity to realign the theory and practice of ecclesiastical power and thus to bridge the chasm that clericalism had opened between them and their congregations.[61] This observation makes clear the faulty logic underlying common notions of the Awakening's essential conservatism. In fact, as Harry Stout has argued, and as has been substantiated above, it is the opponents of revival who ought in fairness to be labeled as "profoundly conservative . . . socially."[62] Characterizations of the revival as benign and even reactionary rest on a dangerously oversimplified typology. While the New Lights were indeed generally quite traditional in their understanding of the work of redemption, opposing the embryonic liberalism of Old Lights such as Chauncy, in Boston most of them combined this with a genuine openness to change and innovation in their view of the church, the one area in which the Old Lights remained dogmatically conservative.

In short, the motive force behind the controversy over the Awakening in Boston was the clash of opposed conceptions of church and ministry embodied in the divergent pastoral styles adopted by Old Light and New Light clergy. Arguments to the contrary reflect a misunderstanding of the importance of the Awakening's pastoral dimension and a failure to grasp the potentially radical

---

59. Michael P. Winship observes: "During the revival, old and by now unfamiliar puritan [sic] motifs emerged with a vengeance . . . and they encountered intense hostility throughout New England society" ("Were There Any Puritans in New England?," 130).

60. For a similar observation regarding Old Light and New Light Presbyterians in the Middle Colonies, see Marilyn J. Westerkamp, *Triumph of the Laity: Scots-Irish Piety and the Great Awakening, 1625–1760* (New York: Oxford University Press, 1988), 183f.

61. On pastoral ministry's function in this regard, see Selement, *Keepers of the Vineyard*, esp. 13–42.

62. Stout, "Ideological Origins," 521.

Chapter 2: The Flourishing of the Kingdom of Christ

implications of the New Lights' ministerial innovations—something of which Chauncy and the Old Lights were certainly not guilty!

Rhys Isaac has observed:

> The strength of anticlericalism in the eighteenth century can only be understood through an imaginative reconstruction of complex inner conflicts. Orthodox Christian doctrine was still generically taught and accepted as the basis for understanding the world, but there was also a mounting sense of the incongruence of doctrine and experience in a society in the process of secularization. Increasing numbers more or less consciously undertook a profound reappraisal of the meaning of life that involved an intensifying search for purposes and for sources of authority contained within the human social order itself. Bitter blows were inevitably struck at the symbols and guardians of orthodoxy—the clergy and their hierarchies of authority.[63]

For pastors who brandished New England's clericalist tradition in an effort to suppress the Awakening, the energies this movement unleashed were largely destructive, ripping apart many congregations, devastating entire communities, and swelling the ranks of the Independents and Baptists, among others. But for those ministers who were willing to rethink their role in the church and their place in society, the Awakening could be a positive force, leading to new growth and vitality.[64]

---

63. Rhys Isaac, *The Transformation of Virginia, 1740–1790* (Chapel Hill, N.C.: University of North Carolina Press, 1983), 182. For a fascinating discussion of the ministry of one New England cleric who struck numerous blows at his fellow clerics' "hierarchies of authority," see Thomas S. Kidd, "Daniel Rogers' Egalitarian Great Awakening," *Journal of the Historical Society*, vol. 7, no. 1 (March 2007): 111–135.

64. Harry S. Stout and Peter Onuf note that the Awakening brought new growth and harmony to some congregations, while for others it "merely exacerbated preexisting tensions and drove an even deeper wedge of contention into the heart of their communities" ("James Davenport and the Great Awakening in New London," *Journal of American History*, vol. 70, no. 3 [December 1983]: 559). Onuf observes: "If the separatists were 'outsiders,' it was because they were alienated from a church that was unable to provide the spiritual sustenance they demanded" ("New Lights in New London: A Group Portrait of the Separatists," *William and Mary Quarterly*, 3d series, vol. 37, no. 4 [October 1980]: 642). For accounts of the Baptists' rapid post-Awakening growth, see C. C. Goen, *Revivalism and Separatism in New England, 1740–1800: Strict Congregationalists and Separate Baptists in the Great Awakening* (New Haven, Conn.: Yale University Press, 1962); and William G. McLoughlin, *New England Dissent, 1630–1833: The Baptists and the Separation of Church and State*, 2 vols. (Cambridge: Harvard University Press, 1971). For discussions of the proliferation of various radical and heterodox groups in the Awakening's aftermath, see Seeman, *Pious Persuasions*, 131–146; and Stephen A. Marini, *Radical Sects of Revolutionary New England* (Cambridge: Harvard University Press, 1982).

Chapter 3:
Tending God's Vineyard

> Perhaps, there never was a town, in any part of the world, since the days of the apostles, more signally blessed than this has been, from its beginning, with skilful, able, faithful gospel ministers.[1]

Introduction

The Great Awakening's active phase in Boston was relatively brief, inaugurated by the arrival in New England of the Anglican itinerant George Whitefield in the autumn of 1740 and aborted scarcely three years later in the firestorm of controversy touched off by the visits of the Presbyterian itinerants Gilbert Tennent and James Davenport.[2] But the pastoral crisis brought to a boil during the Awakening had already been simmering for many years, and for many years more the ecclesiastical kettle remained hot to the touch. The polarization of the local religious community and the subsequent emergence of Old Lights and New Lights as antagonistic parties originated in what was perceived as either an assault on, or a response to the inadequacy of, traditional Congregational clerical elitism.[3]

Since the roots of this crisis lay in the day-to-day interaction of individual ministers with their congregations, and since the effectiveness of that interaction would surely have had consequences for those congregations' vitality, it should have left its mark on their records. All other things being equal, a pastor's competence or ineptitude should have been reflected in his congregation's growth or decline, something that in turn should have been reflected in its record of baptisms and admissions to full membership. In the analysis that follows, membership data will be taken as a pointer to the relative health of a particular church, while baptismal data will serve the same function for its associated parish.[4]

---

1. Charles Chauncy, *A Discourse Occasioned by the Death of the Reverend Thomas Foxcroft, M.A., Late Colleague-Pastor of the First Church in Boston* (Boston: Daniel Kneeland, 1769), 32.
2. See Gaustad, *Great Awakening*, esp. 16–79; and Kidd, *Great Awakening*, 83–137.
3. On this point, see chapter 2 above.
4. Admissions representing transfer of membership from one congregation to another have been excluded from this analysis. It would be a mistake to assume a one-to-one correlation between first-time admissions to communicant status in a given congregation and conversions within the associated parish. As Hall notes in *Worlds of Wonder*, 130 and passim, the choice confronting a New Englander of that era was not black and white, between religion and irreligion, but rather between various sorts of religion, some more

Chapter 3: Tending God's Vineyard 45

Findings will be correlated with narrative indications as to how a congregation's pastor understood and pursued his calling.

Unfortunately, not all ministers kept careful account of matters such as baptisms and changes in membership status.[5] Moreover, although at least a few of them have been the subject of full-scale biographies, too often historians have paid little or no attention to concerns such as visitation and catechesis.[6] Still, satisfactory records do exist for most of Boston's Congregational churches for most of the era in question.[7] Also, even where biographical accounts have nothing to

---

conventionally pious and some less so. Even many who by the standards of that time had evidently experienced the workings of grace in their lives were reluctant to participate more fully in the life of the local church. Pastors commonly went to great lengths in attempting to coax these individuals into applying for full membership or availing themselves of the sacraments, even going so far as to relax the formal requirements for admission to this status. For a consideration of one such case, see Ross W. Beales, Jr., "The Half-Way Covenant and Religious Scrupulosity: The First Church of Dorchester, Massachusetts, as a Test Case," *William and Mary Quarterly*, 3d series, vol. 31, no. 3 (July 1974): 469. Nevertheless, the year-by-year count of first-time, non-transfer admissions to membership in a given church is uniquely valuable as a direct gauge of that congregation's evangelical vitality, just as the tally of baptisms indicates the health of the associated parish.

5. Congregational churches guided by the concept of the church covenant had a theological motive for maintaining accurate records of admissions, transfers, excommunications, etc. Groups that rejected this point of Puritan dogma were left with nothing beyond the purely practical to motivate the keeping of such information. Therefore it comes as no surprise that local Church of England parishes were seriously deficient in this regard. It is more surprising that the records of Boston's First Baptist Church, initially organized in Charlestown in 1665, are totally inadequate, with only the vaguest indication even of adults baptized. This makes for a striking backdrop to the observation that First Baptist Church was initially Arminian in its theological orientation, and that its pastor's opposition to the Great Awakening led to a schism and the organization in 1743 of Boston's Second Baptist Church as a Calvinist congregation with New Light sympathies. See First Baptist Church, Records, City Clerk's Archives, City Hall, Boston; and Nathan E. Wood, *The History of the First Baptist Church of Boston* (Philadelphia: American Baptist Publication Society, 1899), 237–242.

6. The limitations of recent biographies of Cotton Mather by David Levin and Kenneth Silverman have already been noted in chapter 1 above. Just as deficient in this regard are recent biographies of Increase Mather, by Michael G. Hall, cited in chapter 1 above, and of Charles Chauncy, by Edward M. Griffin and Charles H. Lippy, cited below.

7. No records at all survive for Eleventh Church, organized in 1748, and only a few miscellaneous items for Tenth Church, organized in 1742; for Ninth Church, organized in 1737, records prior to 1748 are not specific as to dates of admission to membership; for Third Church, organized in 1667, baptismal records prior to 1717 are unavailable; for Fourth Church, organized in 1698, and Second Church, organized in 1650, records of admission to membership subsequent to 1747 are unavailable, along with baptismal records

contribute to this study, unexpected insights often emerge from a close reading of documentary evidence such as ordination sermons.[8] In short, although the record in this area is admittedly scanty, it is sufficient to shed considerable light on the assertion concerning the impetus behind the controversy over the Awakening that has been advanced in chapters 1 and 2 above.

Accordingly, the remainder of this chapter will be devoted to a close reading of the records of the four Congregational churches organized in Boston prior to 1710; the following chapter will focus on the seven Congregational churches organized there between 1710 and 1760. The aim will be to test claims for a divergence regarding pastoral ministry between the Awakening's supporters and its detractors. Not that Old Lights and New Lights were always polar opposites on this point; as has already been shown, Benjamin Colman, the most prominent local cleric to endorse the revival, was at the same time a stalwart traditionalist in his view of the ministry and its prerogatives.[9] What will more likely be found is a spectrum, with hard-core clerical elitists at one end, radical innovators at the other, and most ministers dispersed between the two extremes.

However, if the position advanced above has merit, the scattering of clergy across this pastoral spectrum ought to be highly uneven, with Old Lights pooled near its elitist terminus and New Lights spread across a much wider expanse, ranging from traditionalists like Colman to activists like William Cooper. Furthermore, a given pastor's precise location on this spectrum ought to be reflected in the relative health of his congregation as documented by its statistics, its year-by-year record of baptisms and first-time admissions to membership.

After all, the thesis being tested holds that Old Light clergy must necessarily have been less effective as pastors, precluded by their own ideology from adopting the tools necessary to meet their congregations' deeply felt needs. All other things being equal, this should have been reflected in a broad pattern of numerical decline in congregation and parish alike in the decades bracketing Boston's years of overt revival. On the other hand, New Light pastors who to one degree or another broke with tradition in favor of an activist pastoral paradigm ought to have seen stability and even a measure of growth in their churches as a result of their labors.

Caught in the middle would have been clergy who sermonized on behalf of the Awakening while nonetheless, whether as a matter of choice or out of neces-

---

for Second Church subsequent to the same date. Originals or copies of all surviving records are held in the City Clerk's Archives, City Hall, Boston. See Harold Field Worthley, *An Inventory of the Records of the Particular (Congregational) Churches of Massachusetts Gathered 1620–1805*, Harvard Theological Studies, vol. 25 (Cambridge: Harvard University Press, 1970), 53–87.

8. This should be clear from the part such documents have played in chapters 1 and 2 above.

9. On this point, see chapter 2 above.

Chapter 3: Tending God's Vineyard   47

sity, clinging to the old clericalist patterns.[10] Their churches were pressure cookers without safety valves; the heat had been turned up by New Light preaching, but the release offered by New Light pastoral practice was denied. Under such conditions, explosions were a definite possibility. In these churches, the record ought to show dissension, division, decline, and even catastrophic collapse. Finally, after this examination of individual congregations, city-wide aggregate figures will be surveyed in an effort to ascertain the Awakening's overall impact on the larger religious community defined by Boston's Congregational churches and their associated parishes.

First ("Old Brick") Church

This church was the town's oldest, organized in Charlestown in 1630 and relocated to Boston two years later.[11] Its senior minister over most of the interval in question was Thomas Foxcroft, who was called to that position in 1717, shortly after his graduation from Harvard College. After 1727, Foxcroft had the assistance of Charles Chauncy, also fresh out of Harvard.[12] Both Foxcroft and Chauncy followed the New England tradition of long (generally lifetime) ministerial tenure, Foxcroft holding his post for fifty-two years and Chauncy for sixty.[13]

In doctrine, Foxcroft was strongly committed to Reformed orthodoxy. This point was made most forcefully by the anonymous author of his obituary, published in the *Massachusetts Gazette* after his death in 1769: "He was then held in high reputation, as one of the best accomplished preachers; and this continued to be the general opinion of him, till there came on a change in the taste of people, and in the vigor of his constitution by repeated disorders of one kind or an-

---

10. For example, Colman apparently acted as he did out of conviction. Poor health forced other local New Light Congregational clergy to give up hope of any substantial ministry beyond the confines of their pulpits. Among those in the latter category were Thomas Foxcroft, of First Church, and Joshua Gee, of Second Church, both discussed below.

11. For a comment on First Church's meetinghouse and its location, see Walter Muir Whitehill, *Boston: A Topographical History*, 2d ed. (Cambridge: Harvard University Press, Belknap Press, 1968), 27, 32.

12. Frederick Lewis Weis, *The Colonial Clergy and the Colonial Churches of New England* (Lancaster, Mass.: Society of the Descendants of the Colonial Clergy, 1936; reprint, Baltimore, Md.: Genealogical Publishing Co., 1977), 53, 88–89, 241.

13. For biographical sketches of Foxcroft, see Arthur B. Ellis, *History of the First Church in Boston, 1630–1880* (Boston: Hall and Whiting, 1881), 181–184; William B. Sprague, *Annals of the American Pulpit*, 9 vols. (New York: Robert Carter and Brothers, 1859–1869), 1: 308–310; and Clifford K. Shipton, *Sibley's Harvard Graduates*, vol. 6: *Biographical Sketches of Those Who Attended Harvard College in the Classes 1713–1721* (Boston: Massachusetts Historical Society, 1942), 47–58.

other.... He was in sentiment a strict *Calvinist*.... [H]e was no TRIMMER, but steadily and uniformly adhered to the *Calvinian* principles, which he took to be the true Scripture ones; making them the chief subjects of his pulpit discourses, as he thought he should thereby 'please God,' if he did not always 'please Men.'"[14]

Regrettably, as this indicates, Foxcroft suffered from poor health for many years. In 1736 he was stricken with a "paralytic shock," evidently a cerebral stroke, from which he never fully recovered. For the rest of his life he struggled with a succession of illnesses that culminated in 1762 with another serious stroke. Consequently, his role in the congregation's day-to-day life was greatly diminished, with most of the pastoral responsibilities that would ordinarily have been his falling instead to Chauncy.[15] This was especially unfortunate for First Church, since the literary evidence suggests that otherwise he would have been quite energetic in his engagement with the congregation. After all, as has already been shown, he ardently embraced an activist understanding of the pastorate, urging that effective ministry required much more than the mere preparation and delivery of carefully crafted sermons, no matter how powerful these might be in themselves.[16]

John Corrigan has claimed Foxcroft as a member of a putative "catholick" party of local clerics whose latitudinarian-influenced view of religion supposedly set them against the doctrinally conservative disciples of another pastoral activist, Cotton Mather.[17] However, this makes too much of some data while ignoring other data entirely. For example, the young Foxcroft's sentiments concerning "the danger of an unconverted ministry" were indistinguishable from those famously articulated by the illiberal Gilbert Tennent at the Awakening's apogee: "The holy Ghost hath given Rules by which to judge of the Meetness of Persons for this Office.... Now the most moral Liver, that is not a thorow Sincere Convert, is notwithstanding all his Refinements under the Power of a *vain* Mind; under the reigning Influence of Pride and Lust, which must needs expose his very

---

14. Foxcroft's obituary is reproduced as an appendix to Chauncy, *Death of Foxcroft*, 34–37; the passage quoted is from ibid., 36.

15. On Foxcroft's stroke and its consequences for Chauncy, see Jones, *Shattered Synthesis*, 165; Charles H. Lippy, *Seasonable Revolutionary: The Mind of Charles Chauncy* (Chicago: Nelson-Hall, 1981), 16; Edward M. Griffin, *Old Brick: Charles Chauncy of Boston, 1705–1787* (Minneapolis: University of Minnesota Press, 1980), 34, 36, 168; and William Emerson, *An Historical Sketch of the First Church in Boston, from Its Foundation to the Present Period* (Boston: Munroe and Francis, 1812), 180.

16. On Foxcroft's understanding of the pastorate, see chapter 2 above.

17. John Corrigan, "Catholick Congregational Clergy and Public Piety," *Church History*, vol. 60, no. 2 (June 1991): 210–222; and idem, *The Prism of Piety: Catholick Congregational Clergy at the Beginning of the Enlightenment* (New York: Oxford University Press, 1991).

mind to Mistakes in his Thoughts about Religion.... Many a good plain Christian has a truer Insight into Divinity, than some of the most learned (but unexperienc'd) Scholars."[18] Foxcroft's exegetical egalitarianism raises questions about any simplistic attempt to divide Boston's Congregational clergy into "two parties, namely the Matherians and those opposed to them," situating him squarely in the latter.[19] The fact is that Mather and Foxcroft had much in common.[20]

For example, like Mather, Foxcroft was anything but an egalitarian when it came to polity: "JESUS CHRIST is Supreme Head of the Church: but he has deputed Ministers to preside over particular Flocks or Families of his People, as his Substitutes and Agents."[21] Foxcroft claimed for clergy both autonomy and a large measure of authority: "[Their] Office indeed, as it is a Ministry, relates more directly and properly to CHRIST, their only Lord and Master. However, in a Sense, they are Servants of the Church.... Yet suffer me to observe, they are not so the Church's Servants, as to be oblig'd only to obey their Orders, and execute their Votes and Decrees. But are call'd *Guides* and *Overseers* of the Flock, and said to have *the Rule* over them."[22] Still, as with Mather, these claims were somewhat tempered: "Yet neither do We pretend to stretch the power of Ministers to the height of Parental Authority. . . . We mean not to assume to our selves a Civil or Temporal Superiority and Dominion: but only assert our status *in the*

---

18. Thomas Foxcroft, *The Importance of Ministers Being Men in Christ* (Boston: D. Henchman, 1728), 18, 35; cf. Gilbert Tennent, *The Danger of an Unconverted Ministry* (Philadelphia: Benjamin Franklin, 1740).

19. Corrigan, "Catholick Congregational Clergy," 210. Corrigan includes in the latter group Colman and Ebenezer Pemberton, Sr., as well as Foxcroft, referring to these alleged anti-Matherians as the "Leverett party" (*Prism of Piety*, 24), the "Leverett camp" (ibid., 25), the "Leverett corner" (ibid., 26), etc., after John Leverett, one of their tutors at Harvard College, who had exposed them to the writings of the English latitudinarians.

20. Corrigan acknowledges that the supposed line of demarcation between his Mather and Leverett "parties" was not "utterly clear," that in fact they were not separated by any "all-encompassing theological opposition," and that the relationship between the two groups was not even "entirely disputatious" (ibid.). This being the case, it seems more appropriate to speak, not of clashing parties, but of shifting affinity groups, and to acknowledge that on many points Foxcroft had a genuine affinity for Mather. Corrigan discusses a number of aspects of doctrine—for example, depravity, regeneration, and vocation—on which Foxcroft's views were much like those of Mather, though he notes their convergence only occasionally; see ibid., 81, 94, 112, 122. For more on this, see below. Corrigan suggests that at some point Mather may have attempted a "whispering campaign" against Foxcroft (ibid., 24), but his notes provide no documentation to support this.

21. Thomas Foxcroft, *Ministers Spiritual Parents, or Fathers in the Church of God* (Boston: B. Green, 1726), 7.

22. Thomas Foxcroft, *A Discourse Preparatory to the Choice of a Minister* (Boston: Gamaliel Rogers, 1727), 4.

Church, and Right of Precedence and Rule in Ecclesiastical Affairs, according to the Word of GOD, that unerring Directory."[23]

According to Foxcroft, the pastor wielded this authority in pursuit of one overriding goal: "'Tis the Business of Ministers to endeavour the *Regeneration and Conversion* of Sinners.... The Work of Ministers is to turn Sinners to GOD thro' the Gospel; and thereby to raise up a spiritual Seed to Christ, their Elder Brother."[24] The pastor had a special responsibility toward those undergoing the terrors commonly considered to prepare the way for conversion: "[W]here any are under Awakenings and preparatory spiritual Dolours, these spiritual Parents should groan earnestly for their Deliverance, and as 'twere *travel* [travail] *in birth*, until Christ be formed in them. They should be inflamed with an holy impatient Thirst for the Conversion of Souls; longing after them all in the bowels of Jesus Christ; that of *Zion* it may be said, *This and that Man was born in her*, under their Ministry.—And they should rejoyce in the Conversion of Sinners."[25]

Again like Mather, Foxcroft saw the distribution of Christian literature as a powerful tool in the pastor's pursuit of this goal: "Moreover, as Parents know how to give good Gifts to their Children,...so should Ministers be ready to impart spiritual Gifts unto their People . . . by spreading Books of Piety among them, as they are able."[26]

Given Foxcroft's strong evangelical sentiments, it comes as no surprise that he welcomed Whitefield to Boston and into First Church's pulpit in the autumn of 1740.[27] The seasoned pastor lavished praise on the young itinerant: "We have in a fresh Instance seen this *Pauline* Spirit and Doctrine remarkably exemplify'd among us. We have seen *a Preacher of Righteousness, fervent in Spirit, teaching diligently the Things of the Lord, ceasing not* even *daily to preach the Kingdom of God*, and *the Things concerning Christ*; and *this with all Confidence*."[28] After controversy had begun to dog Whitefield, Foxcroft remained a loyal supporter,

---

23. Foxcroft, *Spiritual Parents*, 8.

24. Ibid., 13–14.

25. Ibid., 39. For accounts of the place of "preparatory spiritual Dolours" in the Puritan understanding of the conversion process, see Norman Pettit, *The Heart Prepared: Grace and Conversion in Puritan Spiritual Life* (New Haven, Conn.: Yale University Press, 1966); and Charles Lloyd Cohen, *God's Caress: The Psychology of Puritan Religious Experience* (New York: Oxford University Press, 1986), esp. 75–110.

26. Foxcroft, *Spiritual Parents*, 18. On Mather's use of books to this end, see chapter 1 above.

27. Gaustad, *Great Awakening*, 57; Kidd, *Great Awakening*, 85; Shipton, *Sibley's Harvard Graduates*, 6: 52.

28. Thomas Foxcroft, *Some Seasonable Thoughts on Evangelic Preaching; Its Nature, Usefulness, and Obligation* (Boston: G. Rogers and D. Fowle, 1740), 43.

joining in the invitation that brought him back to Boston in 1745.[29] With the Awakening in Boston by then little more than a twilight glow, Foxcroft fondly recalled its noonday splendor:

> [U]pon an impartial Review of the Times which have past over us, I am not able to form any other Judgment, than that some of these later *Years* claim, in spiritual Respects, to be rank'd among the memorable *Years of the Right Hand of the most High*, even Years of merciful *Visitation* to this People...by a more than common Energy of the *Holy Spirit*, accompanying the Word of the Lord *Jesus* unto Numbers of Souls, through the Land, in a Way of Conviction, Conversion, and Edification.—But it's confess'd, while the Husbandman has been sowing his *Wheat*, the Enemy has been busy in sowing his *Tares*: & this Mixture of Mercy and Judgment calls us to temper our Thanksgivings on this Occasion with becoming Humiliations; to *rejoice with Trembling*, and to be cautious that we don't ascribe any Effects or Appearances to the *Spirit of Holiness*, which it would be his Dishonour to be the Author of; while yet we are equally cautious not to deny Him the Glory of his real Operations & genuine Fruits, of whatever kind.[30]

Cotton Mather would certainly have agreed.

One who disagreed was Charles Chauncy, Foxcroft's junior colleague at First Church. Chauncy's views concerning the church and the Christian ministry have already been noted at some length.[31] It is worth pointing out, though, that his allergic reaction to lay itinerants and exhorters eventually led him to the paradoxical assertion that, while a solid theological education was essential to a minister of the gospel, the minister's personal experience of conversion was not. On the one hand, "as the SPIRIT does not *now* furnish persons for preachers, in a *miraculous* manner, but...by *learning* and *study*; those, who han't had the advantage of an *education*...can't, ordinarily, be tho't proper persons, to be employ'd in this sacred business; and to encourage such to engage in it, may be of

---

29. Shipton, *Sibley's Harvard Graduates*, 6: 53; White, "Decline of the Great Awakening," 48 n. 33. See also Kidd, *Great Awakening*, 171; and Thomas Foxcroft, *Apology in Behalf of the Rev^d Mr. Whitefield* (Boston: Rogers and Fowle, 1745).

30. Thomas Foxcroft, *A Seasonable Memento for New Year's Day* (Boston: S. Kneeland and T. Green, 1747), 57.

31. On this point, see chapter 2 above. For biographical sketches of Chauncy, see Sprague, *Annals*, 8: 8–13; Shipton, *Sibley's Harvard Graduates*, 6: 439–467; Ellis, *First Church*, 188–198; and Jones, *Shattered Synthesis*, 165–197. Full-length biographies include Griffin, *Old Brick*, and Lippy, *Seasonable Revolutionary*, cited above. See also Edwin Scott Gaustad, "Charles Chauncy and the Great Awakening: A Survey and Bibliography," *Papers of the Bibliographical Society of America*, vol. 45, no. 2 (Spring 1951): 125–135.

dangerous consequence; especially at present, when *so many* are ready to think themselves *sufficiently gifted* for this great undertaking."[32]

Yet on the other hand, Chauncy insisted, "[n]either *People* who call Men to the Work of the Ministry, nor *Ministers* who separate them to it, can look into their Hearts: nor can they, either of them, make a Judgment of their *State* by any Thing but what is *outward* and *visible*.... Nor can it be *known* of any Minister, on the Earth, that he is the Man *inwardly*, he professes to be *outwardly*.... Thus confining the *Success* of Gospel-Ordinances to the *inward unknown Sanctity* of the Administrators is therefore unreasonable and antichristian."[33] Responding to Tennent, and presumably to Foxcroft as well, Chauncy warned: "I know, the *Instrumentality* of *unconverted* Ministers, in the Business of *Regeneration*, has in these Days, been compared to that of a *naturally dead Man in begetting children*. But this Way of representing the Matter is evidently founded on gross Ignorance of the unavoidable State of the *visible Kingdom of GOD*."[34]

On this point as well as numerous others related to faith and practice alike, the clash between Chauncy's viewpoint and that of Foxcroft is arresting. Indeed, Chauncy's relationship with Foxcroft is something of an enigma. Although the two apparently retained a lifelong respect and even admiration for each other, they crossed swords more often than biographers' references to "the most perfect harmony prevail[ing] between them" might lead one to think.[35] Their fundamental difference of perspective in matters of religion issued in diverging assessments of the Great Awakening which were manifested in matters such as their sharp disagreement over Samuel Mather's dismissal from his position at Second Church.[36] It is striking that although Corrigan deals with Chauncy at length in one book and with Foxcroft somewhat more succinctly in a second, neither book offers any discussion of their decades-spanning interaction at First Church. Foxcroft's name is entirely absent from the first book, while Chauncy's is almost absent from the second.

At any rate, as might have been expected, Chauncy the social elitist was just as much an elitist in his approach to the ministry.[37] In his several published ordination sermons, he concentrated almost exclusively on the preaching office,

---

32. Charles Chauncy, *The Gifts of the Spirit to Ministers Consider'd in Their Diversity* (Boston: Rogers and Fowle, 1742), 36.

33. Charles Chauncy, *Ministers Exhorted, and Encouraged to Take Heed to Themselves, and to Their Doctrine* (Boston: Rogers and Fowle, 1744), 7–8.

34. Ibid., 7.

35. Ellis, *First Church*, 182; see also Walker, *Ten Leaders*, 271.

36. Griffin, *Old Brick*, 58–59; see also the discussion below.

37. On Chauncy's elitism, see Remer, "Old Lights," 571; and Corrigan, *Hidden Balance*, 88–90.

Chapter 3: Tending God's Vineyard 53

making no comment at all about matters such as visitation and catechesis.[38] For the most part, he restricted his own labors to pulpit and study, ruling his congregation with a rod of iron. This heavy-handed approach to congregational oversight was reflected in his treatment by the anonymous author of "The Boston Ministers: A Ballad," a manuscript dating from the mid-1770s.[39] Although the composer demonstrated appreciation and even a measure of affection for almost every other local pastor, he or she derided Chauncy as "[i]n church a tyrant great." Moreover, contemporary accounts indicate that on those few occasions when Chauncy ventured forth into the community, he displayed a surprising degree of ineptitude:

> The Doctor was accustomed to make his pastoral visits (so tradition says) in an ancient chaise, driven by a colored servant equally ancient, who used to amuse himself at such times, when his master indulged in a nap or in profound reflection, by driving from one side of the street to the other and snapping up with the end of his whip any persons of his own shade who happened to be passing by at the time. These parish calls, although short and far between, were generally made on a Monday morning, interrupting, on that account, in most families at all events of the humbler sort, "the pressing domestic engagements peculiar to that season." They were not seldom also attended with more or less constraint, arising, it might be, from a habit of absent-mindedness, which sometimes got the better of him, or worse still, from an irritable state of mind incident to a press of work.[40]

In short, with Foxcroft an invalid and Chauncy less than competent, First Church lacked effective pastoral oversight through most of the era under examination. This is reflected in its disappointing record of first-time admissions to full membership during these two ministers' long, overlapping tenures.[41] Aside from sharp peaks in 1715, 1727–1728, and 1756, first-time admissions were in broad decline throughout the interval. For example, more new members were admitted in 1715 alone than over the entire span from 1742 to 1760. Were it not for the surge of first-time admissions following the earthquakes of 1727 and 1755, the picture would have been even bleaker.[42]

---

38. For example, see Chauncy, *Ministers Exhorted*; idem, *The Duty of Ministers to "Make Known the Mystery of the Gospel"* (Boston: Edes and Gill, 1766); and idem, *A Sermon Preached May 6, 1767, at the Ordination of the Reverend Simeon Howard, M.A., to the Pastoral Care of the West-Church in Boston* (Boston: R. Draper, Edes and Gill, and T. and J. Fleet, 1767).

39. A photostatic copy of this document is held in the Massachusetts Historical Society Archives, Boston.

40. Ellis, *First Church*, 194; see also Walker, *Ten Leaders*, 272.

41. See Chart 1; and Appendix, Table 1, column 1.

42. On the so-called "Earthquake Revival" of 1727, see Youngs, *God's Messengers*, 110–112; and Seeman, *Pious Persuasions*, 149–154. As will be noted below, this earthquake had a dramatic impact on all of Boston's Congregational churches. I have not seen

It is significant that First Church's membership was largely female throughout the period under consideration.[43] Between 1710 and 1760, a total of 661 people were admitted to full membership; 444 of these, about 67%, were women, while 217, about 33%, were men. During the period of the Awakening, between 1740 and 1743, a total of just 33 were admitted to full membership; 22, again about 67%, were women, while 11, again about 33%, were men. This followed a pattern that had begun to emerge as early as the 1640s.[44] Over the initial decade of the congregation's existence, 447 were admitted to full membership, just 209 of these, about 47%, being women; however, over its second decade, 344 were admitted to full membership, 192 of these, about 56%, being women, and over succeeding decades, the preponderance of women over men among admissions to full membership steadily grew. The pattern was much the same in most other New England Congregational churches of that era.[45]

The congregation's numerical decline was likely associated with Foxcroft's withdrawal from active pastoral ministry following his stroke in 1736. This observation provides a striking context for Chauncy's complaints, later in life, about members' tardiness and absenteeism at ecclesiastical functions—at the Thursday lectures long held at First Church, and finally even at Sunday worship: "That prayer was never more pertinent, than at this day; 'revive thy work, O Lord', in these declining churches! And should it please God to do this, I may venture to say, without pretending to the spirit of prophecy, that there will not then be so thin, and scandalous an appearance at our FIFTH-DAY-LECTURE."[46] "Do not suffer yourselves to be needlessly absent from the house of God, but attend there in a steady, uniform course, on the institutions of divine

---

any recent discussion of the similar though smaller impact of the earthquake of 1755. Seeman mistakenly claims that New England experienced only four revivals during the eighteenth century: "the Earthquake Revival of 1727, the Connecticut River Valley Revival of 1735, the Great Awakening, and the Seacoast Revival of the early 1760s" (*Pious Persuasions*, 148). For a comment on other revivals, see Youngs, *God's Messengers*, 113.

43. See Chart 2; and Appendix, Table 2, columns 1, 2, and 3. Note that deciding whether those whose names are recorded in First Church's membership rolls were male or female occasionally involves some educated guesswork. Note also that figures for admission by gender do not exclude those transferring their membership from other churches.

44. Figures for men and women admitted prior to 1710 are based on my own tabulations; see First Church, Records, City Clerk's Archives, City Hall, Boston.

45. For comments on this phenomenon, see Hall, *Worlds of Wonder*, 14, 241; and Bonomi, *Under the Cope of Heaven*, 111–112.

46. Charles Chauncy, *A Discourse Occasioned by the Death of the Reverend Dr. Joseph Sewall, Late Colleague Pastor of the South-Church in Boston* (Boston: Kneeland and Adams, 1769), 33–34.

Chapter 3: Tending God's Vineyard

Chart 1: First Church, first-time admissions to membership and baptisms

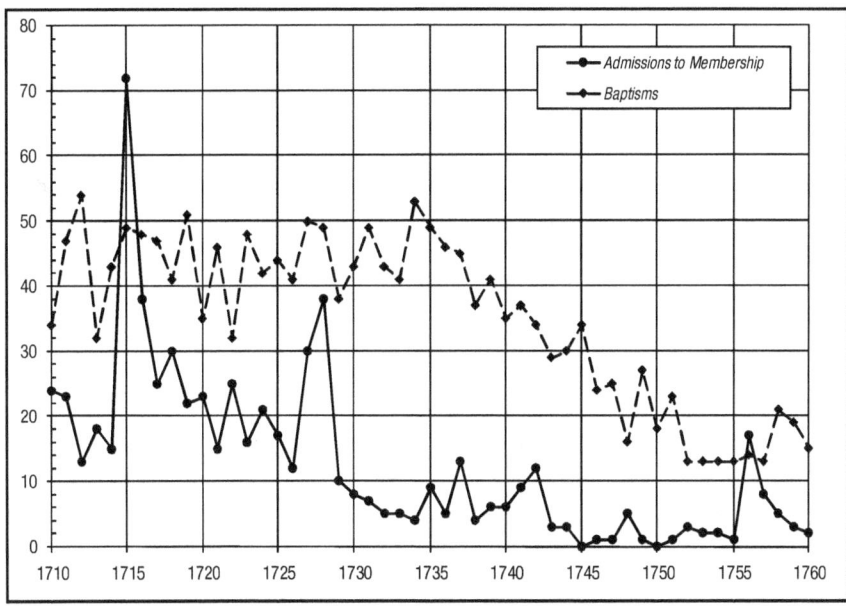

Chart 2: First Church, admissions to membership by gender

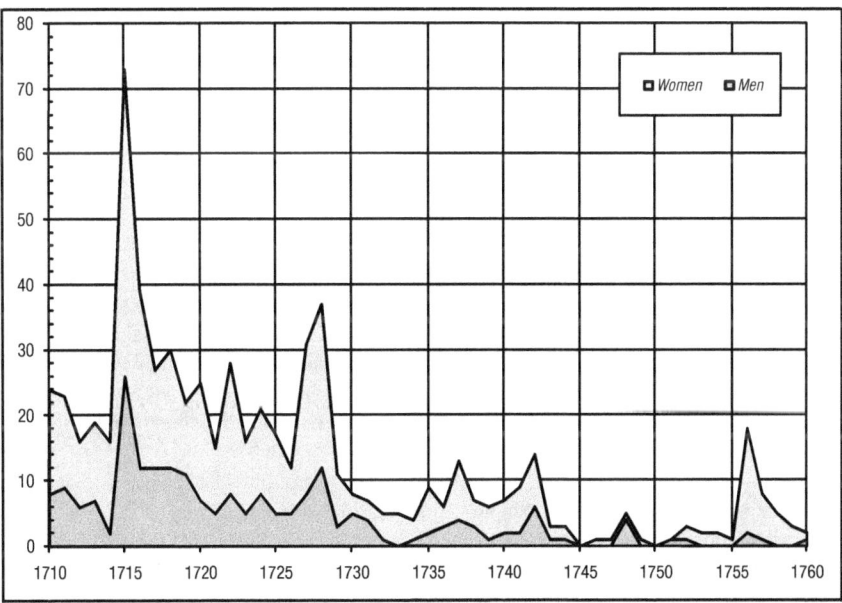

worship.... Be advised...to come seasonably to the house of worship, from sabbath to sabbath.... Too common a fault this, in all our churches, and it were to be wished it might be generally amended."[47] Probably many of the empty pews that elicited Chauncy's protest would have remained vacant even had all of First Church's members arrived on time.[48]

Second ("Old North") Church

This church was organized in 1650. From very modest beginnings, the Mathers—Increase and his son Cotton—built it into the town's largest parish. Cotton's dynamic approach to pastoral ministry, and the congregation's consequent vitality, have already been noted.[49] After Increase's death in 1723, Cotton was joined by Joshua Gee, a son of the church and a recent graduate of Harvard who was ordained and installed as his assistant that same year.[50]

Like Cotton, Gee was a Calvinist by conviction and an evangelical by temperament: "Now then be perswaded, O Sinner, to regard the solemn warnings of GOD; while Life and Death are set before you for your Choice, and you are compassionately called upon to chuse Life.... And O that we [ministers] might be the happy Instruments of saving your Souls from Death and Destruction.... We beseech you to forsake your sinful Ways, how alluring soever they be.... We beseech you to renounce your own Righteousness, to embrace the LORD JESUS CHRIST by a living Faith, and resign up your selves to GOD through him.... We beseech you to maintain a Life of Holiness and new Obedience.... And we

---

47. Charles Chauncy, *A Sermon Delivered at the First Church in Boston, March 13th, 1785: Occasioned by the Return of the Society to Their House of Worship, after Long Absence, to Make Way for the Repairs That Were Necessary* (Boston: Greenleaf and Freeman, 1785), 20–21.

48. See the description of his third wife's funeral: "In the afternoon of the day on which his wife was to be buried, the religious services were appointed to begin at three o'clock. When that precise hour arrived, Chauncy turned to his colleague, [John] Clarke, who was to conduct the exercises, and said, '*It is time to begin.*' Clarke said, 'Will it not be well to wait a little while, as so few persons are present?' Dr. Chauncy answered in a very decided tone, '*Mr. Clarke, she is to be buried. Begin!*'" (Ellis, *First Church*, 194).

49. On this, see chapter 2 above. For a comment on Second Church's meetinghouse and its location, see Whitehill, *Boston*, 28, 32, 37.

50. Weis, *Colonial Clergy*, 91, 136, 241. For biographical sketches of Gee, see Sprague, *Annals*, 1: 312–314; Shipton, *Sibley's Harvard Graduates*, 6: 175–183; and Chandler Robbins, *A History of the Second Church, or Old North, in Boston, to Which Is Added a History of the New Brick Church* (Boston: John Wilson and Son, 1852), 115–119.

beseech you to make sure of a real unfeigned Conversion to GOD in CHRIST."[51]

But the ties binding Gee to Cotton were stronger than theology alone could account for, as Gee attested in his sermon on Cotton's death: "The LORD hath taken up my master from my head, and heard me cry after him, *my father, my father*!... I have extraordinary reason to lament his death, and to love his memory. He was an instrument of spiritual good to me, in his ministry, from my early days; and very much assisted and directed my youthful studies: He excited me to publick service in the ministry; and accepted me to serve with him, as a son in the gospel: He bore with my infirmities; and helped me under difficulties: He quickened me to my work; and shewed me an example: He instructed, admonished, and exhorted me as a father; while by his condescending goodness he raised me to the level of a friend and brother."[52]

However, there was one crucial difference between them. Where Cotton had been a clerical activist, always ready to innovate for the sake of the flock, Gee took relatively little part in parish life. This was at least partly because of his poor physical condition.[53] His health began to fail after his first wife's death in 1730, and he suffered a succession of debilitating diseases in the years prior to his own death in 1748: "First a grievous Head-ache, and then a frequent Bleeding, seized him; which impaired his Eye-sight, broke his Constitution, and brought on a growing Languishment, that for these three or four Years has exceedingly disabled him . . . till he died."[54]

Such chronic illness would have made it a strain for him simply to prepare and deliver sermons. But his disposition may also have played a part in his disengagement: "Mr. Gee is represented on all hands as having been a very superiour man—not possessing popular talents, but of great profoundness and learning, excelling in argument, and capable of rising to any height of excellence; but unhappily of an indolent habit, which prevented his making that use of his advantages, which would have secured to him the ascendancy for which he seems

---

51. Joshua Gee, *The Strait Gate and the Narrow Way, Infinitely Preferable to the Wide Gate and the Broad Way* (Boston: D. Henchman, 1729), 83–85.

52. Joshua Gee, *Israel's Mourning for Aaron's Death* (Boston: S. Gerrish and N. Belknap, 1728), 24.

53. For discussions of Gee's health, see Robbins, *History*, 118–119; and Shipton, *Sibley's Harvard Graduates*, 6: 178.

54. From Gee's obituary, reprinted in Shipton, *Sibley's Harvard Graduates*, 6: 182. John Eliot, in *A Biographical Dictionary, Containing a Brief Account of the First Settlers, and Other Eminent Characters among the Magistrates, Ministers, Literary and Worthy Men, in New-England* (Boston: Edward Oliver, 1809), 216, identifies the fatal malady as tuberculosis.

to have been formed."[55] Charles Chauncy seems to have been grateful for small favors: "'Twas a mercy to this town Mr. Gee was of this indolent turn; otherwise he would have made mad work among us, as his zeal was fiery hot, his principles rigid to the highest degree, and his charity as cold as death in regard of all but those who tho't as he did. His loving ease more than any thing kept him from being [a] most mischievous man."[56]

In 1732 the church called Samuel Mather, Cotton's son and Increase's grandson, to serve as Gee's assistant.[57] However, this appointment, which should have been a source of strength for the congregation, instead became a wellspring of controversy with the coming of revival. Gee's sympathies were clear and consistent. In the autumn of 1740, he welcomed George Whitefield into his pulpit;[58] three years later, he jousted with Nathanael Eells, moderator of the Old Light assembly that produced *The Testimony of the Pastors of the Churches* against the Awakening;[59] also in 1743, he took the lead in convening the New Light assembly that issued *The Testimony and Advice of an Assembly of Pastors of Churches* in the Awakening's defense;[60] and that same year, he joined with Benjamin Colman, Thomas Prince, John Webb, William Cooper, and Thomas Foxcroft in signing the preface to Gilbert Tennent's book, *The Necessity of Holding Fast the Truth*.[61] This preface paid lavish tribute to Tennent's ministry: "When this our dear BROTHER, whose *Praise* is in our *Churches* thro' the *Provinces*, visited us at *Boston* two years ago ... it pleased GOD in a wonderful Manner to crown his abundant Services with *Success*, in the *Conviction* and (we trust) *Conversion* of many Souls."[62]

---

55. Henry Ware, *Two Discourses Containing the History of the Old North and New Brick Churches, United as the Second Church in Boston* (Boston: James W. Burditt, 1821), 22.

56. Quoted in Ezra Stiles, *Extracts from the "Itineraries" and Other Miscellanies of Ezra Stiles, D.D., LL.D., 1755–1794, with a Selection from His Correspondence*, ed. Franklin Bowditch Dexter (New Haven, Conn.: Yale University Press, 1916), 445–446; see also Robbins, *History*, 118.

57. Weis, *Colonial Clergy*, 137; Robbins, *History*, 119–120; Shipton, *Sibley's Harvard Graduates*, 6: 222.

58. Shipton, *Sibley's Harvard Graduates*, 6: 179; Ware, *Two Discourses*, 22; George Whitefield, *Journals* (Carlisle, Penn.: Banner of Truth Trust, 1960), 461.

59. Joshua Gee, *A Letter to the Reverend Mr. Nathanael Eells, Moderator of the Late Convention of Pastors in Boston; Containing Some Remarks on Their Printed Testimony against Several Errors and Disorders in the Land* (Boston: J. Draper, 1743).

60. Gaustad, *Great Awakening*, 63–65; Kidd, *Great Awakening*, 160–161; Shipton, *Sibley's Harvard Graduates*, 6: 180–181.

61. Joshua Gee et al., Preface to *The Necessity of Holding Fast the Truth*, by Gilbert Tennent (Boston: S. Kneeland and T. Green, 1743), i–vi.

62. Ibid., v.

Chapter 3: Tending God's Vineyard 59

The younger Mather, on the other hand, soon showed himself to be a foe of the Awakening. The result was a controversy that finally drove the church to summon an ecclesiastical council, in response to whose findings he issued a telling statement: "I shall endeavor to be more frequent and distinct in preaching on the nature, and pressing the necessity, of regeneration by the Spirit of grace.... I shall endeavor to beware of any thing in my sermons or conversation which may tend to discourage the work of conviction or conversion among us. I shall be cautious and watchful in this respect; and, in public and private, encourage the said good work of God."[63] When he failed to carry through on his pledge to the church's satisfaction, the council was summoned yet again. In December of 1741, it decided for his dismissal, Chauncy and Colman being the lone dissenters. The church voted by a narrow margin to accept the council's results, upon which about a quarter of the members withdrew and organized Tenth Church, to which they called Samuel as pastor.[64]

Gee's hand in Samuel's ouster from Second Church won him the lasting animus of local liberals, who laid on him the blame for the resulting schism: "He was bigotted in his opinions, which were in favour of high *supralapsarian* doctrines. He was somewhat bitter in controversy.... His passions led him to imprudence in his ministerial conduct[, so that during] his ministry a division was made in the church."[65] Afterward, his difficulties with Samuel over the Awakening continued. Although the pastor of Tenth Church avoided a direct assault on the New Lights such as Chauncy was mounting at First Church, he freely expressed his opinions to several European correspondents who later quoted him at length in their own publications. For example, two of his letters, subsequently issued in Scotland as a single pamphlet, described the revival as mere "mechanical and passionate religion" which opened the way for "Antinomianism and Familism" without any impact on the decline of "Modesty, Sobriety, Industry, Frugality, Honesty, [and] Charity."[66] Gee responded furiously, deriding these

---

63. Quoted in Shipton, *Sibley's Harvard Graduates*, 6: 224.

64. Ibid.; Cooper, *Tenacious of Their Liberties*, 203. Alexander McKenzie, in "The Religious History of the Provincial Period," in *The Memorial History of Boston, Including Suffolk County, Massachusetts*, ed. Justin Winsor, vol. 2, *The Provincial Period* (Boston: Ticknor and Co., 1881), 229, says that ninety-three withdrew while 263 remained with Gee. See also Robbins, *History*, 122–123; and Lippy, *Seasonable Revolutionary*, 37. Chauncy not only cast one of two dissenting votes on the council but rendered himself odious to local New Light clerics by composing a rebuttal to the charges against Mather which the latter then read to the congregation. For a discussion of this incident, see Griffin, *Old Brick*, 58–59. For more on Tenth Church, see chapter 4 below.

65. Eliot, *Dictionary*, 215. Ware's allowance that Mather's ouster was "on account of some dissatisfaction with his preaching," and "possibly had some connexion with the religious excitements of that period" (*Two Discourses*, 23) is disingenuous.

66. Samuel Mather, *The State of Religion in New England* (Glasgow: Robert Foulis, 1743), 107–112, quoted in Shipton, *Sibley's Harvard Graduates*, 6: 225.

comments as "shameful Misrepresentations of the State of Religion among us."[67]

With Samuel's departure from Second Church, the congregation once again had to face the problem of providing an assistant for Gee. Having evidently learned from their previous mistake, they prefaced the new search with a resolution that the person to be chosen "shall appear to the church to be a person of experimental piety, who embraces the doctrines of grace according to the gospel, and the Confession of Faith of the churches of New England."[68] With Samuel Checkley, Jr., installed as Gee's junior colleague in 1747 and succeeding to the senior pastorate upon Gee's death the following year, they got exactly what they were seeking.[69] Checkley, son of the pastor of Sixth Church, displayed his revivalist sympathies with his subscription for Jonathan Edwards's *Life of David Brainerd*.[70] Nor was he averse to preaching on Calvinism's finer points: "We are afraid there are many that talk of Justification by Christ's Righteousness, that know not what they say, nor whereof they affirm. For the Help of such we would say, that by the Righteousness of Christ is meant, his active and passive Obedience to the Law; it is this that God imputes to the Sinner."[71]

Checkley complemented his Calvinist head with a warmly evangelical heart: "[Our] Hope is founded upon the Mercy of God, thro' Christ, and a comfortable Sense that we have been enabled to comply with the Terms of Salvation. The Work of Redemption, and the Application of it to the Souls of Sinners, is all of Free Grace.... The Condition is, Believing in Christ, accepting Him as a Prophet, Priest, and King. This Method of Salvation is every Way worthy of the Perfection of God; and suited to Man's reasonable Nature. We dare not say, that God could not have found out any other Way; but as he hath seen fit to pitch upon this Method, we ought to conclude that it is the best Way."[72] Even a funeral gave him the chance to offer an extended evangelistic appeal: "Make haste to the Lord Jesus Christ, who hath 'abolished death' and delivers from the 'wrath to come.' Look to him in earnest to turn you from all your sins, to interest you in his perfect righteousness, and satisfy you by the holy Ghost. Look to him that a day of divine power may come upon your souls, that you may know by happy experience, what it is to be raised from spiritual death, by having a divine and spiritual principle implanted in you, that shall habitually and powerfully dispose

---

67. Gee, *Letter to Eells*, 8.
68. Quoted in Robbins, *History*, 124.
69. Weis, *Colonial Clergy*, 54.
70. For a short biography of Checkley, see Clifford K. Shipton, *Sibley's Harvard Graduates*, vol. 11: *Biographical Sketches of Those Who Attended Harvard College in the Classes 1741–1745* (Boston: Massachusetts Historical Society, 1960), 189–191.
71. Samuel Checkley, Jr., *The Character and Hope of the Righteous Consider'd* (Boston: J. Draper, 1748), 5.
72. Ibid., 8–9.

you to walk in newness of life and new obedience."[73] Obviously he was much like Gee both in his theological orientation and in his approach to spirituality.

Unhappily, Checkley was also like Gee in his lethargy, leaving "the records of the church so imperfect, that little can be learned from them of its state and fortunes during his connection with it."[74] He neglected to record not just baptisms and admissions to membership but deaths, minutes of church meetings, and even births, a matter required by law.[75] However, for the period prior to 1748, membership statistics set forth Second Church's "state and fortunes" in painful detail, with a pattern much like that of First Church.[76] This should come as no surprise. Gee may have had good pastoral instincts; for example, one author speaks of "his great fondness for 'revivals' [which] led him to multiply prayer-meetings in his own church."[77] Yet his frailty, like that of Foxcroft, limited his options. Moreover, Samuel Mather, like Chauncy and unlike his father Cotton, was both a clerical elitist and an inept pastor.[78] Accordingly, although figures for first-time admission to membership show a surge during the so-called "Earthquake Revival" of 1727, this is superimposed on an underlying pattern of steady decline. Ironically, the Great Awakening brought more new members into even First Church—Chauncy's church—than into Second Church—the Mathers' church, the church of Gee the ardent New Light.

One pastoral tool with which Second Church under Increase and Cotton Mather came to be closely associated was the practice of "owning the covenant." In this time-hallowed ceremony, one or more persons would renew the vows that had been taken on their behalf at the time of their baptism as infants, giving their assent to orthodox doctrine and agreeing to live under the church's discipline. A parishioner who had not been admitted to a church's membership roster would often be required to take this step before presenting his or her own infants for baptism under the terms of the Halfway Covenant; for this reason, the practice was most closely associated with churches offering baptism on that basis.

Yet members too might avail themselves of this rite. In fact, beginning in the 1670s, Increase campaigned on behalf of mass ceremonies in which the goal was that all of a congregation's members and parishioners would own the

---

73. Samuel Checkley, Jr., *The Christian Triumphing over Death through Christ* (Boston: Kneeland and Adams, 1765), 23–24.

74. Robbins, *History*, 124.

75. Shipton, *Sibley's Harvard Graduates*, 11: 190.

76. See Chart 3; and Appendix, Table 1, column 2.

77. Robbins, *History*, 116. It is difficult to reconcile this activist image with the same author's claim that Gee "shrunk from working" (ibid., 118).

78. On his clerical elitism, see chapter 2 above; on his pastoral ineptitude, see chapter 4 below.

Chart 3: Second Church, first-time admissions to membership and baptisms

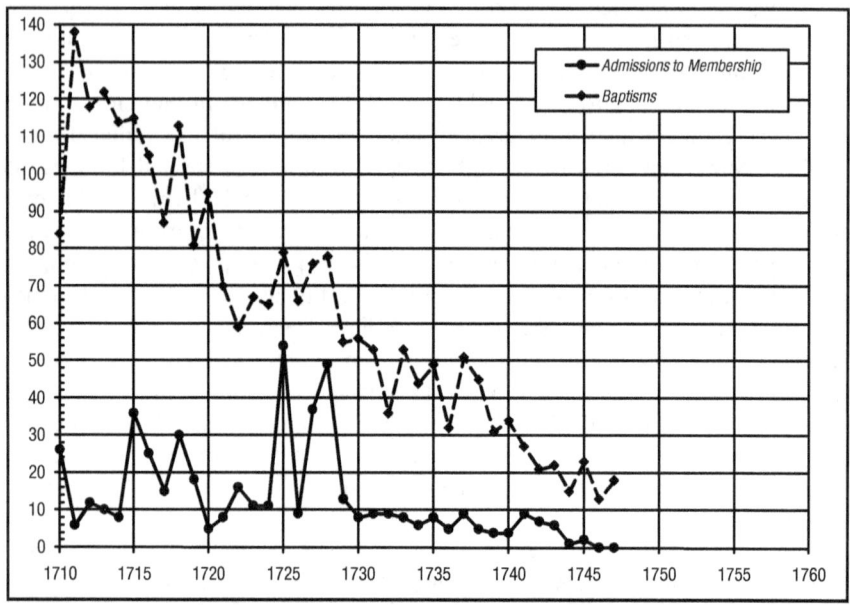

Chart 4: Second Church, covenant renewals

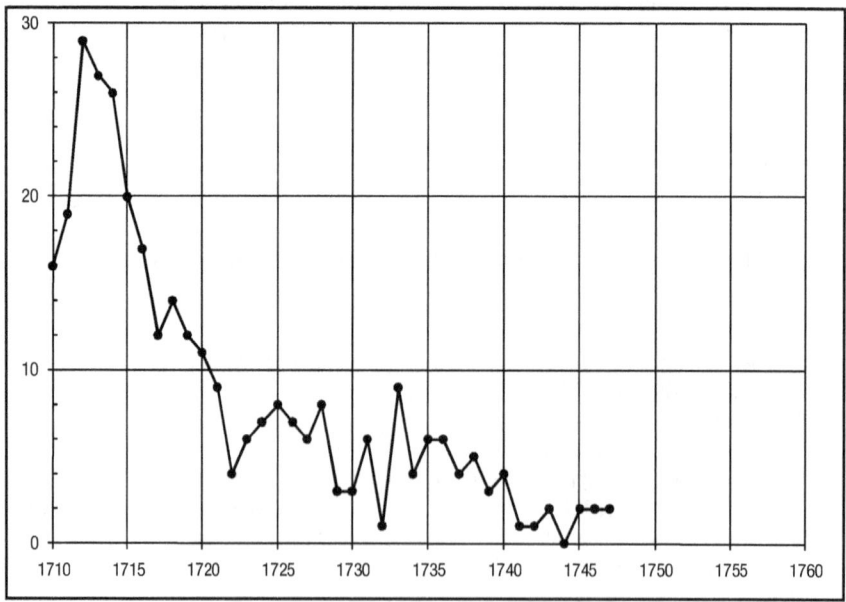

covenant together. He saw this as a means of promoting not just the church's revival but society's reform, and his position was given official sanction by the so-called "Reforming Synod" of 1679.[79] Covenant renewal was practiced at Second Church throughout Increase's pastorate as well as that of Cotton, by both individuals and larger groups, their number tracking loosely with the number of those admitted to membership.[80] After Cotton's death in 1728, the number of those owning the covenant declined noticeably, but this does not seem to have reflected any turning away from the practice as such, since the number of those joining the church declined even more noticeably. Instead, it merely offers further documentation of the church's rapidly deteriorating health.

Baptismal figures document the deterioration even more clearly.[81] After a precipitous plunge late in Cotton's tenure, they stabilized during the early years of Gee's pastorate. A subsequent sharp drop, probably related to his failing health after 1730, was followed by another plateau associated with Samuel Mather's early ministry. The shock of the Awakening and the internecine strife that followed in its wake, which led to Samuel's discharge and the subsequent withdrawal of a considerable number of members, apparently led to a final collapse.

Doubtless exacerbating the problem was the fact that after 1714 Second Church had to face the competition of Fifth ("New North") Church, a flourishing congregation whose meetinghouse stood just two blocks away.[82] But to note their proximity is to raise the question of why a person might have preferred one over the other. The answer to that question is likely to have had more than a little to do with the disparate ways in which the two churches' pastors went about their business. Second Church's experience provides clear documentation of the dangers confronting churches in which loyalties were divided. Pastors who preached revival but were unwilling, or simply unable, to implement an activist pastoral model were playing with fire.

Third ("Old South") Church

This church was organized in 1669 by former members of First Church frustrated at that congregation's refusal to implement the terms of the Halfway Covenant, which would have made baptism available to the children of baptized non-

---

79. Miller, *From Colony to Province*, 115–118; Hall, *Faithful Shepherd*, 243–244; Hall, *Last American Puritan*, 148, 152; Kidd, *Great Awakening*, 3; Carpenter, "New England's Puritan Century," 55–56. For the text of the Reforming Synod's statement on covenant renewal, see Walker, *Creeds and Platforms of Congregationalism*, 435–437.
80. See Chart 4; and Appendix, Table 3, column 1.
81. See Chart 3; and Appendix, Table 5, column 2.
82. On Fifth Church, see chapter 4 below.

communicants.[83] First Church's membership had originally been rather pluralistic, with the range of theological perspectives taken by its members even reflected in the somewhat different doctrinal stances of its earliest pastors, John Wilson and John Cotton.[84] However, thanks to the congregation's "continuing contact with English Puritanism," notes Mark A. Peterson, "the radicalization of English Puritanism in the years after 1630" in turn led to the radicalization of a majority of the members.[85]

One clear demonstration of this point came in 1667, when First Church called John Davenport, pastor of the Congregational church in New Haven, Connecticut, and a leading opponent of the Halfway Covenant, to assume its own pastorate. His call was controversial, opposed by a substantial minority at First Church who saw the Halfway Covenant as allowing them "to look inward to the needs of the godly . . . as well as outward" to the needs of noncommunicants.[86] Eventually the minority decided to withdraw and organize a new congregation, though the majority fought their withdrawal, not reconciling with them until 1682.[87] First Church was the only congregation in Massachusetts to experience such a schism.[88]

Although the Halfway Covenant's opponents have sometimes been caricatured as hidebound conservatives and its supporters as forward-looking liberals, it would be more accurate to describe the former as stressing the tribal over the evangelical and the latter as stressing the evangelical over the tribal.[89] The differences between these two groups were not absolute, as though the minority who organized Third Church concerned themselves only with proclaiming the gospel while the majority they left behind at First Church concerned themselves

---

83. On this, see above. See also Walker, *Ten Leaders*, 133; Foster, *Long Argument*, 200–204; Peterson, *Price of Redemption*, 23–50; Benjamin B. Wisner, *The History of the Old South Church in Boston* (Boston: Crocker and Brewster, 1830), 2–10; Hamilton Andrews Hill, *History of the Old South Church*, 2 vols. (Boston: Houghton Mifflin, 1890), 1: 1–204; Robert G. Pope, *The Half-Way Covenant: Church Membership in Puritan New England* (Princeton, N.J.: Princeton University Press, 1969), 152–184; and Ola Elizabeth Winslow, *"And Plead for the Rights of All": Old South Church in Boston, 1669–1969* (Boston: Nimrod Press, 1970), 1–15. For a comment on Third Church's meetinghouses and their locations, see Whitehill, *Boston*, 32, 37.

84. Peterson, *Price of Redemption*, 25–26.

85. Ibid., 25.

86. Ibid., 29. Davenport was the great-grandfather of the controversial New Light itinerant James Davenport.

87. Ibid., 31–50; Foster, *Long Argument*, 246.

88. Cooper, *Tenacious of Their Liberties*, 98.

89. For two applications of the conservative/liberal typology, one classic and the other contemporary, see Miller, *From Colony to Province*, 93–104; and Cooper, *Tenacious of Their Liberties*, 98. One recent study making a strong case for the tribal/evangelical typology is Peterson, *Price of Redemption*, 23–35.

only with edifying the saints; after all, as has been shown, Thomas Foxcroft, later one of First Church's pastors, put great stress on outreach to the unregenerate.[90] However, what was often peripheral at First Church was always central at Third Church. From the very outset, its members took "a more evangelical approach to the church's relationship to the larger world," one that encouraged them to "cultivat[e] their religion as widely as possible."[91] This approach was certainly reflected in the labors undertaken by their pastors over the interval in question here.

Though none of Boston's richest men were counted among Third Church's members, many of those on its rolls were socially prominent or materially affluent or both.[92] This enabled the church to offer its ministers generous financial support, freeing them from the concerns that, as has been seen, were so disruptive elsewhere.[93] The church first came to prominence in the community during the lengthy pastorate (1678–1707) of Samuel Willard.[94] Its pastors during the early and mid-eighteenth century were Ebenezer Pemberton, Sr. (1700–1716), Joseph Sewall (1713–1769), and Thomas Prince (1718–1758).[95] Though the ministry of Pemberton, "a notorious and hot-headed liberal" and a clerical elitist, is not of great significance to this discussion, it is worth noting that he opposed the election of Sewall, who had been chosen at least partly as a "counterbalance."[96] In spite of Pemberton's doubts, the younger Sewall, son of Justice Sam-

---

90. Peterson goes too far when he describes English Puritanism as "to a certain degree, an exclusive movement [in which] godly Puritans withdrew from their profane neighbors into private conventicles rather than seeking to convert them," so that the evangelical impulse animating the founders of Third Church could even be described as "something new" (ibid., 229, 230). On this point, see J. I. Packer, *A Quest for Godliness: The Puritan Vision of the Christian Life* (Wheaton, Ill.: Good News Publishers, Crossway Books, 1990), 291–308; and idem, "The Puritan View of Preaching the Gospel," in *Puritan Papers, Volume One: 1956–1959*, ed. D. Martyn Lloyd-Jones (Phillipsburg, N.J.: P&R Publishing, 2000), 255–269.
91. Peterson, *Price of Redemption*, 20, 3.
92. Ibid., 69–74.
93. Ibid., 122–125.
94. For a brief biography of Willard, see John Langdon Sibley, *Biographical Sketches of Graduates of Harvard University, in Cambridge, Massachusetts*, vol. 2 (Cambridge: Harvard University Press, 1881), 13–36. See also Ernest Benson Lowrie, *The Shape of the Puritan Mind: The Thought of Samuel Willard* (New Haven, Conn.: Yale University Press, 1974), esp. 9–19; and Seymour Van Dyken, *Samuel Willard, 1640–1707: Preacher of Orthodoxy in an Era of Change* (Grand Rapids, Mich.: William B. Eerdmans, 1972).
95. Weis, *Colonial Clergy*, 161–162, 170, 184, 241.
96. Clifford K. Shipton, *Sibley's Harvard Graduates*, vol. 5: *Biographical Sketches of Those Who Attended Harvard College in the Classes 1701–1712* (Boston: Massachusetts Historical Society, 1937), 381; Cooper, *Tenacious of Their Liberties*, 183–184. Sewall set aside any ill feelings he might have harbored toward Pemberton to deliver a gracious ser-

uel Sewall, soon showed himself to be an extremely effective pastor—"more remarkable for his piety than his learning," perhaps, but held in the highest respect by his fellow clergy and hailed by Cotton Mather as "a dear Son."[97]

As a child, Sewall had presumably been influenced by his father's participation in religious societies such as Mather championed.[98] Later, while a student at Harvard, Sewall himself had become involved in a society of the sort that Mather recommended for would-be ministers.[99] Mather described this particular group in glowing terms: "On the Evening of the *Lords Dayes*, they met, and Pray'd together, and Read Instructive Treatises, and communicated unto each other their thoughts on proper Subjects and Sang the Praises of God. On *Saturdayes* before the *Communion*, they spent the Afternoons together, in preparing for the Interviews with Heaven, which they had before them. And sometimes they spent *whole Dayes* in Prayer with Fasting before the Glorious God; particularly to obtain Blessing for the *Colledge* whereof they were the Members."[100]

Later, as Third Church's pastor, Sewall continued to follow Mather's example, urging his parishioners as well to involve themselves in such societies: "Let the more private Meetings of Christians be encouraged, and well regulated. Exercise your selves in such Duties as are proper for you, and let good Hours be observed."[101] His diary for the early years of his ministry attests to his own con-

---

mon on his death, published as *Precious Treasures in Earthen Vessels* (Boston: B. Green, 1717).

97. The disparaging assessment is by Eliot, in his *Dictionary*, 423. On Sewall as Mather's "Son," see Cotton Mather, *Diary*, 2: 436, entry for February 14, 1717. For brief biographies of Sewall, see Sprague, *Annals of the American Pulpit*, 1: 278–280; Shipton, *Sibley's Harvard Graduates,* 5: 376–393; and Henry M. Dexter, "Joseph Sewall," *Congregational Quarterly*, vol. 5, no. 3 (July 1863): 201–205. See also Hamilton Andrews Hill, *The Rev. Joseph Sewall: His Youth and Early Manhood* (Boston: David Clapp and Son, 1892).

98. See Samuel Sewall, *The Diary of Samuel Sewall, 1674–1729*, ed. M. Halsey Thomas, 2 vols. (New York: Farrar, Straus and Giroux, 1973), 1: 28–29, entry for December 13, 1676; 1: 30, entry for December 20, 1676; 1: 31, entry for December 27, 1676; 1: 33, entry for January 17, 1677; 1: 34, entry for January 24, 1677; 1: 34–35, entry for February 7, 1677; 1: 36, entry for February 21, 1677; 1: 37, entry for March 7, 1677; 1: 38, entry for March 14, 1677; and passim. See also Peterson, *Price of Redemption*, 81. On Mather's advocacy of religious societies, see chapter 1 above.

99. For more on Mather's recommendation of such societies for students, see chapter 1 above. For further discussion of student religious societies at Harvard, see Youngs, *God's Messengers*, 17–18; and Stout, "Great Awakening Reconsidered," 29.

100. Cotton Mather, *Golgotha* (Boston: B. Green, 1713), 44.

101. Joseph Sewall, *God's People Must Enquire of Him to Bestow the Blessings Promised in His Word* (Boston: D. Fowle, 1742), 28.

Chapter 3: Tending God's Vineyard 67

tinuing participation: "I was at a Private Meeting, at Mr. Bromfield's."[102] "At ye Private Meeting I had communion with God. Pr[aise] God. I made ye last prayer."[103] "Several of ye Private Meetings were there. L[or]d, hear."[104] "At night I preach't at a Priv[ate] Meeting of young men fr[om] Luke 2.49. I hope I had God's gracious presence with me. Praise G[od]. Oh [tha]t some may be quicken'd to engage in G[o]d's service betimes. L[or]d help me to be more diligent in thy business."[105]

Among the factors motivating Sewall to lay such stress on these societies was the unique opportunity they afforded for spiritual solidarity: "You must seek the Fellowship and Acquaintance of such as Serve the LORD with their Houses, and be ready to Encourage, Strengthen, and Confirm you in this Excellent Service. It would be very Beautiful, very Profitable, if such Houses as are Households of Faith, would cultivate an Intimate Acquaintance, and Endearing Friendship each with [an]other. And that, among other Things, for this very End, that they might strengthen each other in Family-Piety, by their Amicable Union, and by their Communion in Offices of Kindness and Love."[106]

Sewall waxed eloquent about the importance of "Family-Piety" in terms he might almost have borrowed from Mather: "*The Heads of Families should take care to Instruct their Houses, and to Teach them the good Knowledge of the LORD, His Mind and Will. . . . They should take care to Catechise their Children and Servants. . . . The Heads* of Families must take care that the Worship of GOD be kept up, and maintain'd in them. . . . In this way they must use their Endeavours that their Houses may be *Bethels*, Houses of GOD, Houses devoted to His more immediate Service; That they be Temples Consecrated to the Worship of GOD. Every Family is a distinct Society, and as such, they ought to worship GOD together, and the Heads of Families should lead herein."[107]

Of Sewall's Calvinist theological orientation there was no doubt, though some questioned the consequences: "He was a genuine disciple of the famous John Calvin. He dwelt upon the great articles of the christian faith in preaching and conversation; and dreaded the propagation of any opinions in this country, which were contrary to the principles of our fathers. Hence he was no friend to free inquiries, or to any discussion of theological opinions, which were held true by the first reformers. . . . Though he so often preached the doctrines of the gos-

---

102. Joseph Sewall, "Diary, November 15, 1711 – July 30, 1716," 78, entry for January 16, 1713, Massachusetts Historical Society Archives, Boston.
103. Ibid., 129, entry for August 5, 1713.
104. Ibid., 148, entry for December 14, 1713.
105. Ibid., 32, entry for April 13, 1712.
106. Joseph Sewall, *Desires That Joshua's Resolution May Be Revived: Or, Excitations to the Constant and Diligent Exercise of Family-Religion* (Boston: B. Green, 1716), 77.
107. Ibid., 26–31.

pel, he never entered into any curious speculations; his object was to impress upon people what they should believe, and how they must live to be eternally happy."[108] In this as well, he was much like Mather: "We are all of us Condemned Malefactors, as we are by nature Sinners; and there's but one way whereby we can be delivered from the righteous Sentence and Curse of the Law. And that is by Faith in that Glorious Redeemer who is Appointed by GOD to be the Judge of the World. . . . If we can't in that Day plead that we have received CHRIST by Faith; if we do not then appear Cloathed with His Righteousness, we shall have no valid Plea to make why a Sentence of Condemnation should not pass upon us. We must now believe in Christ, that we may be justified by Faith in His Name, or we shall not be openly acquitted in the Great Day."[109]

Sewall was dubbed "the weeping prophet," and one source identifies the evident emotion with which he engaged in ministry as the key to his effectiveness: "He was distinguished above almost any other man of his time for devotional fervour, and simple and earnest engagedness in his work."[110] He was above all an evangelist par excellence who sounded the call to conversion again and again over the course of half a century in the ministry: *"We must seek after a saving Conversion to GOD, and not be at rest until we have closed with the Lord JESUS CHRIST, as offered to us in the Gospel. . . . We must be born again, born from above, of the Spirit of GOD, or we can't enter into the Kingdom of Heaven, and therefore are not fit to die. There must be a saving change wrought on all the powers of our Souls; we must be turned from all Sin, unto GOD, or this great change will find us unprepar'd."*[111] "What are we by our first Birth? Dust and Ashes. Frail impotent Creatures, that have deserved to be consumed in the Fire of God's Wrath. . . . O then let us lie down in deep Abasement before the Lord, and cry to him that we may be born again, born from above."[112] "May such as have not yet been perswaded to close with Christ . . . now hear the loud Calls of God's Word and Rod; and fly for Refuge to lay hold on the *Hope* set before them in Him, who hath *abolished* Death. . . . O cry for the Holy Spirit, that you may turn."[113]

---

108. Eliot, *Dictionary*, 422–423.

109. Joseph Sewall, *The Certainty and Suddenness of Christ's Coming to Judgment, Improved as a Motive to Diligence in Preparing for It* (Boston: B. Green, 1716), 7–8.

110. Shipton, *Sibley's Harvard Graduates*, 5: 387; Sprague, *Annals*, 1: 279. See also Wisner, *Old South Church*, 22; and Winslow, *"Rights of All,"* 72, 75.

111. Joseph Sewall, *The Duty of Every Man to Be Always Ready to Die* (Boston: B. Green, 1727), 4.

112. Joseph Sewall, *All Flesh Is as Grass, but the Word of the Lord Endureth Forever* (Boston: S. Kneeland and T. Green, 1741), 15–16.

113. Joseph Sewall, *The Character and Reward of the Faithful Ministers of Christ* (Boston: S. Kneeland, 1763), 18.

Sewall's evangelistic appeals rang with urgency because, at least from his perspective, not many of his listeners seemed to grasp the gravity of their plight. In the years prior to the Great Awakening, he cast a concerned eye over New England's spiritual landscape: "I suppose few, if any, can remember the time when People were so generally Awakened, and brought to say with trembling, *What must we do to be saved.*"[114] Since revival came at the initiative of God's Spirit, its absence demonstrated that the Spirit was grieved with New England and its churches: "We have in a dreadful manner vexed the Holy Spirit that hath been striving with us by Ordinances and Providences. And now it seems as if the Holy Spirit did in a great measure cease striving with Men. Few comparatively have any remarkable Convictions under the Preaching of the Word. Conversions are rare, and dubious."[115] He responded, though, not with despair but with a call to prayer: "O then let us seek of God His Holy Spirit to revive His Work among us! and that importunately and incessantly, being sensible of our great need of His saving Influences."[116] "O let us then lift up the hands that hang down, let us continue instant in Prayer to the God of all Grace that He would by His Spirit carry on this Work 'till a sincere Repentance and thorough Reformation be wrought among this People."[117]

Sewall held out hope of a happier time to be inaugurated by the longed-for outpouring of God's Spirit: "And is not the Day near when the Fountain . . . shall be in a signal manner opened in the extensive Preaching of the Gospel, and the abundant Effusions of the Spirit of Grace[?] . . . Let us then pray and wait; believe and not make haste. . . . And in our Prayers, let us be earnest with God that He would pour out His Spirit upon us, and His Blessing upon our Offspring."[118] When that time finally arrived, he stressed the contrast between the lean years that had gone before and this new day of harvest: "At sometimes the Spirit is awfully restrain'd, and then Conversions are rare and doubtful. At other Seasons, God is pleas'd to pour out His Spirit upon his People, and then his Works of Grace, are as the Light which goeth forth. . . . Convictions and Conversions become more frequent and apparent, so far as our Judgment reacheth. It is true, the saving Conversion of others can't be certainly known by us in the ordinary Way, because we are not able to look directly into the Heart, but must judge by outward Appearances. And therefore we ought to exercise Judgment

---

114. Joseph Sewall, *Repentance the Sure Way to Escape Destruction* (Boston, D. Henchman, 1727), 29.

115. Joseph Sewall, *The Holy Spirit the Gift of God Our Heavenly Father, to Them That Ask Him* (Boston: D. Henchman, 1728), 25.

116. Ibid., 26.

117. Sewall, *Repentance*, 29.

118. Ibid., 30–31.

with Charity. But then there are sometimes Fruits of the Spirit so evident, that they can't be conceal'd or denied."[119]

It should come as no surprise that Sewall not only welcomed George Whitefield into his pulpit in 1740 but continued to back him throughout the ensuing controversy.[120] Sewall surely winced at the revival's irregularities, but he joined other New Light clergy in judging these to be either benign or, at worst, peripheral: "As for the *Out-Cries, Tremblings*, and *Faintings* which have been experienced in some Places, I apprehend the Cause must be judged of by the Effect.... If such Persons therefore have an holy Awe of God, a deep Humiliation under the Sense of Sin, and earnest Concern about Deliverance from it; here is the Finger of God.... But then, if any would indulge themselves in these Out-Cries, especially in time of publick Worship, when there is no real Necessity for it, and they might restrain themselves; I think they are disorderly, and do that which has a Tendency to disturb the quiet attentive hearing of God's Word. Nor may we make a Judgment of a Work, whether genuine or no, meerly by such extraordinary Commotions."[121]

Such "Commotions" ought to motivate God's people, not to reject the revival, but to pray that it be strengthened and purified: "In this remarkable Season, let us be earnest with God for the more plentiful Effusions of his Spirit, that there may stand up an *exceeding great Army* to fight the Battles of the Lord, and take the Kingdom of Heaven with an holy Violence.... And let us avoid every Thing that has a Tendency to quench the Spirit, and so to hinder the Success of the Gospel."[122] Indeed, the very coming of the Awakening ought to demonstrate that such prayers were not in vain: "We have formerly once and again observed such Days of Prayer to seek the Lord for spiritual Blessings, the comprehensive sum of which is the *Gift of the Holy Ghost*. And may we not hope that God is now giving a gracious Answer to the Supplications which have in this Way been offered to him in Years past? And ought not this to encourage us now to pray the more earnestly? Yes surely."[123]

Ever the evangelist, Sewall offered the same motivation to those hesitating on the brink of commitment: "The Fountain is still open, and full as ever. The Merits and Righteousness of CHRIST have lost nothing of their Virtue, by being communicated to such vast Numbers; and the Influences of the blessed Spirit of GOD are as powerful to cleanse and refresh your Souls, as ever they were. And I may add, that the present *remarkable Day of Grace*, in which GOD is giving

---

119. Sewall, *Convincing the World*, 17.
120. Whitefield, *Journals*, 459, 464, 469, 472, 528, 531–532, 534; Shipton, *Sibley's Harvard Graduates*, 5: 387; Wisner, *Old South Church*, 28–29; Hill, *Old South Church*, 1: 506; Kidd, *Great Awakening*, 85, 96, 169.
121. Sewall, *God's People Must Enquire*, 25–26.
122. Sewall, *Convincing the World*, 131.
123. Ibid., 19–20.

spiritual Blessings with a liberal Hand, may well encourage you to go to GOD as to a Fountain opened in CHRIST for the Supply of all your Wants. O be persuaded then to hearken and consider, to hear and obey the Calls of the Gospel, that your Souls may live!"[124] For those already enlisted in the ranks, there was the further call to cooperation in the cause of Christ: "And let us then all unite in our diligent and prudent Endeavours to promote this Work, each one keeping within his own line. . . . And let us unite our Endeavours in this great and difficult Work, as Fellow-Helpers to the Truth. . . . And let the Success which God hath of late given to the Ministry of the Word above what we have known in Times past, animate us to labour more abundantly. . . . And let us all unite in seeking the advancement of Christ's Kingdom among us."[125]

Sewall himself constantly strove to that end. His obituary recalled his unceasing labors, not just from the pulpit, but in pastoral ministry among the members of his congregation: "He discharged the other parts of his sacred trust with prudence and fidelity, diligence and impartiality, warning every man and teaching every man in all wisdom, not only publicly but from house to house, that he might present every man perfect in Christ Jesus. . . . There is reason to believe, that no small number, now among the spirits of just men made perfect, are blessing and praising God for him, as the instrument of that happiness they now enjoy; and that there are many yet living, who are the seals of his ministry, and will be his crown and joy in the day of the Lord."[126]

Sewall's co-laborer for most of his tenure at Third Church was Thomas Prince, his friend and Harvard classmate.[127] While in college, Prince had been a member of the same religious society that had so affected Sewall and impressed Cotton Mather.[128] Like Sewall, Prince was bound to Mather by ties of love and admiration: "For *my self*, I must always account the particular Intimacy [Mather] was pleased to favour me with, as one of the richest Blessings of all my Life. And I can't but reflect with the deepest Regret on the precious Advantages I

---

124. Joseph Sewall, *The Thirsty Invited to Come, and Take the Waters of Life Freely* (Boston: Rogers and Fowle, 1742), 23.

125. Sewall, *God's People Must Enquire*, 20–21, 30.

126. The obituary, from the July 3, 1769, issue of the Boston *Evening-Post*, is reprinted as an appendix to Chauncy, *Death of Sewall*, 35–39; the quoted passage is from ibid., 37.

127. For biographical sketches of Prince, see Shipton, *Sibley's Harvard Graduates*, 5: 341–368; Sprague, *Annals*, 1: 304–307; John Alden, "The Reverend Thomas Prince Recollected; or, The Early Libraries of the Old South Church Reviewed," typewritten ms in the Congregational Library, Boston; and Francis Everett Blake, *History of the Town of Princeton in the County of Worcester and Commonwealth of Massachusetts*, 2 vols. (Princeton, Mass.: By the Town, 1915), 1: 109–121. For a comment on Prince's long-standing friendship with Sewall, see Peterson, *Price of Redemption*, 135.

128. Shipton, *Sibley's Harvard Graduates*, 5: 341–342; on this society, see above.

have carelessly lost, thro' a fond expectation of his continuing longer."[129] Prince was perhaps a bit more tolerant than Sewall and Mather of other theological viewpoints. One source notes: "Although Cotton Mather once warned him to be less complacent with heretics, he continued to regard toleration as a virtue."[130] Yet, like Sewall and Mather, he himself was a committed Calvinist; doubtless this led him to sponsor the young Jonathan Edwards and to facilitate, together with William Cooper of Fourth Church, the printing of Edwards's forthright Calvinist sermon, *God Glorified in Man's Dependence*, his first published work.[131]

Prince held firmly to the Calvinist perspective on humanity's plight apart from Christ, responding, like Sewall, Mather, and Edwards, with ardent evangelistic appeals: "Death and Hell are open before us, eternal Destruction has no covering, and now may be the only Season we may have to escape them. To morrow, yea to night may be too late for ever.... Now therefore, Hearken to the Calls of GOD, and no longer dare to harden your Hearts thro' the Deceitfulness of Sin. Now is the only certain accepted Time: and Now, if you Improve it, is the certain happy Day, the Hour of your Eternal Salvation."[132] "But O! how shall we come to know that we are of the Blessed Number [of the redeemed]? Why, we must Receive the Words of CHRIST, and Keep them, Believe in, Embrace and Follow Him.... Now *this Word* ... is the *glorious Gospel*. And O! how long and often, has it been Preached to You.... But O! how many are there that are yet unperswaded? ... Yet, thro' the Riches of his Grace and Patience, You have now another Opportunity and Invitation more: O! *today, if Ye will hear his Voice, harden not your Hearts!*"[133]

---

129. Prince, *The Departure of Elijah Lamented*, 23; this sermon was a memorial to Mather after his death. See also Mather's many letters to Prince collected in his *Diary*: 2: 512, 596, 681, 683, 684, 685, 686, 688, 792, 811, 812, 813, 815, 816. For yet another pointer to Mather's influence, see *The Prince Library: A Catalogue of the Collection of Books and Manuscripts Which Formerly Belonged to the Reverend Thomas Prince, and Was by Him Bequeathed to the Old South Church, and Is Now Deposited in the Public Library of the City of Boston* (Boston: Alfred Mudge and Son, 1870), which lists titles by Pietists like August Hermann Francke, many volumes by Richard Baxter, and page after page of books by Cotton Mather himself. See also Silverman, *Life and Times*, 401; Shipton, *Sibley's Harvard Graduates*, 5: 350; and Alden, "Thomas Prince Recollected."

130. Shipton, *Sibley's Harvard Graduates*, 5: 352. See also Winslow, *"Rights of All,"* 74–75; and Peterson, *Price of Redemption*, 136.

131. Iain H. Murray, *Jonathan Edwards: A New Biography* (Carlisle, Penn.: Banner of Truth Trust, 1987), 107–108; George M. Marsden, *Jonathan Edwards: A Life* (New Haven, Conn.: Yale University Press, 2003), 141–142.

132. Thomas Prince, *Morning Health No Security against Sudden Arrest of Death before Night* (Boston: D. Henchman, 1727), 24–25.

133. Thomas Prince, *The Dying Prayer of Christ, for His People's Preservation and Unity* (Boston: S. Kneeland and T. Green, 1732), 21–22.

Chapter 3: Tending God's Vineyard 73

As a preacher, Prince was unquestionably less effective than Sewall, reading his sermon texts in a droning monotone and encumbering them with more learning than his parishioners could readily digest.[134] In his later sermons he began to set aside the scholarly apparatus in favor of a more forthright, emotional appeal, but this likely remained a weakness, as is suggested by his daughter Deborah's dying words to him: "*O Sir, . . . that you may be more fervent in your Ministry, and in exhorting and expostulating with Sinners!*"[135] However, he showed the influence of Cotton Mather in his recognition that the pulpit was only one aspect of a pastor's ministry.[136] For example, like Mather, he published extensively, and during the era of the Great Awakening he even turned to journalism, editing and publishing *The Christian History*, America's first religious periodical, as a conduit for news of revival that was itself intended to foster further revival.[137] Predictably, Charles Chauncy saw Prince's publication instead as "the grand Engine of fomenting Divisions, and making Separations in our Churches, and continuing the false Spirit of Error and Delusion in the Land."[138]

Another aspect of ministry on which Prince, like Mather, put much stress was in-home visitation and catechesis. He spoke of the importance of such hands-on pastoral care in words he might almost have borrowed from Mather: "We must endeavour to know and be familiarly acquainted with You. We must *be with You at all seasons, and go from House to House*. . . . We must not only *Teach You Publickly*, but *also from House to House, Testifying—Repentance towards GOD and Faith towards Our* LORD JESUS CHRIST. . . . We must watch over You, and give an Account of You to CHRIST that imploys Us, and commits the Care of You to Us. . . . We must give an Account of the Success and Consequence of Our painful Ministry."[139]

Prince's embrace of such pastoral tools gave his ministry a breadth and depth that mere sermonizers could not match, as Sewall noted: "He was an able Minister of the New-Testament; a *Scribe* instructed to the Kingdom of Heaven,

---

134. Thus Wisner, *Old South Church*, 24. See also Winslow, *"Rights of All,"* 74; and Shipton, *Sibley's Harvard Graduates*, 5: 347.

135. Quoted in Thomas Prince, *The Sovereign God Acknowledged and Blessed, Both in Giving and in Taking Away* (Boston: Rogers and Fowle, 1744), 31; this was a funeral sermon for his daughter. For more on Deborah, see Hill, *Old South Church*, 1: 547–549; and see below.

136. For a discussion of Prince's daily schedule, which was much like that of Mather, see Peterson, *Price of Redemption*, 128.

137. Gaustad, *Great Awakening*, 58; Peterson, *Price of Redemption*, 139–141.

138. Chauncy's comments are from the October 15, 1744, issue of the Boston *Evening-Post*, quoted in Shipton, *Sibley's Harvard Graduates*, 5: 357.

139. Thomas Prince, *A Sermon Delivered by Thomas Prince, M.A., on Wednesday, October 1, 1718, at His Ordination to the Pastoral Charge of the South-Church in Boston, N.E. in Conjunction with the Reverend Mr. Joseph Sewall* (Boston: J. Franklin, 1718), 31, 40.

who could bring forth out of his Treasure, Things old and new.... His *private Conversation* was entertaining and instructive. As a tender and faithful Pastor, he was ready to warn them that are unruly, to comfort the feeble-minded, and resolve the doubting Believer.... I trust there are a Number of you who will be found the Seals of his Ministry, his Crown and Joy, in the Day of Christ's Appearing."[140]

As might be expected, the Awakening's arrival found Prince positioned on the side of Whitefield and the New Lights, serving locally as one of the Awakening's most effective, albeit provocative, champions.[141] When the flood tide of revival first swept over Boston in the fall of 1740, he and other local ministers used religious societies as channels to contain and direct the torrent: "[P]rivate societies for religious exercises, both of younger and elder persons, both of males and females by themselves, in several parts of the town, now increased to a much greater number than ever, viz. to near the number of thirty, meeting on Lord's Day, Monday, Wednesday, and Thursday evenings; so that the people were constantly employing the ministers to pray and preach at those societies, as also at many private houses, where no formed society met: and such numbers flocked to hear us as greatly crowded them."[142] Prince's own daughter Deborah was involved in one of these groups; after her untimely death, he gave thanks for "the Female *Society* to which she join'd for the most indearing Exercise of social Piety."[143]

Sewall and Prince worked well together because they pursued a common task with complementary skills.[144] As Third Church weathered the storm and stress of the next century's religious controversies, their joint pastorate lingered in parishioners' memories as a time of wonderful tranquility. One early historian of Old South referred to the "great religious prosperity" the congregation had enjoyed under their leadership.[145] According to another, their ministry was practically unique in that regard: "Forty years were these excellent men ... associated in

---

140. Joseph Sewall, *The Duty, Character, and Reward of Christ's Faithful Servants* (Boston: S. Kneeland, 1758), 15; Sewall delivered this sermon the Sunday after Prince's death.

141. Eleazar Wheelock, the Connecticut itinerant, hailed him as "dear Mr. Prince"; see the extract from Wheelock's journal reprinted in Tracy, *Great Awakening*, 203. See also Sprague, *Annals*, 1: 304; Shipton, *Sibley's Harvard Graduates*, 5: 355–356; Eliot, *Dictionary*, 391–391; Wisner, *Old South Church*, 28–29; Kidd, *Great Awakening*, 115; and Whitefield, *Journals*, 528 and passim.

142. Thomas Prince, *An Account of the Revival of Religion in Boston, in the Years 1740–1–2–3* (n.p., n.d.; reprint, Boston: Samuel Armstrong, 1823), 21–22; this volume is a multi-year compilation of individual issues of Prince's religious newspaper, *The Christian History*.

143. Prince, *Sovereign God*, 25.

144. Hill, *Old South Church*, 2: 41.

145. Ibid., 1: 395.

Chapter 3: Tending God's Vineyard 75

the responsibilities and labors of the pastoral office in this congregation; furnishing an example of mutual affection and union of purpose and pursuit, to which the annals of collegiate charges will be searched for a parallel, I fear, almost in vain."[146] As has been seen, the "union of purpose and pursuit" binding them together had two components: their shared theological stance of evangelical Calvinism that enabled them to present a united front in support of the Great Awakening, thus warding off the strife and schism that bedeviled so many other churches; and their shared ministerial stance of pastoral activism that enabled them not only to control but to deepen the course of the revival in their congregation. As a result, it flourished while others declined, eventually outgrowing its old meetinghouse and in 1730 moving into the larger facility that still stands today.[147]

Membership statistics corroborate Third Church's robust health during the era under consideration.[148] First-time admissions surged not only following the earthquakes of 1727 and 1755, as in the other congregations already examined, but also during the Great Awakening.[149] One history of the congregation notes: "Within six months from the end of January 1740–1 were three score joined to our communicants ... [and] many more ... would have entered [but for their scruples concerning communion]."[150] These sharp spikes were superimposed on an underlying pattern that began a very shallow decline only after the establishment in 1719 of Sixth ("New South") Church, whose meetinghouse stood just three blocks away.

As with First Church, more women than men were admitted to first-time membership during the period under consideration, though at Third Church, women's preponderance was somewhat less marked.[151] Between 1710 and 1760, a total of 750 people were admitted to full membership, 479 of them, about 64%, being female. During the Great Awakening, between 1740 and 1743, the gender gap narrowed still further, 120 being admitted to full membership, just 67

---

146. Wisner, *Old South Church*, 24.
147. Winslow, *"Rights of All,"* 79–86; Hill, *Old South Church*, 1: 437, 439–441, 446–451; McKenzie, "Provincial Period," 227.
148. See Chart 5; and Appendix, Table 1, column 3.
149. For discussions of the effect of the earthquakes of 1727 and 1755 on Third Church, see Peterson, *Price of Redemption*, 140–141; and Hill, *Old South Church*, 1: 422–423, 2: 21–22. For a description of the Awakening's numerical impact on Third Church, see ibid., 1: 519.
150. Ibid.
151. See Chart 6; and Appendix, Table 2, columns 4, 5, and 6. Again, note that deciding whether those whose names are recorded in Third Church's membership records were male or female occasionally involves a bit of guesswork. Note also that figures for admission by gender do not exclude those transferring their membership from other churches.

Chart 5: Third Church, first-time admissions to membership and baptisms

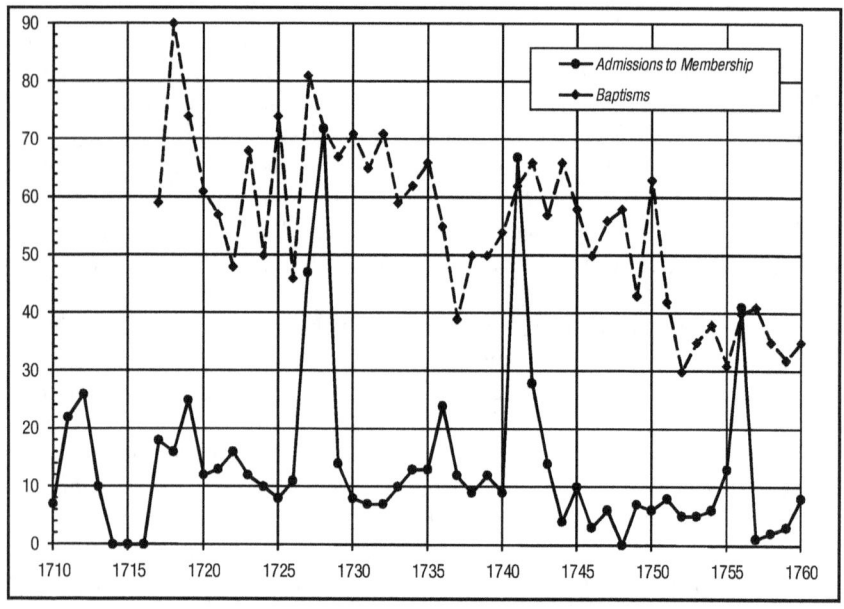

Chart 6: Third Church, admissions to membership by gender

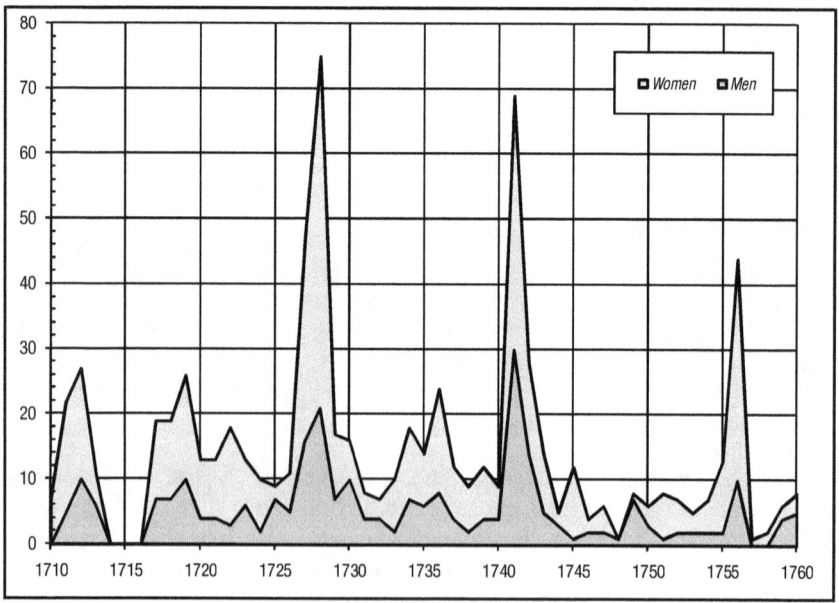

Chapter 3: Tending God's Vineyard

of whom, about 56%, were female. This documents what several scholars have identified as the Awakening's effect of narrowing the gender gap in at least some New Light congregations.[152]

Though Pemberton seems to have made no use of covenant renewal, his predecessor, Willard, encouraged it throughout his tenure; on Friday, April 30, 1680, he even led the entire congregation in owning the covenant, members and parishioners alike.[153] During this era, covenant renewal, like membership, was relatively feminized; between 1669 and 1706, a total of 653 people owned the covenant, 417 of them, about 64%, being female.[154] Pemberton's successors, Sewall and Prince, encouraged the practice as well, though during their era, it became relatively masculinized; between 1717 and 1760, a total of 269 people owned the covenant, only 127 of them, about 47%, being female.[155] For the duration of the Awakening, this masculinization became even more pronounced; between 1740 and 1743, a total of 46 people owned the covenant, just 20 of them, about 43%, being female. It seems that even in such a New Light bastion, many men who might otherwise have applied for full membership preferred covenant renewal instead; perhaps they were put off by the creeping feminization of terminology and imagery associated with the evangelical conversion narrative.[156] The total number of those owning the covenant or admitted to first-time membership between 1740 and 1743 was 166; of these, 87, about 52%, were female, while 79, about 48%, were male. This demonstrates more clearly yet the Awakening's impact even on the relatively narrow gender gap at Third Church.

The congregation's baptismal figures remained stable several decades longer than did its figures for first-time admission to membership.[157] A slow downward trend started only after about 1750, by which time several other Congregational churches had been organized and both Sewall and Prince were well advanced in years. The experience of Third Church demonstrates that the Awakening was as much about ecclesiology as about soteriology, that consequently what a pastor did was just as important as what he said, and that pastors who grasped this

---

152. For discussions of this point, see Cowing, "Sex and Preaching"; Walsh, "Great Awakening"; Minkema, "Old Age and Religion," 701; and Seeman, *Pious Persuasions*, 149.

153. For more on Willard's mass ceremony of covenant renewal, see Peterson, *Price of Redemption*, 48, 137; and Kidd, *Great Awakening*, 4.

154. See Chart 7; and Appendix, Table 4.

155. See Chart 8; and Appendix, Table 3, column 2, and Table 4. As in nn. 43 and 155 above, decisions as to the gender of those owning the covenant occasionally involve an element of conjecture.

156. Seeman, *Pious Persuasions*, 149.

157. See Chart 5; and Appendix, Table 5, column 3.

Chart 7: Third Church, covenant renewals by gender, 1669–1709

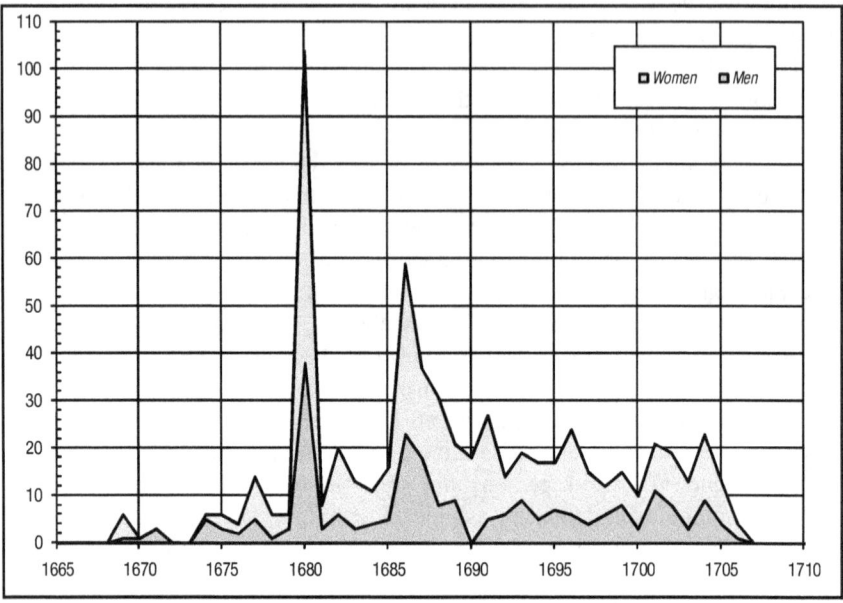

Chart 8: Third Church, covenant renewals by gender, 1710–1760

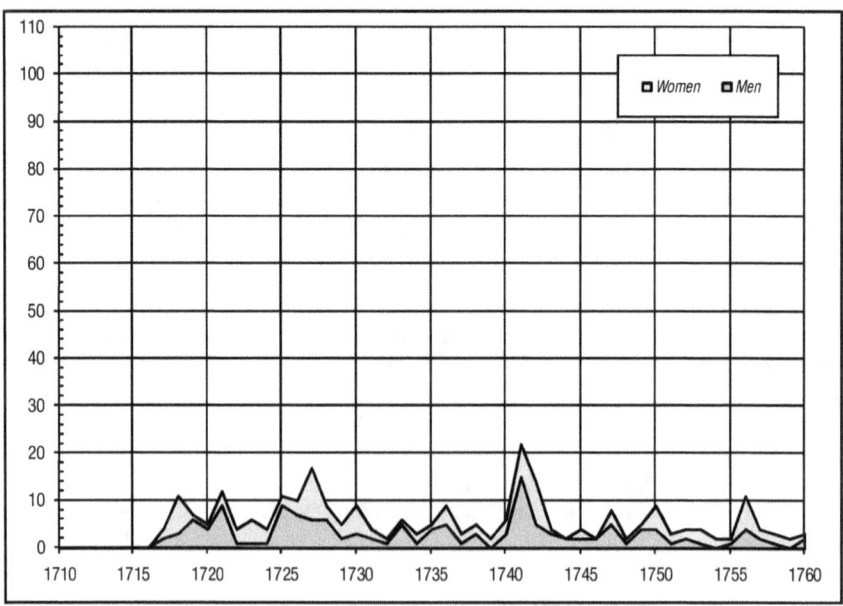

point were positioned to reap real benefits. All in all, Third Church during the era of Sewall and Prince seems to have been a model New Light congregation. These years are well deserving of their designation as "a golden age."[158]

Fourth ("Brattle Street") Church

This church was organized in 1698 by a group of progressives uncomfortable with certain aspects of traditional Massachusetts Congregationalism.[159] They granted their pastors unusually sweeping authority in matters such as admission to membership and administration of the sacraments, though they retained for themselves at least some of the "lay liberties" traditionally associated with this form of church government.[160] The church's pastors during the era under examination included Benjamin Colman (1699–1747), William Cooper (1716–1743), and Samuel Cooper (1746–1783).[161] Colman began his tenure crossing swords with the Mathers as the embodiment of the local Congregational establishment; however, their antagonism was only temporary.[162] As one source notes, "[Colman and Cotton Mather] had long been at variance, but their friendship was renewed several years before Dr. Mather died, and then they wondered how they could so long disagree."[163] Indeed, in several respects—their love of learning,

---

158. Winslow, *"Rights of All,"* 71.

159. See John G. Palfrey, *A Sermon Preached to the Church in Brattle Square, in Two Parts, July 18, 1824* (Boston: Phelps and Farnham, 1825), 5–9; Samuel Kirkland Lothrop, *A History of the Church in Brattle Street, Boston* (Boston: William Crosby and H. P. Nichols, 1851), 1–53; idem, *Memorial of the Church in Brattle Square* (Boston: John Wilson and Son, 1871), 9–17; McKenzie, "Provincial Period," 204–209; Miller, *From Colony to Province*, 240–244, 254–255, and passim; Middlekauff, *Mathers*, 219, Youngs, *God's Messengers*, 82–83; and Corrigan, *Prism of Piety*, 27–31. For a comment on Fourth Church's meetinghouse and its location, see Whitehill, *Boston*, 30.

160. Holifield, *Covenant Sealed*, 192; Foster, *Long Argument*, 282; Cooper, *Tenacious of Their Liberties*, 158, 180–181.

161. Weis, *Colonial Clergy*, 59–62, 242.

162. On Colman's transition from establishment-challenging outsider to establishment-leading insider, see Thomas S. Kidd, *The Protestant Interest: New England after Puritanism* (New Haven, Conn.: Yale University Press, 2004), 29–50.

163. Eliot, *Dictionary*, 125–126. For brief biographies of Colman, see Sprague, *Annals*, 1: 223–229; and Clifford K. Shipton, *Sibley's Harvard Graduates*, vol. 4: *Biographical Sketches of Those Who Attended Harvard College in the Classes 1690–1700* (Boston: Massachusetts Historical Society, 1933), 120–137. See also Chapman, "Benjamin Colman." For an older, rather filiopietistic account, see Ebenezer Turell, *The Life and Character of the Reverend Benjamin Colman, D.D.* (Boston: Rogers and Fowle, 1749). On Colman's elitist social outlook, see Anthony Gregg Roeber, "'Her Merchandize . . . Shall Be Holiness to the Lord': The Progress and Decline of Puritan Gentility at the Brattle Street Church, Boston, 1715–1745," *New England Historical and Genealogical Register*, vol. 131, no. 3 (July 1977): 176. For an intriguing study of his pulpit style, see Teresa

their predilection for society's upper crust, and even their deep-seated theological conservatism—Colman and Cotton were much alike.[164]

Colman's fundamental commitment to moderate Calvinism was never in doubt.[165] When it came to soteriology, this ecclesiological radical was very much a traditionalist: "By the Sin of our *first Parents* we have left our first State, and how are we *fallen*! Our Nature is corrupted, our Souls enfeebled and *disabled*, indisposed and *averse* to what is holy and good. Our moral and spiritual Powers are gone from us, and as it were *wither'd* away.... The Representation of this *moral Impotence* you see is indeed a *will not*, rather than a *cannot*; but the being disabled to *will* that which is good is the *worst* kind of Inability, and the most lamentable Degree thereof.... Here is a wretched *Disability* indeed; a *wither'd* Mind and Will that cannot so much as meditate heartily and purpose, *of it self*, the Thing that is good."[166] But he urged that a sinner's "moral impotence" was no excuse for spiritual apathy: "*Impotent as we are, the Lord expects that we try to exert ourselves, as well as we can, and in whatsoever we can, under the Call of his Word.* ... Believe it, that Christ says to *You* this Day, as to the impotent *Man* of old, 'Stand forth now in the midst!' ... What! will you not *try*? ... Altho' your Strength and Limbs are utterly gone, yet can you *ly and look* up unto God on High, to perform all things for you.... Only *look to Jesus*, and he can give thee *Faith to be healed*."[167] On the other hand, he tended to soft-pedal his presentations of such doctrine, preferring honey to vinegar.[168]

Nevertheless, seeing conversion as the indispensable introduction to the Christian life, Colman stressed that evangelism must be the pastor's central calling: "This, *this* is *saving* Grace and Mercy! what *Sinners* should seek, and what *Saints* may triumph in! what *Ministers* should preach, and *People* hear for. Else *what go ye forth to see?* ... For what a *Farce* is the Solemnity of a preached *Christ* and his unsearchable *Riches* turned into, if it have *no Effect* upon the Hearts and Lives of Men? if it effect no change of Souls here, nor turn to their

---

Toulouse, "Benjamin Colman and the Shaping of Balance," in *The Art of Prophesying: New England Sermons and the Shaping of Belief* (Athens: University of Georgia Press, 1987), 46–74. For an examination of life in the Colman household, see Clayton Harding Chapman, "Benjamin Colman's Daughters," *New England Quarterly*, vol. 26, no. 2 (June 1953): 169–192.

164. See Jones, *Shattered Synthesis*, 92–93.

165. Harry S. Stout describes Colman as "staunchly Calvinist in theology" (*The Divine Dramatist: George Whitefield and the Rise of Modern Evangelicalism*, Library of Religious Biography [Grand Rapids, Mich.: William B. Eerdmans, 1991], 117). See also Carpenter, "New England's Puritan Century," 55.

166. Benjamin Colman, *The Wither'd Hand Stretched Forth at the Command of Christ, and Restored* (Boston: J. Draper, 1739), 5–6; this popular sermon went through several editions. See also Corrigan, *Prism of Piety*, 80.

167. Colman, *Wither'd Hand*, 11–14.

168. Palfrey, *Church in Brattle Square*, 14.

Chapter 3: Tending God's Vineyard 81

Salvation in the Life to come? Let us throw up our *Sabbaths*, and cast away our *Bibles*, and lay aside the Order and Work of a *Ministry*; if they be not for the *Conversion of Souls*."[169]

Indeed, like Tennent and Foxcroft, and unlike Chauncy, Colman saw evangelism as so paramount among the pastor's pursuits that would-be clergy who had yet to experience regeneration for themselves ought to seek it without delay—or look for another line of work: "More particularly, I must take the Opportunity now given me of God to admonish those that are *Candidates for the Ministry*: Before and above all their preparatory Studies . . . that they do in the first place seek of God *this* more necessary Foundation for a Gospel Minister, and more abundant Qualification for One; namely, *a blessed Regeneration*, and a *sound Conversion* to God. . . . And as for the *People of God*, here is a plain but most important *Direction* to them, in their *Choice of a Pastor*; Chuse One whom you have Reason to esteem a *Saint*, a converted and sanctified Person, who will follow after *Holiness*, and labour for *your Conversion* and Salvation."[170]

To New Englanders of that era, no one more typified the evangelist than Solomon Stoddard, long-time pastor of the Congregational church in Northampton, Massachusetts. Colman's own clerical elitism and consequent detachment from the day-to-day lives of his parishioners have already been noted.[171] That he was a social elitist as well was noted by one of Fourth Church's early historians, along with the consequences for his ministry: "With all his excellences and valuable public services, Colman was not popular, that is, he was not a general favorite with the community."[172] Yet though this must have hobbled his own efforts at evangelism, he invoked Stoddard's example as motivation to further such efforts, arguing that not only "in our whole public Ministry" but "in all our more private Applications to Souls," ministers must act "as dying Men with dying People."[173]

In fact, so indispensable was regeneration that all legitimate ministerial means to that end ought to be pursued: "The Conversion of any one Soul is a Thing to be admired. The *Rarity* of the Thing makes it admirable. What a Pity 'tis to give this as a Reason! a true Conversion to GOD is a *singular* Thing in a World lying in Wickedness: Abundance of Conversions then must be wonder-

---

169. Benjamin Colman, *Ministers and People under Special Obligations to Sanctity, Humility, and Gratitude; for the Great Grace Given Them in the Preached Gospel* (Boston: S. Kneeland and T. Green, 1732), 17.
170. Ibid., 6. On Tennent's and Foxcroft's views in this regard, see above.
171. Turell, *Benjamin Colman*, 182; see also chapter 2 above.
172. Lothrop, *Church in Brattle Street*, 84.
173. Benjamin Colman, *The Faithful Ministers of Christ Mindful of Their Own Death* (Boston: D. Henchman, 1729), 25; this was originally delivered as a lecture to mark Stoddard's death.

ful."[174] When such abundance finally came to Boston with the arrival of George Whitefield in the fall of 1740, Colman was moved to flights of poetic fancy: "My *Brethren*, . . . We have *rejoiced* to see you as *Clouds* in our *Streets*, and as *Doves* about the Windows of your Places of *Resort for worship* in the Weeks past. . . . [A]nd you seem'd earnestly to hearken to [Christ], as if you would, as if you were ready, and even on the Wing!"[175]

Colman had played a pivotal role in arranging Whitefield's visit, and his pulpit was the first in Boston to be graced by the Anglican itinerant's oratory.[176] Writing to a Mr. Parsons, of Lyme, Connecticut, he could scarcely restrain himself: "We have had a week of Sabbaths."[177] In the fall of 1741, the fiery Connecticut itinerant Eleazar Wheelock preached in Fourth Church's meetinghouse "with considerable freedom."[178] In the ensuing months, as controversy first arose, Colman remained a supporter of the revival: "I . . . [give] *Glory* to GOD for the *Great and good Work of his Grace*, which he has so *visibly begun*, spread and is *carrying on*, in every *Part* almost of our *Provinces*."[179]

Eventually, though, as a rift began to open in the ranks of clergy and laity alike, with Old and New Lights squaring off and countless churches racked by dissension, his love for order and stability led him to view the Awakening through different eyes.[180] This shift of perspective was apparent in 1743, when he attended but declined an invitation to moderate the conference of clergy that issued the pro-revival *Testimony and Advice of an Assembly of Pastors of Churches*; he signed the conference's final document only with reservations.[181] In the end he repented of his first unqualified approbation: "[W]hoever of us went early and *too suddenly* into a good Opinion of the *Transports* of weak People and *Children*, in the Beginning of the *Work of God* which we still judge has been among us in many Places; let us look *back* with *Humility*, even in the Conscience of our *Integrity* therein, and not be asham'd to confess our *Inadvertence*

---

174. Benjamin Colman, *Souls Flying to Jesus Christ Pleasant and Admirable to Behold* (Boston: G. Rogers and D. Fowle, 1740), 19.

175. Ibid., 22.

176. See Whitefield, *Journals*, 457, 459; Tracy, *Great Awakening*, 88; Gaustad, *Great Awakening*, 26; Stout, *Divine Dramatist*, 118; Chapman, "Benjamin Colman," 229, 233; Kidd, *Protestant Interest*, 98; idem, *Great Awakening*, 85; and Arnold Dallimore, *George Whitefield: The Life and Times of the Great Evangelist of the Eighteenth-Century Revival*, 2 vols. (Carlisle, Penn.: Banner of Truth Trust, 1970), 1: 528.

177. Quoted in Hill, *Old South Church*, 1: 512.

178. Tracy, *Great Awakening*, 203.

179. Benjamin Colman, *The Great God Has Magnified His Word to the Children of Men* (Boston: T. Fleet, 1742), 32.

180. Kidd, *Great Awakening*, 136.

181. Tracy, *Great Awakening*, 300; Roeber, "'Holiness to the Lord,'" 191–192. See also chapter 2 above.

Chapter 3: Tending God's Vineyard

and Imprudence in not being more aware of the *Tendency* of those *Extraordinaries* and irregularities, unto these *Errors* and Extravagances of others."[182]

William Cooper, Colman's associate at Fourth Church, was an unabashed Calvinist who stressed the sovereignty of God in the redemption of the elect: "Fallen Man would never seek after GOD, if GOD did not seek after him; but go farther and farther from him, and keep at an everlasting Distance. . . . And this Grace of GOD in bringing Sinners Home to himself is *distinguishing*. These are taken, while others are *left*. . . . [T]hus it is to this Day. The Gospel Net encloses some, and lets others go."[183] What set Cooper apart from Colman, also a Calvinist, was more the manner than the content of his proclamation. One early source contrasted Colman's style of preaching, in which "the orthodox doctrines are . . . implied, and, as occasion required, explicitly stated," with that of Cooper, in which "they are introduced on system and with relish."[184] More bluntly, though also more pejoratively, another early source described Cooper as "a man in whom the rigid Calvinism of that day, in its austerity, its repulsiveness, and its strength, was fitly represented."[185]

Colman himself commented in his funeral sermon for Cooper: "You all know that CHRIST has been the *Alpha* and *Omega* to him in all his *Sermons*. . . . And this led him strong into the *Calvinistic Scheme* betimes, because he judg'd it to be the very Scheme of the *Gospel*: He soon grew much a Master in it, and accordingly has been very *zealous* for it, as the *Doctrine according to Godliness*, and the *Truth in JESUS*."[186] Cooper had a knack for presenting Calvinist orthodoxy in a way that moved as well as enlightened his listeners. One source notes: "When Dr. Colman preached, the people went away highly gratified. . . . But when his colleague [Cooper] had performed the pulpit exercises, he had such a way of addressing the heart, and giving a solemnity to their spirits, that each man had a look of concern, and went home silent as the grave. Death, judgment,

---

182. Benjamin Colman, *A Letter from the Reverend Dr. Colman of Boston, to the Reverend Mr. Williams of Lebanon, upon Reading the "Confessions" and "Retractations" of the Reverend Mr. James Davenport* (Boston: Rogers and Fowle, 1744), 4. Chapman goes too far with his claim that Colman thereby "declared that he was at last for peace even at the risk of opposing the revival" ("Benjamin Colman," 251).

183. William Cooper, *One Shall Be Taken, and Another Left* (Boston: T. Fleet, 1741), 10, 12. Cooper's role in the publication of Jonathan Edwards's defense of Calvinist soteriology, *God Glorified in Man's Dependence*, has already been noted.

184. Palfrey, *Church in Brattle Square*, 14.

185. Lothrop, *Church in Brattle Street*, 75–76. Cooper's leading role in the ordination of the heterodox Robert Breck demonstrates that, for all his warmth to Calvinist orthodoxy, he was not as rigid as Lothrop claimed. For more on the Breck controversy, see ibid., 73–75; and Chapman, "Benjamin Colman," 217–222.

186. Benjamin Colman, *Jesus Weeping over His Dead Friend, and with His Friends in Their Mourning* (Boston: Rogers and Fowle, 1744), 29.

and eternity were the subjects of his preaching."[187] In short, according to Colman's biographer, Cooper was "what is thought of today as a good evangelistic preacher."[188]

When the Great Awakening arrived, Cooper the pastor-evangelist became Cooper the itinerant evangelist, visiting Portsmouth, New Hampshire, in the winter of 1741–1742 "for nearly three weeks, preaching almost every evening, with remarkable success."[189] He rejoiced at what he saw as a genuine spiritual awakening: "I make no doubt but all of you think what has led me to these Words at this Time; the remarkable *Work of Grace* begun, and I hope going on amongst us; the eminent Success which GOD has been pleas'd to give to his preached Gospel of late; the surprizing Effusion of the Holy Spirit, as a Spirit of *Conversion* to a blessed Number, I doubt not; as a Spirit of *Conviction* unto many."[190] One early source observed: "No one of the clergy was more engaged in defending and keeping up what was called the awakening of 1741–1743."[191] Nor did the Awakening's excesses trouble him as they did his colleague: "What man! Have the Spirit of Christ, without *light* in the understanding, or *heat* in the heart, or *holiness* in the life, or *heavenliness* in the affections? . . . It is impossible!—It is as impossible as that there should be fire without light, or heat, and the other sensible effects of it."[192] In Colman's funeral sermon for Cooper, he noted that to the end his colleague had remained "immoveably *determined*, as we all know, that there *has been a remarkable work of* GOD going on among us."[193]

As has already been noted, Cooper was an unusually effective spiritual counselor who saw the demand for his services soar with the coming of revival: "[T]he Rev. Mr. COOPER greatly rejoyced in the late remarkable Revival of Religion among us, declaring that since the Year 1740, more people had sometimes come to him in Concern about their Souls in one Week's Time than in the whole twenty[-]four Years of his preceeding Ministry."[194] Colman remarked on "the *Resort* to [Cooper during the Awakening] . . . of a *Multitude* of Persons, younger and older, under strong *Convictions*."[195] Cooper was diligent as well in pastoral visitation, an activity that bore much fruit: "[H]e . . . visited them in their Sick-

---

187. Eliot, *Dictionary*, 128.
188. Chapman, "Benjamin Colman," 258–259.
189. Tracy, *Great Awakening*, 181.
190. Cooper, *One Shall be Taken*, 14.
191. Palfrey, *Church in Brattle Square*, 15.
192. William Cooper, *The Sin and Danger of Quenching the Spirit* (Boston: G. Rogers, 1741), 12.
193. Colman, *Jesus Weeping*, 32.
194. Prince, *Christian History . . . for the Year 1743*, 341. Cooper's reputation as a counselor has already been noted in chapter 2 above.
195. Colman, *Jesus Weeping*, 32.

nesses, received their Visits, directed your Consciences, *warn'd the unruly, comforted the Feeble-minded, supported the weak*, [and so] is known to many of You. . . . God pleas'd greatly to *own* his Ministry, publick and private, for saving Good to Souls, and gave him many *Seals* of it, more especially (as he judg'd) of late Years; in *whom* he had much Joy, and *they* a vast Honour and Reverence for him:—And may they be his Crown in the Day of CHRIST."[196] As a means of furthering the work begun in pastoral counseling and house-to-house visitation, Cooper looked to religious societies. In this regard, he cited the example of a recently deceased teenager's growth in grace: "He now [after his conversion] chose for his Companions those that fear'd the Lord; and associated with some such who meet every Lord's day Evening for the Exercises of Religion, and found it of Advantage to him."[197]

It might have been expected that there would be great interest in such societies among the members of Second Church and Third Church; after all, their pastors were members of the Mather family or disciples of Cotton Mather himself. More surprising is the interest in such societies shown by the members of this congregation, largely drawn as they were from Boston society's upper crust. Their interest is attested by a resolution set down in the congregation's records, dated May 30, 1728, and bearing the signatures of ten heads of households:

> [W]e propose (with God's leave and help) to sett up and attend a private meeting for religious Exercises with the advice and countenance of our Pastors, agreeable to the practice of many of the best Christians formerly in this Place and which we apprehend sufficiently warranted from the Word of God. Mat.:18.20. Mal:3.16. I Thes:5.11. Heb:10.24.25. –
>
> We therefore whose Names are here[in]after sett down, do agree and resolve as follows. –
>
> 1 That we will meet (with our Wives) at each other[']s Houses, at least once in a Month, viz. on the Tuesday after every Sacrament day, in or towards the Evening, and spend a convenient portion of time, about two hours[,] in the Exercises of Religion, to begin at or before seven o'clock according to the time of the Year. –
>
> 2d The Exercises to be performed are: first a prayer to be made by one of us in his turn; then a Sermon to be read or repeated; next a Prayer made by another of the Brethren; and then a Psalm to be sung; to which may be added Godly conference as the time shall allow. –
>
> 3d In the Evening prayers there shall be some special Articles, to ask the pouring out of the Spirit of God, not only upon ourselves, but upon our Children and families, very particularly the family whose we then are, and upon the

---

196. Ibid., 29–31.

197. Cooper, *Service of God*, 28. This example has already been cited in chapter 2 above.

Church we belong to[198] and the Pastors of it, that the work of God may be greatly carried on in it.—The conference may arise from what has been just before read, or what we heard the Lord[']s-day before, or the providences of God that may have occur'd.

    4 That we will look upon ourselves as oblig'd in very close and strong Bonds, to be serviseable to one another in all christian offices, more especially that we will upon all occasions, lovingly give, and as lovingly take, mutual admonition of any thing that we may see amiss in one another.[199]

The phrasing suggests that this entry may have been drafted, in part or more likely in its entirety, by one of the church's pastors—probably by William Cooper himself. But the signatures affixed to it demonstrate that interest in religious societies, at least among a certain element of the congregation, was sincere and profound.

After William Cooper's death in 1743, his son Samuel began an involvement with Fourth Church that led to his ordination and installation three years later as Colman's junior associate.[200] By bent and upbringing, the younger Cooper was closer to Fourth Church's senior pastor than to his own father. One early source noted: "[Samuel's] diction was more chaste and correct [than William's], and his gift in prayer peculiar, and very excellent. . . . His religious sentiments were liberal, and he was a friend to free inquiry."[201] More recently, the younger Cooper has been described as building "a temporary bridge between the evangelical Calvinism of [his father] and the rational Christianity of . . . Jonathan Mayhew and other liberal ministers of the area."[202]

Strikingly, Samuel's progressive theology was joined to a disengaged ecclesiology. Where William had described ministers as *"sowers, whose business it is to sow the seed of the word, in preaching the gospel of the kingdom,"*[203] his son argued that "[t]he principal Business of a minister is to do good to the Souls of

---

    198. At this point in the text, an asterisk directs the reader to a marginal note: "NB The Society is to consist only of Persons in full communion with the Church." This is a remarkable stipulation, given the fact that one of the impulses behind the founding of Fourth Church was the minimization of the prerogatives exercised by full communicants at the expense of members of the associated parish. For more on this, see Lothrop, *Church in Brattle Street*, 25.

    199. Fourth Church, Records, City Clerk's Archives, City Hall, Boston.

    200. For biographical sketches of Samuel Cooper, see Sprague, *Annals*, 1: 440–444; and Shipton, *Sibley's Harvard Graduates*, 11: 192–213. For a full-length account, see Charles W. Akers, *The Divine Politician: Samuel Cooper and the American Revolution* (Boston: Northeastern University Press, 1982).

    201. Eliot, *Dictionary*, 130.

    202. Akers, *Divine Politician*, 15; see also Roeber, "'Holiness to the Lord,'" 192.

    203. William Cooper, *The Work of Ministers Represented under the Figure of Sowers* (Boston: J. Draper, 1736), 3.

Chapter 3: Tending God's Vineyard   87

Men; and to lay himself out to enrich them with all spiritual Blessings."[204] Where William had been diligent in visitation, his son went no further than to suggest that a pastor ought to be "easy of access to all who desire his private Instructions and Counsels."[205] Where William had been a white-hot evangelist, his son could summon very little passion for experimental religion, even in the context of an ordination sermon: "You are I trust no stranger to internal Devotion, and the sensations of true Piety; and having experienced the Comfort and Joy of Heart which attend these Sensations, you will be encouraged to cultivate and improve them."[206] It might be wondered how such a thoroughly secularized individual could hope—or want—to succeed as a Christian minister.[207] Unfortunately, so seriously did Samuel neglect the keeping of the church's records that it is difficult to say how the church fared during his lengthy tenure as sole pastor.[208]

For the era preceding Colman's death, though, the record is sufficient to allow the making of observations and the drawing of conclusions. On the one hand, it must be admitted that Fourth Church had its share of struggles during those years. For example, Colman's incessant efforts to curry favor with society's elite left him with more than his share of detractors.[209] This made for

---

204. Samuel Cooper, *A Sermon Preach'd April 9, 1760, at the Ordination of the Reverend Mr. Joseph Jackson to the Pastoral Care of the Church in Brooklin* [sic] (Boston: John Draper, 1760), 26.

205. Ibid., 31.

206. Ibid., 43. Even this rather cool articulation came far down Cooper's list of priorities for the young minister.

207. Shipton, in *Sibley's Harvard Graduates*, 11: 199, remarks on the thoroughly secular tone that pervades Cooper's correspondence. Out of over 400 pages in *The Divine Politician*, Akers devotes no more than a handful to a consideration of Cooper's pastorate.

208. Several early historians of Fourth Church expressed their frustration at the younger Cooper's deficiencies in this regard, and at the consequences for scholarship. Palfrey commented: "Unhappily, the Church records do not furnish materials for estimating the success of his ministry, having been almost totally neglected by him in the midst of his various cares" (*Church in Brattle Square*, 17). Lothrop echoed the sentiment: "We are compelled . . . to resort to other sources than the records of the church during his pastorship to learn any thing of the condition and progress of our affairs. Twenty lines on one half page of the records, and about as many more on a loose sheet of paper, comprise all that stands recorded in his own hand of his ministry of thirty-nine years' duration" (*Church in Brattle Street*, 93).

209. See above on Colman's clerical and social elitism. Even the titles of several of his published sermons—for example, *The Merchandise of a People Holiness to the Lord* (Boston: J. Draper, 1736)—demonstrate his eagerness to ingratiate himself with the members of the local business community.

Chart 9: Fourth Church, first-time admissions to membership and baptisms

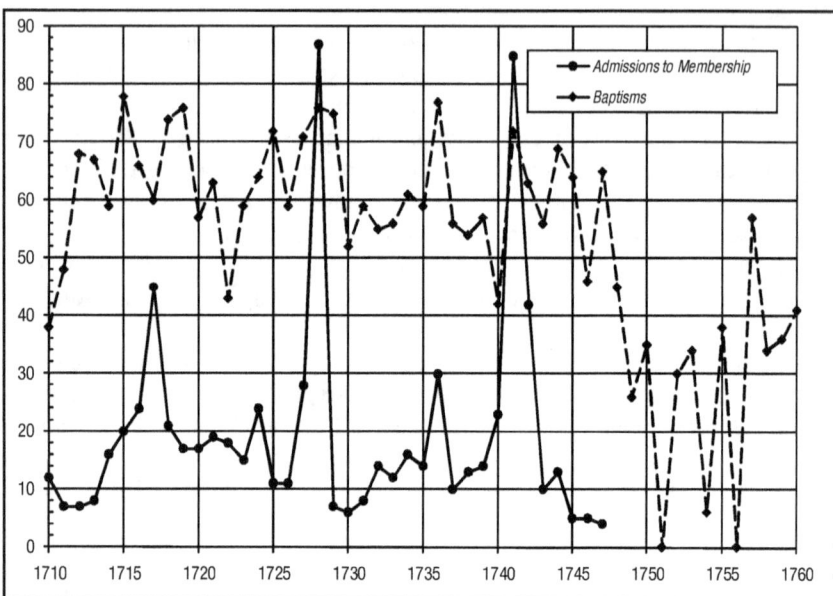

quite a contrast with William Cooper, whose popularity was attested by the fact that after his death a newspaper advertisement offered likenesses for sale to grieving parishioners.[210] Moreover, although Colman and the elder Cooper seem to have worked together quite harmoniously throughout the period of their collaboration, the increasing hesitance about the Awakening that the former seems to have felt after about 1741, clashing with the latter's unbridled enthusiasm, was apparently reflected in a division of sentiment in the congregation itself.[211] One early history of the church addressed this problem in painfully circumspect language: "From all that can be ascertained upon the subject, it is evident that, in relation to the Great Awakening, ... this difference of opinion extended to the congregation also; and it is to the credit of all the parties concerned, that no schism took place,—that the unity of the parish and of the pastors was unbroken."[212]

On the other hand, Fourth Church did experience considerable growth under Colman and William Cooper's joint pastorate, even finding it necessary to

---

210. Akers, *Divine Politician*, 15.
211. Lothrop, *Church in Brattle Street*, 67–68.
212. Ibid., 69–70. Roeber, in "'Holiness to the Lord,'" devotes considerable space to a discussion of the sources and consequences of such tension in Fourth Church; see also Remer, "Old Lights," 572–573.

enlarge its meetinghouse a few years after the latter's arrival.[213] In fact, the statistics demonstrate that, at least through the mid-1740s, this church was as healthy as any in Boston. Figures for admission to membership show spikes at the time of the 1727 earthquake as well as during the Great Awakening, overlying a pattern of gradual decline between 1710 and 1730 and equally gradual growth between 1730 and 1740.[214] Baptismal figures are essentially stable throughout the period of Colman's pastorate, beginning a sharp drop only after his death and stabilizing again by the mid-1750s.[215] Although Colman and William Cooper were by no means as smoothly synchronized in their ministries as were Sewall and Prince at Third Church, neither were they as jarringly out of step as were Foxcroft and Chauncy at First Church. Moreover, the elder Cooper's hands-on, in-the-trenches approach to pastoral care was rivaled locally only by that of Sewall himself. All of this evidently paid dividends in a robust, resilient congregation.

---

213. Lothrop, *Church in Brattle Street*, 66.
214. See Chart 9; and Appendix, Table 1, column 4.
215. See Chart 9; and Appendix, Table 5, column 4.

Chapter 4:
Nurturing New Vines

A very great Number of the Flock, whereof I have been all along hitherto, a trembling servant, imagine our large Meeting-house to be overstock'd with people; and that they mightily want larger Accommodations for themselves and their Families. They are therefore violently sett upon building a new Meeting-house.... I am jealous, lest it be a meer Design of Satan, to ruine the North Church; and furnish ill-humoured Men, with an Engine to break in peeces this flourishing and envied Society.[1]

Introduction

In colonial New England, a community's physical growth had spiritual consequences. For example, since residents were expected to live within half a mile of their church's meetinghouse, sooner or later the community's territorial expansion would lead to the subdivision of its original parish. Furthermore, since there was a limit to the number of members and parishioners who could be adequately cared for by one or two pastors, the community's numerical expansion would necessarily have the same effect, even if its territory remained the same.[2] Yet in spite of the fact that this process was inevitable, the dividing of old parishes and the creating of new churches often led to conflict as established congregations and their ministers took offense at the perceived slight. In addition, new parishes and churches might be created even apart from the dictates of growth where dissension over some point of faith or practice made it impossible for "brethren to dwell together in unity" (Psalm 133:1, AV). Of Boston's three Congregational churches established after 1630 but before 1710, just one—Second—owed its origin to the community's expansion, while two—Third and Fourth—were born of doctrinal discord. Of the seven churches established during the era under consideration, four—Fifth, Sixth, Eighth, and Ninth—were products of expansion, while three—Seventh, Tenth, and Eleventh—resulted from further clashes. As will be seen in the Conclusion, this proliferation of churches had important consequences. What remains at this point is to examine those latter seven churches individually.

---

1. Mather, *Diary*, 2: 181, entry for February 21, 1713; 2: 183, entry for February 28, 1713.
2. See Winslow, *Meetinghouse Hill*, 118–141.

Fifth ("New North") Church

This church was organized in 1714 in response to the steady increase in population of Boston's North End and the consequent overcrowding of the Mathers' Second Church.³ Fifth Church's pastors during the era under examination included John Webb (1714–1750), Peter Thacher (1720–1739), and Andrew Eliot (1742–1778).⁴ Webb came to the position after Increase Mather had intervened to block the election of John Barnard, Jr., a young protégé of Benjamin Colman; Webb's own election may have been facilitated by Cotton Mather.⁵

Although Webb stood somewhat to the Mathers' left in matters of politics, in matters of theology he and they stood side by side.⁶ A traditional Calvinist, he insisted that the atonement was limited in its scope and definite in its application: "JESUS CHRIST has *actually paid the Price of his Blood* for the Redemption of all that do or shall believe in Him. . . . [T]he Sufferings and Death of the SON of GOD, as they were all in our Nature, so they were also in our Stead. . . . So that Christ has actually paid the Price of his Blood for our Redemption."⁷ From this he derived the doctrine of the perseverance of the saints: "Hence learn *the Safety and Happiness of every true Believer*. . . . [The elect] meet with many *outward* Troubles here; but with a great many more *inward* and spiritual Distresses. . . . And they are e'en ready sometimes to give up all for lost, and so to despair of ever being saved. But after all, they are redeemed, and kept free from the *Dominion* of their spiritual Enemies. . . . And therefore their State is *safe*, amidst the greatest Storms of Temptation and Distress they can meet withal."⁸ In all of this, of course, he also stood side by side with most of his ministerial colleagues.

---

3. See McKenzie, "Provincial Period," 220–221. On early tensions between these two congregations and their ultimate resolution, see Silverman, *Life and Times*, 332–333; and Hall, *Last American Puritan*, 344–345. See also Mather, *Diary*, 2: 616, entry for May 1, 1721; 2: 622, entry for May 31, 1721; and passim. For a comment on Fifth Church's meetinghouse and its location, see Whitehill, *Boston*, 28.

4. Weis, *Colonial Clergy*, 77–78, 201, 216, 242.

5. Hall, *Last American Puritan*, 345; Chapman, "Benjamin Colman," 186–187; Corrigan, *Prism of Piety*, 42.

6. For a biographical sketch of Webb, see Shipton, *Sibley's Harvard Graduates*, 5: 463–471. Shipton observes: "In many ways Mr. Webb was further to the political left than were his patrons" (ibid., 465–466). For an illustration of this point, see his sermon, *The Believer's Redemption in the Precious Blood of Christ* (Newport, R.I.: J. Franklin, 1728), which is studded with references to "spiritual Liberty," "a State of Freedom," "a State of spiritual Liberty," and similar terms, albeit in a religious context (ibid., 14, 15, 16, and passim).

7. Ibid., 25–26.

8. Ibid., 38.

One matter on which Webb stood somewhat to Cotton Mather's right—and certainly to the right of innovative figures from his own generation like Sewall, Prince, and William Cooper—was his outlook on pastoral care. His first publication, *The Young-Man['] s Duty, Explained and Pressed upon Him*, originated as a presentation to a young men's religious society, its members presumably drawn from the ranks of his own congregation, "and now *Published* at their *Request*." Yet although in the course of this sermon on spiritual priorities he found time to address such familiar concerns as the study of the Bible, the shunning of evil company, the careful observance of the Lord's Day, and the cultivation of private prayer, he had absolutely nothing to say about religious societies themselves.[9]

In a later sermon on the ministry, Webb worked within the most conventional of frameworks: "What is the *Work* which CHRIST has given his Ministers to do? ... *First*, They must *Preach* the everlasting Gospel to those they are sent unto. This is the Chief Article they have in their sacred Commission. ... *Again*, They must be much in *Prayer* to God with and for their particular Flocks. ... And *then*, They must Administer the *Seals* and *Censures* of the Gospel to the proper subjects of them. ... And then *Finally*, They must *imitate* the *Life* of CHRIST, and exemplify the *Duties* of Christianity in holy Lives and Conversations."[10] Again, his silence was as eloquent as his speech.

Webb certainly felt the need of renewal for church and community alike: "While Religion is losing Ground among us, we must pray, that God wou'd *revive his Work in our CHURCHES*. ... Indeed, God has now and then by his Word and Providences, been somewhat reviving his Work among us. ... But alas! ... we are at this time, fallen into as dead a sleep as ever. ... For now 'tis but seldom indeed, any Sinner is so far awakened by the Word, as to go to his Minister, and inquire of him, *What he must do to be saved?* ... This is certainly one of the darkest signs we have of the HOLY SPIRIT'S withdrawal from us: and we of this Church, have had reason to lament after a departing God in this respect."[11]

When revival finally came, Webb turned to the imagery of Revelation 3:20 to sound a note of urgency: "[T]ho' the Lord Jesus has been waiting upon most of you for a long Time; yet he has not been alike urgent in his Request to you at all Times. ... [But] *in this Time of the OUTPOWRING of the SPIRIT from on High*: He comes as a Lover that is impatient of any further Delay. ... Nay, when thou

---

9. John Webb, *The Young-Man['] s Duty, Explained and Pressed upon Him* (Boston: S. Kneeland, 1718), 31–34.

10. John Webb, *The Duty of Ministers to Work the Works of Him That Sent Them, While It Is Day* (Boston: S. Gerrish, 1727), 8–10.

11. John Webb, *The Duty of a Degenerate People to Pray for the Reviving of God's Work* (Boston: S. Kneeland and T. Green, 1734), 21–24. See Kidd, *Protestant Interest*, 165.

lyest down to take thy Rest in the Seasons of the Night, does not Sleep oftimes depart from thine Eyes by the loud and urgent Calls of the Lord Jesus Christ, instantly to open to him? . . . O, arise, and open to him immediately, least [lest] this hot Love, by thy obstinate Refusals, should quickly turn into fearing Wrath."[12]

Yet although Webb employed such arresting imagery to press his listeners for an immediate response, he drained his argument of its power by falling back on the time-hallowed terms of Puritan preparationism in order to point out that this was actually impossible: "[B]y Christ's *knocking at the Door*, we are . . . to understand all the *Convictions* of Conscience which he brings the Sinner under, by his *Word*, . . . by his *providential Dispensations* towards him, and more especially by the *inward strivings of his Holy Spirit*. Of these *Knocks* of Christ, some are more loud and awakening, . . . Others again, are more gentle and alluring. . . . And whereas Christ is said in the Text to *stand at the Door*, and knock; this supposes that Christ's *Treaty* with Gospel Sinners is not a *transient Act*, begun or concluded in one Day or Hour only; but a *continued Act*, which for the most Part, takes up a considerable Space of Time."[13]

Whatever Webb's consequent theological concerns about the mass evangelism of his day, he welcomed George Whitefield into his pulpit in 1740 and again in 1745.[14] Moreover, always vigorous in the practice of pastoral visitation, he redoubled his efforts during the era of the Awakening. Andrew Eliot, his colleague, recalled: "When out of the Pulpit, as he naturally cared for your State, so he laboured to promote your best Interests. . . . With what Condescension and Goodness would he go from House to House to extinguish a Flame he has seen to be kindling? Especially he was willing to spend and to be spent for the Good of your Souls. You had a peculiar Opportunity of observing this, in the late Day of awakening; when he exerted himself in so extraordinary a Manner, that some have thought, he exhausted his Strength and hastened a Dissolution. However this was, he herein discovered his sincere Desire to advance the Interest of the Redeemer, and to do good to the Souls of Men. It was a constant Principle with him, as he sometimes express'd himself, rather 'to wear than to rust out.'"[15]

The payoff for such strenuous efforts was striking: "God peculiarly honoured him, by encreasing the Number of his Hearers: So that for a long Time he has had one of the largest Assemblies in the Town and Land. But, which is vastly

---

12. John Webb, *Christ's Suit to the Sinner, While He Stands and Knocks at the Door* (Boston: S. Kneeland and T. Green, 1741), 29–30.

13. Ibid., 6–7.

14. Whitefield, *Journals*, 460, 469; Tracy, *Great Awakening*, 88, 369; Chapman, "Benjamin Colman," 252; Kidd, *Great Awakening*, 85, 135, 169.

15. Andrew Eliot, *A Burning and Shining Light Extinguished* (Boston: Daniel Fowle, 1750), 32–33; Eliot preached this sermon at Fifth Church on the Sunday after Webb's funeral.

more desirable, God was pleased to crown his Faithful Labours, with remarkable Success: Great Numbers were awakened, under his Ministry.... No small Number have owned to me that he was their spiritual Father."[16] Plainly Webb was more astute as a practitioner than as a theoretician of pastoral ministry. At some point in the 1740s—the precise year is not recorded—he suffered a stroke that left him partially incapacitated for the remainder of his life.[17]

Webb's associate at Fifth Church after 1720 was Peter Thacher.[18] Unfortunately, Thacher's arrival plunged the congregation into a new round of controversy. For some years he had been the pastor of the parish church in Weymouth, Massachusetts; with that congregation resisting his departure, and with a considerable number at Fifth Church sympathetic to their plight, the local ministerial association refused to sanction his installation.[19] One unfortunate consequence of Fifth Church's insistence on exercising its prerogative in this regard was the withdrawal of a group opposed to Thacher's call and its move to establish in the North End that same year yet another congregation, Seventh Church.[20] Such controversy and escalating ecclesiastical competition did no one any good.

In theology, by all reports, Thacher's views were quite conventional: "[T]he Principles in which he fixt himself were strictly *Calvinistical*. These he had been train'd up in under the Ministry of the renowned Mr. *Willard*. But as he had too large a Soul to call any Man Master on Earth; his Establishment in these Principles, was the Result of indefatigable Study, Prayer, and great Experience. And being thus confirmed in his religious Principles, he always discovered a Christian *Zeal* and *Warmth* in the Defence of them, to his dying Day."[21] This suggests that he may have had something of a temper, even in the pulpit. Apparently his "Zeal and Warmth" generated a fair bit of homiletical smoke, as William Cooper suggested in his cautious description of Thacher's sermonic style: "[H]is utterance was not the most clear, and his Method and Train of Reasoning were not so easily taken by common Hearers, which might bring his preaching under a

---

16. Ibid., 34.

17. Shipton, *Sibley's Harvard Graduates*, 5: 468.

18. For biographical sketches of Thacher, see Sprague, *Annals*, 1: 266–268; and Shipton, *Sibley's Harvard Graduates*, 4: 303–308.

19. Cooper notes "an angry pamphlet war" (*Tenacious of Their Liberties*, 186); Shipton, in *Sibley's Harvard Graduates*, 4: 305–306, describes a near-riot on the day of the ceremony.

20. See the discussion in McKenzie, "Provincial Period," 222–223; Robbins, *History*, 169–178; Chapman, "Benjamin Colman," 188–190; Silverman, *Life and Times*, 332–333; and Hall, *Last American Puritan*, 348–350. For more on Seventh Church, see below.

21. John Webb, *The Duty of Survivors to Remember and to Follow the Faith of Their Godly Deceased Pastors* (Boston: J. Draper, 1739), 25; Webb delivered this sermon the Sunday after Thacher's death.

Chapter 4: Nurturing New Vines

Disadvantage with some. But the attentive and judicious ... were his greatest Admirers."[22] Reading between the lines, it seems likely that he was not the most persuasive of pulpiteers.

This is not to say that Thacher could not occasionally sound an evangelistic appeal as well as any of his fellow clergy: "NOW, NOW is our Time to procure a Change of State; to obtain a Deliverance from that Sin and Guilt which thus expose us. GOD hath, by the Gospel, in His infinite Mercy given us a precious Day of Grace, and opened a Treaty of Peace with His Rebels. If we hear and comply with His Terms; we shall be received to Mercy, and find infinite Advantages. But we must remember that GOD, the Sovereign, hath set bounds to this Day. There will, Sinner, there will certainly be a last Call, a last Offer."[23] But his asthma, one of the motivations behind his move from Weymouth to Boston, rendered it increasingly difficult for him to take an active part in the life of the parish.[24] Significantly, although William Cooper was a leading pastoral activist, his eulogy for Thacher praised the late minister's learning and oratorical prowess while saying absolutely nothing about any putative efforts in regard to pastoral visitation or catechesis.[25]

After Thacher's death, Andrew Eliot was ordained and installed in 1742 as Webb's associate.[26] Even late in his career, Eliot could still sound a note of urgency in regard to the gospel: "[H]owever innocent you may be according to the law of man, yet you stand condemned by the law of God.... You are every moment exposed to everlasting destruction, which is worse than death. Oh! fly to Christ now, while there is hope.... Make haste, make no delay; you run a dreadful venture every moment you put off this important concern, because the next moment may finish your time of probation, and begin your everlasting doom."[27] Nevertheless, with regard to the Great Awakening, his views were quite caustic, even to the point of appropriating language originally directed against James Davenport for application to George Whitefield himself: "As to Mr. Whitefield's being the ringleader of these things of bad and dangerous tendency which have prevailed among us, I am really at a loss what to say. In

---

22. William Cooper, *Compendium Evangelicum* (Boston: T. Fleet, 1739), 30; this was originally delivered as a lecture to mark Thacher's death.

23. Peter Thacher, *Man's Frailty Practically Exhibited in His Life and Death* (Boston: S. Kneeland and T. Green, 1730), 20.

24. Shipton, *Sibley's Harvard Graduates*, 4: 305, 308.

25. Cooper, *Compendium Evangelicum*, 29–31.

26. For short biographies of Eliot, see Sprague, *Annals*, 1: 417–421; and Clifford K. Shipton, *Sibley's Harvard Graduates*, vol. 10: *Biographical Sketches of Those Who Attended Harvard College in the Classes 1736–1740* (Boston: Massachusetts Historical Society, 1958), 128–161.

27. Andrew Eliot, *Christ's Promise to the Penitent Thief* (Boston: John Boyle, 1773), 29.

one sense he seems to be the *accidental* cause, as he was an instrument of stirring up a religious concern in the minds of great numbers, which concern the devil has unhappily improved to lead many astray, and give them a false and enthusiastical peace. But you'll say, has he not been the *direct cause*? Has not a vein of enthusiasm run through his writings, his preaching, and his conduct? ... [T]o call him a *rank enthusiast*, is, I think, carrying the matter too far. ... The modest expression which the united ministers used in their Testimony against Mr. Davenport, suits me better,—that he is 'tinctured with enthusiasm.'"[28]

Eliot could certainly ring the changes on the theme of pastoral ministry: "A faithful Minister will dispense that spiritual Food which shall be most profitable and seasonable to his People. ... In private he will seek to know the State of the Souls that are committed to his Charge, and to give the best Advice and Direction he is able. When any are under Awakenings he will not immediately apply Comfort, but will search the Wound to the Bottom; lest he be found to daub with untempered Mortar."[29] But what he gave with one hand, he took away with the other: "I am sensible, how difficult it is, in the present situation of things, to manage pastoral visits to any valuable purpose; and that people are apt to expect too much from their ministers in this respect, more than they are able to perform, without neglecting the business of the study, which, in general, is of greater importance. ... [T]he duty of a minister, with respect to private inspection, depends on so many circumstances, that it cannot easily be determin'd. ... That something is to be done, is evident from many passages of scripture, and from the nature of the office. But how much, and in what way, the scripture has left to every one's reason and conscience."[30] Thus pastoral visitation died the death of a thousand cuts.

Indeed, at times Eliot lapsed into language that would have brought a smile to the lips of Increase Mather himself: "Be much in retirement, for devotion, for reading, and for meditation. There is scarce any time spent more profitably both for a minister and for his people, than that which he spends in his *study*."[31] Given such ministerial priorities, a steadily widening chasm between this pastor and his parish was inevitable. Eliot's son Ephraim commented on his father's ministry in words heavy with possibly unintended irony: "His tone of voice was bold and positive, as though he would not be contradicted; nor indeed did he

---

28. This quotation is from Eliot's letter to the Rev. Richard Salter, of Mansfield, Conn., dated April 15, 1745, quoted in Sprague, *Annals*, 1: 417–418.

29. Andrew Eliot, *The Faithful Steward* (Boston: T. Fleet, 1742), 21; Eliot preached this sermon at his own ordination.

30. Andrew Eliot, *A Sermon Preached at the Ordination of the Reverend Mr. Joseph Roberts, to the Pastoral Care of a Church in Leicester, October 23d 1754* (Boston: D. Fowle, 1754), 18–19.

31. Ibid., 39. For a discussion of Increase Mather's views on visitation, see chapter 1 above.

bear contradiction tamely out of the pulpit. Over an highly irascible temper he had acquired a remarkable command.... His influence over his parishioners was great; so that, although there were a number very inimical to him, yet he never was openly opposed by them. They, out of derision, used to style him POPE."[32]

Whatever Eliot's deficiencies as a pastor, plainly Webb was quite effective. In fact, congregational statistics appear to bear out Eliot's enthusiastic assessment of his senior associate noted above. Figures for first-time admission to membership in Fifth Church show surges following the earthquakes of 1727 and 1755 as well as the Great Awakening, superimposed on an underlying pattern of slow growth followed by equally slow decline.[33] Figures for covenant renewal show even greater strength, trending upward fairly steadily throughout the interval.[34] Baptismal statistics reflect an upward trend as well, peaking in 1741 and stabilizing after 1750.[35] All this was in spite of the schism of 1720 and the consequent fact that after 1722 Fifth Church had to compete with not just one but two other congregations in the same small neighborhood.

Another pointer to Fifth Church's vitality under Webb's ministry was the strength of its lay leadership. In most local congregations, the post of ruling (lay) elder was filled only intermittently if at all; First Church's last ruling elder died in 1713, for example, and Fourth Church, Sixth Church, Eighth Church, and Ninth Church ordained no one at all to that position. But from 1720 until Webb's death in 1750, Fifth Church always had at least two and usually three lay elders. In fact, the last person to be elected to that office in any of Boston's Congregational churches was Fifth Church's William Parkman, installed in 1743 and holding the post until his death in 1775.[36]

It is tempting to associate the church's passage from expansion through equilibrium to contraction in the decades after the Awakening with Webb's stroke and subsequent incapacitation that left Eliot to carry the pastoral burden

---

32. Quoted in Sprague, *Annals*, 1: 420.
33. See Chart 10; and Appendix, Table 1, column 5.
34. See Chart 11; and Appendix, Table 3, column 3.
35. See Chart 10; and Appendix, Table 5, column 5.
36. See Worthley, *Inventory*, 53–54, 59, 63, 70, 72–73, 75, 77, 81, and 84. For more on the function of this office and the factors leading to its near-universal neglect, see Youngs, *God's Messengers*, 68, 96–97; Murray, *Jonathan Edwards*, 344–346; and Harold Field Worthley, "The Lay Offices of the Particular (Congregational) Churches of Massachusetts, 1620–1755: An Investigation of Practice and Theory" (Th.D. dissertation, Harvard Divinity School, 1970). For a comment on the resurrection of the office of ruling elder in one New Light parish, see Christopher M. Jedrey, *The World of John Cleaveland: Family and Community in Eighteenth-Century New England* (New York: W. W. Norton, 1979), 55.

Chart 10: Fifth Church, first-time admissions to membership and baptisms

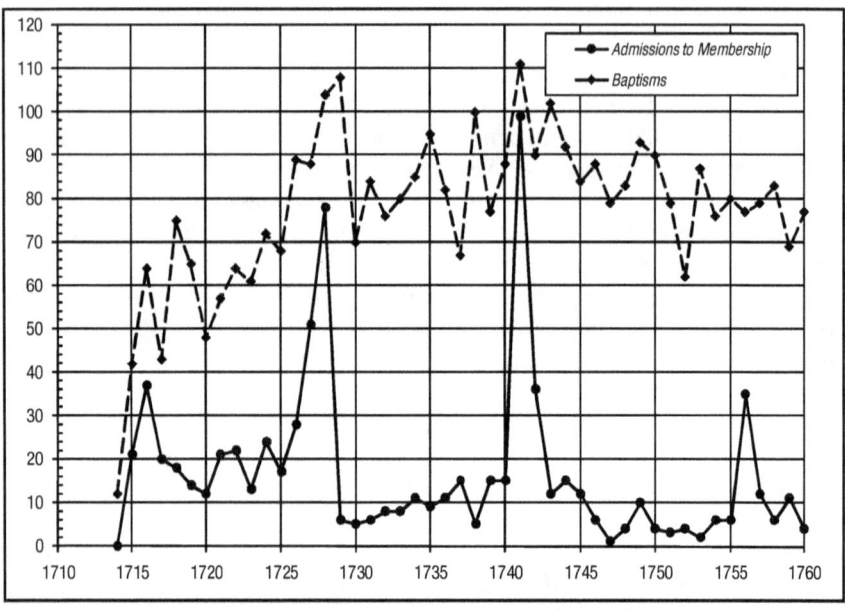

Chart 11: Fifth Church, covenant renewals

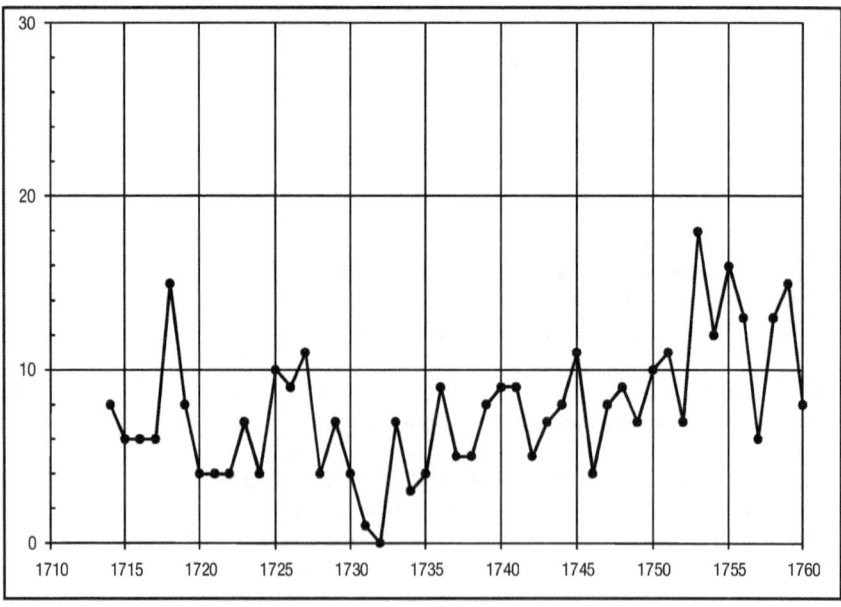

unaided. Comparing these statistics with those of Second Church, whose meetinghouse was located just two blocks down the street, drives home the point being made here about the nature of the revival. Joshua Gee, minister at Second Church and a leading New Light spokesman, was nonetheless pastorally inept; consequently, his congregation experienced catastrophic decline. John Webb may not have been the most innovative of theologians, nor even a particularly astute pastoral theorist, but as a pastoral practitioner he had few peers; reflecting this, his flock saw steady growth. In short, taming and channeling the forces of revival surging through mid-eighteenth-century religious structures required that a pastor do more than just mouth the right theological formulas, be they New or Old Light. The course of the Great Awakening was driven at least as much by ecclesiological as by soteriological concerns.

Sixth ("New South") Church

This church, organized in 1719, had Samuel Checkley, Sr., as its sole pastor during the period under examination.[37] Checkley's evangelical Calvinism was thoroughly conventional: "Conviction is antecedent to Conversion: and Sinners in order to Pardon, must have their Eyes opened, and be made to see ... how they were shapen in iniquity, and conceived in Sin, and are by Nature Children of Wrath.... They must not only see their Vileness, but under the Sense of it, be deeply humbled and abased, and lay themselves low before God.... Would such obtain Mercy at the Hands of God, they must confess and acknowledge their Sins to him, and that freely, particularly.... Would they obtain Mercy, they must believe in Jesus Christ. Faith in Christ is a saving Grace, which must be wrought in Sinners, and without which all their hopes of Pardon and Salvation will be in vain."[38]

The certainty of final judgment and the uncertainty associated with its delay made Checkley's call to repentance all the more urgent: "The Door of Mercy is now open, and the glorious God, whom you have affronted and provoked, offers Peace and Reconciliation to you: But all this will soon be over, the Door will be shut; and then tho' you beg and plead for Mercy, God will be deaf to your cries.... Let Sinners then ... be exhorted with all speed to seek to God for Mercy.... O be quickened, to seek and cry for Pardon. You see God is willing

---

37. McKenzie, "Provincial Period," 222; Weis, *Colonial Clergy*, 54, 242. For a biographical sketch of Checkley, see Shipton, *Sibley's Harvard Graduates*, 6: 74–78. For a comment on Sixth Church's meetinghouse and its location, see Whitehill, *Boston*, 33.

38. Samuel Checkley[, Sr.], *Mercy with God for the Chief of Sinners* (Boston: T. Fleet, 1733), 16, 18–21. On the other hand, the fact that Checkley was willing to accept Robert Breck's liberal Arminianism as falling within the pale of orthodoxy demonstrates that he was hardly doctrinaire; see Shipton, *Sibley's Harvard Graduates*, 6: 76.

Chart 12: Sixth Church, first-time admissions to membership and baptisms

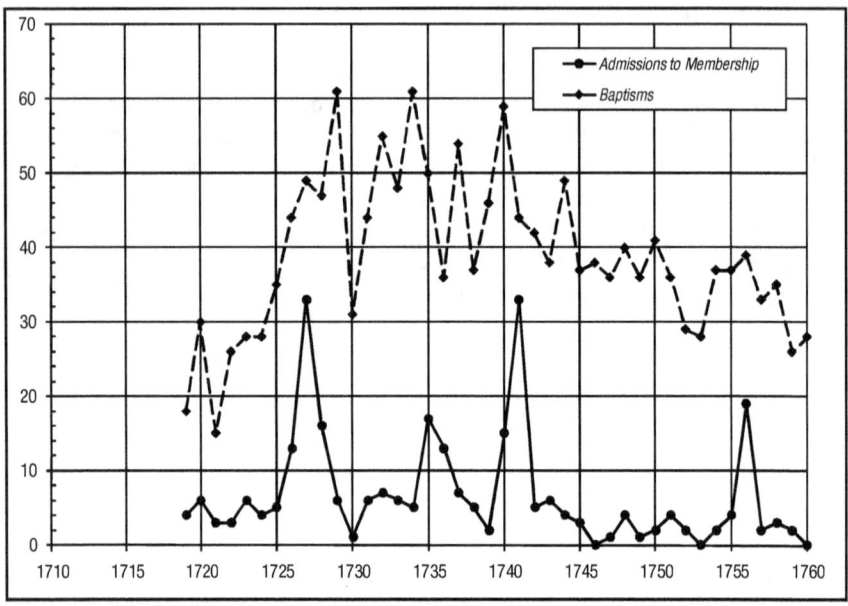

Chart 13: Sixth Church, covenant renewals

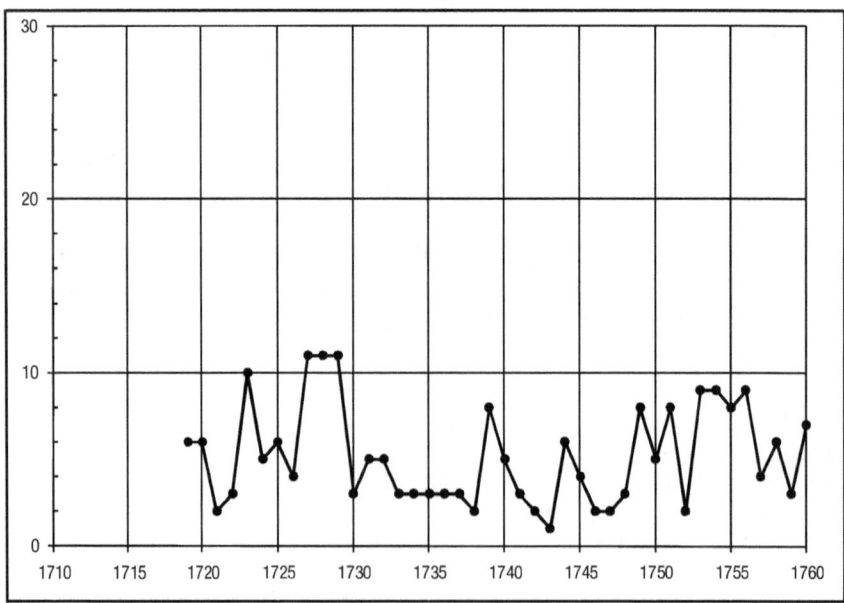

Chapter 4: Nurturing New Vines

to pardon you, will you not then come to him for it? Don't sit down . . . but seek God's Favour with your whole Heart. . . . And don't delay in this Work."[39]

Checkley's special concern for the young reflected the early death of nine of his twelve offspring: "And now, dear Children! . . . [H]ow short your Time may be, you know not, This night your Soul may be required of you. This Sabbath may be your last, and before another your Grave may be made. This call to come to CHRIST may be the last, don't fight it then but hearken to it; do so for GOD's sake, and your Souls sake."[40] The quickened interest in religion that so many young people showed during the Awakening moved him to issue a challenge: "It is a Time wherein, we hope, many Children are seeking CHRIST; may you all do so, and seek as to find him. Your Parents (we trust) have often carried you to JESUS, and many and many a Time pray'd for you, even before you were able to pray for your selves. But do not think this eno', and depend upon what they have done for you: but now you are come to these Years, go to CHRIST your selves, and beg of him to lay his Hands upon, and bless you—Their Prayers, and their Tears won't convert and save you."[41]

Checkley welcomed George Whitefield into his pulpit in 1740 and again in 1745.[42] The Awakening made itself felt at Sixth Church, as elsewhere, with the burgeoning of religious societies, noted in Checkley's preface to his treatise, *Little Children Brought to Jesus Christ*: "The following Sermon was first preached in private, at the Desire of some young Persons who (in this Day of general Awakening) were thoughtful of their Souls, and concerned about the Salvation of them."[43] His hands-on approach to the pastorate was reflected in his charge to Penuel Bowen at Bowen's ordination and installation in 1766 as his associate: "[V]isit the flock, the poor as well as the rich, not preferring one before another, and doing nothing by partiality—all souls are precious to Christ—let them be so to you also, and be ready to spend and be spent for them—Deal tenderly with distressed and quickened souls, leading them to Christ also for rest, strengthen also, comfort and edify believers."[44] This pastoral dynamism is reflected in Sixth

---

39. Ibid., 24–27.
40. Samuel Checkley[, Sr.], *Little Children Brought to Jesus Christ* (Boston: Rogers and Fowle, 1741), 24.
41. Ibid., 22.
42. Whitefield, *Journals*, 461, 534; Kidd, *Great Awakening*, 85, 169.
43. Checkley, *Little Children*, 4.
44. Checkley's charge was printed as an appendix to the sermon preached at Bowen's ordination, Charles Chauncy's *Duty of Ministers*; the quoted passage is from ibid., 35. Checkley's perspective on the pastorate and his exhortation that Bowen "assert, explain and defend the great doctrines of the Gospel, such as the trinity of persons in the Godhead, the divinity of Christ, and also of the blessed spirit—the imputation of Adam's sin to his posterity, regeneration, and justification by faith alone, as therein revealed" make

Church's statistics, which show a long period of growth and stability extending through the first quarter-century of Checkley's ministry.[45] Unfortunately, the early loss of so many of his children greatly diminished his effectiveness in later years. One source notes: "As a result of these repeated shocks he wept much of the time, even in the pulpit, and otherwise showed signs of mental collapse," eventually dying "a shattered man."[46] This likely accounts for the congregation's slow decline that seems to have begun in the mid-1740s.

Seventh ("New Brick") Church

This church was organized in 1722 by dissidents who had withdrawn from Fifth Church in protest over the settlement there of Peter Thacher as pastor.[47] Its ministers during the interval under consideration here included William Waldron (1722–1727), William Welsteed (1728–1753), Ellis Gray (1738–1753), and Ebenezer Pemberton, Jr. (1754–1777).[48]

Waldron acquired a reputation for piety during his student days at Harvard.[49] William Cooper observed: "While at the *College* I know he was one of those *young Students* who us'd to meet on the Evenings of the Lord's-Days, for Prayer and other Exercises of private social Religion."[50] Similarly, Cotton Mather noted: "[W]hen he came in his ... Adolescence to sojourn at the *Colledge*, he was one who not only *Assisted*, but also *Revived* a SOCIETY of *Scholars*, that held their private and weekly Meetings, for the Service of *Religion*."[51] This was the same religious society in which Joseph Sewall and Thomas Prince had once been involved.[52] Like Sewall and Prince, Waldron had close ties to the Mathers,

---

for quite a contrast with the views of Chauncy and raise questions about Bowen's own outlook.

45. See Charts 12 and 13; and Appendix, Table 1, column 6, Table 3, column 4, and Table 5, column 6.

46. Shipton, *Sibley's Harvard Graduates*, 6: 77.

47. See above. For this reason, it was sometimes called the "Revenge Church"; see Corrigan, *Prism of Piety*, 28. For a comment on Seventh Church's meetinghouse and its location, see Whitehill, *Boston*, 27–28.

48. Weis, *Colonial Clergy*, 95–96, 162, 213, 219, 242.

49. For biographical sketches of Waldron, see Shipton, *Sibley's Harvard Graduates*, 6: 214–219; and Sprague, *Annals*, 1: 316–318.

50. William Cooper, Preface to *Divine Providence Ador'd and Justify'd in the Early Death of God's Children and Servants*, by Thomas Foxcroft (Boston: S. Gerrish, S. Kneeland, N. Belknap, and B. Love, 1727), ix; Foxcroft's lecture was originally delivered at First Church on the day of Waldron's burial.

51. Mather, *Hor-Hagigdad*, 22.

52. On this, see chapter 3 above; see also Shipton, *Sibley's Harvard Graduates*, 6: 214.

Cotton preaching at his ordination and Increase giving the charge.[53] A host of telling details—his presence at Increase's deathbed and subsequent remark, "I could have rejoyced to have obtained his Mantle"; his subscription toward the publication of Cotton's *Ratio Disciplinae Fratrum Nov-Anglorum*; and even his intimate friendship with William Cooper—further document his position in the Mathers' inner circle.[54]

Presumably Waldron's theological perspective was similar to that of the Mathers. Certainly his approach to the pastorate was closely attuned to that of Cotton, as Cooper reminded Waldron's parishioners: "*YOU* who were his *peculiar Charge* lay very near his Heart. . . . When any were awakened under his Ministry, profess'd to receive good Impressions by it, and were wro't upon to give themselves to CHRIST and to his People, nothing was a greater Joy to him."[55] Even the manner in which he went about his work reflected Cotton's influence: "As he taught you publickly, *so from House to House*. Sometime before his Death, he had set apart *Tuesdays* in the After-noons, for *Pastoral Visits* properly so called. He has sometimes noted down the Families he visited, adding, 'The Design was to serve the best Interests; GOD grant that it may be so!'"[56] Cotton himself praised Waldron's eagerness to foster family devotions: "*Remember how you have received and heard* . . . very particularly, the Excitations to FAMILY-RELIGION: Among the Inculcations whereof, you have not forgotten the part he had."[57] The result of all this, one source comments, was that he "gain[ed], in a high degree, the affections of his people."[58]

Unfortunately, Waldron's premature death denied him the chance to set the congregation on a firm footing. An early history of Seventh Church lamented: "If he had lived longer, there is no doubt that he would have exerted a powerful influence in the community, and have left more conspicuous memorials upon the records of this church. But Providence had another destiny in store for him."[59] As a result, his ministry would be remembered more for its promise than for its actual record of accomplishments. That the promise was great, and hence the

---

53. Ibid., 1: 316. Cotton's sermon was published as *Love Triumphant*, with Increase's charge as an appendix.

54. Shipton, *Sibley's Harvard Graduates*, 6: 216; Robbins, *History*, 182. Mather referred to "the RATIO DISCIPLINAE, whereof [Waldron] was one of the publishers" (*Hor-Hagidgad*, 23). Cooper cited his "Intimate Friendship [with Waldron] of several Years Continuance" (Preface to *Divine Providence*, iv).

55. Ibid., ix.

56. Ibid., x.

57. Mather, *Hor-Hagidgad*, 26.

58. Sprague, *Annals*, 1: 317.

59. Robbins, *History*, 183.

church's loss as well, is attested by the list of his pallbearers: Sewall, Prince, Cooper, Foxcroft, Checkley, and Gee.[60]

William Welsteed cut a much less imposing figure.[61] He certainly shared the common view of his community's spiritual declension, and of the only hope for its transformation: "Let us then cry mightily to God, for the plentiful Effusion of his Spirit and Grace, on all Orders, Ranks and Ages of Men, to recover us to himself.... Let none be at Ease and Rest, 'till they have attained to a good Hope thro' Grace, that such a regenerating Change is pass'd upon them, and they brought to live unto God by Jesus Christ."[62] Moreover, maintaining Waldron's concern for family devotions, he highlighted widespread deficiencies in this area as a major cause of the problem: "To a criminal Remissness in Family Worship, Instruction and Government, as much as to any one Thing whatever, is owing that dreadful Defection and Degeneracy in the rising Age, that rudeness and dissoluteness of Manners manifestly present among our Children and Youth, which affords but a melancholy Prospect of future Times."[63]

On the other hand, as even the latter passage demonstrates, Welsteed placed a great premium on social order. As a result, although he welcomed Whitefield into his pulpit in 1740, five years later he refused to extend the itinerant that same courtesy.[64] He may not have joined Chauncy in open opposition to the Awakening, but neither did he sign *The Testimony and Advice of an Assembly of Pastors of Churches* vindicating it against its detractors. Edwin Scott Gaustad identifies him as one of a handful of "wavering neutrals" among the local clergy.[65] Like the Old Lights and certain socially conservative New Lights already noted, he was more concerned to enforce orthodoxy in regard to ecclesiology than soteriology.

Tellingly, Samuel Mather observed that on the one hand, Welsteed "was careful not to insist on those Points, about which wise and good Protestants have different Sentiments and various Ways of explaining themselves," while on the other hand, he "very much liked *the Ecclesiastical Constitution* of his Country: And [was greatly troubled] when any of the Children of this Land went off from the *Congregational Way*: For He thought, that *They* changed for the worse."[66] As Mather noted, he did occasionally call on his people in their homes: "Those of

---

60. Shipton, *Sibley's Harvard Graduates*, 6: 218.
61. For a biographical sketch of Welsteed, see Shipton, *Sibley's Harvard Graduates*, 6: 153–158. In Shipton's estimate, "he was not a man of great ability"(6: 156).
62. William Welsteed, *The Dignity and Duty of the Civil Magistrate* (Boston: S. Kneeland, 1751), 56.
63. Ibid., 57.
64. Whitefield, *Journals*, 464; Shipton, *Sibley's Harvard Graduates*, 6: 156–157.
65. Gaustad, "Society and the Great Awakening," 574.
66. Mather, *Walk of the Upright*, 28–29. See chapter 2 above for further comment on this quotation.

Chapter 4: Nurturing New Vines

You, who were under his more immediate Care and Charge, can bear Witness ... how kindly He *visited* you all, especially in the Times of your Trouble."[67] However, this was not done in the systematic manner that had characterized Waldron's ministry. In Welsteed's conception of the pastoral office, other aspects—especially preparation for public worship—took clear precedence.[68] The consequences for Seventh Church were dire.

In 1738 Ellis Gray was ordained and installed as Welsteed's junior associate.[69] Gray was just as lackluster as his senior colleague.[70] His theology was quite conventional: "The Consciences of Sinners must be awakened, they must find and feel themselves guilty before GOD, and obnoxious to his Wrath, before they'll inquire after Relief. . . . Being brought to a Sight and Sense of its miserable undone State by Nature, the Sinner, with Soul trembling and astonished, is brought to the Foot of Christ, saying, *Lord, What wilt thou have me to do?*. . . And being brought to see the Insufficiency of every Thing in himself, and of every Thing without him, through the whole Compass of created Nature, to free him from Guilt and from the Wrath to come, he has the Discoveries of the Saviour made to him in his Beauty, Fulness and Alsufficiency."[71]

Gray even offered the usual word of warning to the unregenerate: "[H]ow many of you are there[,] my Brethren, who have long sat under the preached Gospel in a state of unrenewed Nature and Sin, of carnal Security and Blindness, shutting your Eyes against the Light of the glorious Gospel[?] . . . What can such expect, but to be finally rejected of GOD, to be given up to Blindness of Mind, Hardness of Heart, and Searedness of Conscience, and so bring on themselves swift Destruction? . . . If thus seeing we will not see, and hearing we will not hear, our Destruction is inevitable."[72]

But Gray followed Welsteed and other traditionalists in embracing a narrow view of the ministry that stressed preaching above all and made no place for pastoral tools such as visitation and catechesis. In one ordination sermon he expressed these priorities quite plainly: "Now there are several Ways by which ... Nourishment is conveyed to the Soul[:] By preaching the Word[,] ... by

---

67. Ibid., 29.

68. Mather commented that Welsteed was "conscientious in preparing for the public Offices of Religion" (ibid., 28).

69. For a short biography of Gray, see Clifford K. Shipton, *Sibley's Harvard Graduates*, vol. 9: *Biographical Sketches of Those Who Attended Harvard College in the Classes 1731–1735* (Boston: Massachusetts Historical Society, 1956), 400–404.

70. Shipton notes: "As a clergyman, Gray never shone as his friends anticipated, [although] he had all the virtues suitable to the office" (ibid., 402).

71. Ellis Gray, *The Design of the Institution of the Gospel-Ministry, Fidelity in the Discharge of It; and the Obligation upon the Ministers of the Gospel Thankfully to Acknowledge the Power and Grace of God towards Them* (Boston: G. Rogers, 1741), 9.

72. Ibid., 15.

administering the Seals of the Covenant, Baptism and the Lord's Supper[,] ... by [ministers'] ... fervent Prayers to God[,] ... [and] by [ministers'] own pious and heavenly Examples."[73] Note the telling omissions. Samuel Mather observed: "[H]is public Performances, like his moral Behaviours, were well approved; ... indeed, both in his Praying and Preaching, He shewed himself to be a Scribe, well instructed unto the Kingdom of Heaven."[74]

Not surprisingly, as the Great Awakening proceeded, Gray the "Scribe" became increasingly alarmed at its course: "He must be a stranger in our Israel, who has not heard of, or observed the almost general Concern, that has been awaken'd upon the Minds of People through the Land, about their Souls and Eternity. And a goodly Number have given clear and bright Evidences of a saving Conversion to God.... But Oh at the same Time the busy Adversary has been very active, in sowing his Tares the Seeds of Discord and Division in our Churches.... Our great Danger ... lies here, lest we should damp the Work of God on the one Hand, by a misguided Zeal because of Imprudences and Infirmities, and should overlook that which is substantial and valuable; or on the other should put the divine Stamp upon those Things which will give the Scoffer Occasion to speak reproachfully of our most holy Religion, and which cannot without the greatest Dishonour be attributed to the Holy Spirit."[75]

Jonathan Edwards would not have disagreed with Gray on this point, and Gray's subscription for Edwards's *Life of David Brainerd* demonstrates that even in the late 1740s he retained a measure of sympathy for the Awakening.[76] But with the passing years, its "Imprudences and Infirmities" weighed more and more heavily in his estimate against "that which [was] substantial and valuable." According to Gaustad, he was another of the handful of "wavering neutrals" among the local clergy.[77] His church paid the price.

The nails were driven into Seventh Church's coffin by Ebenezer Pemberton, Jr., the fourth and last of its pastors during the interval under consideration.[78] Pemberton was the son of a pastor of Boston's Third Church and a graduate of Harvard, ordained in 1727 and dispatched to New York City in response to a request from its lone Presbyterian church that Boston's Congregational clergy provide them with a minister.[79] He spent the next twenty-six years in New York;

---

73. Ellis Gray, *The Fidelity of Ministers to Themselves, and to the Flock of God, Consider'd and Enforc'd* (Boston: G. Rogers, 1742), 22–25.

74. Mather, *Walk of the Upright*, 22.

75. Gray, *Fidelity of Ministers*, 31–32.

76. Shipton, *Sibley's Harvard Graduates*, 9: 403.

77. Gaustad, "Society and the Great Awakening," 574.

78. For biographical sketches of Pemberton, see Sprague, *Annals*, 1: 336–337; and Shipton, *Sibley's Harvard Graduates*, 6: 535–546.

79. Leonard J. Trinterud, *The Forming of an American Tradition: A Re-Examination of Colonial Presbyterianism* (Philadelphia: Westminster Press, 1949), 68.

in 1739 he was the only one of that city's ministers who welcomed George Whitefield into his pulpit, and later he played a leading part in the Presbyterians' post-Awakening civil war.[80] He was brought back to Boston by an invitation from Seventh Church in the aftermath of the deaths of Welsteed and Gray in quick succession in early 1753. Much more of a New Light than either of his immediate predecessors, he was a committed Edwardsian whose orthodox Calvinism sharply differentiated him from his theologically liberal father.[81]

Pemberton's preaching always had an evangelical thrust: "Let us sincerely endeavour after a saving acquaintance with [the] Mystery of Godliness. Our blessed Saviour is propos'd unto us in the Gospel as the proper Object of our Faith. . . . It is not enough that we yield a naked assent unto the Gospel, but our Faith must purify the Heart, and produce the works of sincere Obedience, if we would be entitled to the favour of Christ, and own'd as his faithful Servants."[82] "[T]here is a knowlege by which we may be delivered, from the ruins of our Apostate state and recover our forfeited felicity.—This is not an acquaintance with the secrets of Nature or the intrigues and policies of Art, but a knowlege *of Christ and him crucified*. . . . [T]ho' a doctrinal knowlege is an essential part [of this], yet it is by no means the whole. . . . [What is called for is a] knowlege that is not produc'd by the powers of human reason or the common methods of education or instruction, but is the effect of a divine illumination, a spiritual discovery of Christ to the Soul."[83]

Pemberton saw George Whitefield as having mediated just such an experience to those stirred by his sermons: "We heard with Pleasure from a Divine of the *Episcopal Communion*, those great Doctrines of the Gospel, which our venerable Ancestors, brought with them from their native Country. . . . While He preached the Gospel, the *Holy Ghost was sent down*, to apply it to the Consciences of the Hearers—The eyes of the blind were opened, to behold the Glories of a Compassionate Saviour—The Ears of the Deaf were unstopped, to attend to the Invitations of incarnate Love—The dead were animated with a divine Principle of Life—Many in all Parts of the Land, *were turned from Dark-*

---

80. Ibid., 86, 116; Shipton, *Sibley's Harvard Graduates*, 6: 538; Whitefield, *Journals*, 349, 359–360, 484; Dallimore, *George Whitefield*, 1: 434, 486; Stout, *Divine Dramatist*, 96; Westerkamp, *Triumph of the Laity*, 159; Thomas H. L. Cornman, *Caterpillars and Newfangled Religion: The Struggle for the Soul of Colonial American Presbyterianism* (Lanham, Md.: University Press of America, 2003), 135, 137.

81. Shipton, *Sibley's Harvard Graduates*, 6: 538. On Ebenezer Pemberton, Sr.'s theological liberalism, see chapter 3 above.

82. Ebenezer Pemberton[, Jr.], *Sermons on Several Subjects* (Boston: T. Fleet, 1738), 14–15.

83. Ebenezer Pemberton[, Jr.], *The Knowlege of Christ Recommended* (New London, Conn.: T. Green, 1741), 2, 4–6.

ness to Light, and *from the Power of Satan unto God.*"[84] However, he well knew that there were those, even in the church, who were less than sympathetic to such an understanding of faith: "How many are contented with a bare profession, and flatter themselves that they shall be saved, because they are the visible *Children of the Kingdom*? How many *seek to enter in, but shall not be able,* because they seek with a fatal *coldness* and *indifference,* as if they only beg'd a denial?"[85]

Much of the blame for this he laid at the feet of the church and its ministers: "Alas! in this degenerate Age, Religion is wounded in the House of its Friends, the Professors of the Gospel are often Enemies to the Cross of Christ, and the venerable Name by which we are called, is insulted and blasphemed by reason of the scandalous miscarriages of those who enroll their Names among the number of his followers."[86] "O my Brethren! to what Difficulties are the Ministers of Christ reduc'd, that in these Temples dedicated to the Honor of his Name; in these Assemblies design'd for the edification of the Saints; among the Professors of the holy Gospel; We have Reason to fear, there are those, who are the Enemies of the *Son of God.* . . . [A]llow me to ask—Are you indeed the Servants of Christ? . . . Do you receive him in the united Characters of a Prince and a Saviour[?] . . . If not, you are the Enemies of Christ."[87]

In 1741, following the example Whitefield had set the previous year at Harvard, Pemberton even sounded the call to conversion before a gathering of students at Yale: "Every Soul in this Assembly, that has not an experimental knowledge of Christ, is under the condemning sentence of the divine Law, and exposed to an infinitely more terrible execution, than any human power can inflict; there remains but a short and uncertain time to fly from the amazing danger and escape the vengeance of eternal fire. . . . Rouse up your selves therefore, My Dear Brethren,—Awake out of this fatal Security—Cry earnestly to God that he

---

84. Ebenezer Pemberton[, Jr.], *Heaven the Residence of the Saints* (Boston: D. Kneeland, 1770), 21–23; Pemberton delivered this sermon as a tribute to Whitefield after the evangelist's sudden death in Newburyport earlier that year.

85. Ebenezer Pemberton[, Jr.], *Practical Discourses on Various Texts* (Boston: T. Fleet, 1741), 70.

86. Pemberton, *Several Subjects,* 14.

87. Ebenezer Pemberton[, Jr.], *All Power in Heaven, and in Earth Given unto Jesus Christ* (Boston: D. Fowle, 1756), 12–13. That this sermon was intended as a direct responce to the incipient Arianism of such local figures as Ebenezer Gay and Jonathan Mayhew is attested by its preface, bearing the signatures of Joseph Sewall, Thomas Prince, and Thomas Foxcroft and describing Pemberton's essay as "of excellent Service to guard many of the Readers from those most dangerous and pernicious Suggestions against [Christ's] adorable Deity which have been of late unhappily publish'd, to the great Grief and Offence of many among us" (ibid., iv).

would bestow upon you the spirit *of wisdom and revelation, That you may know him—whom to know is Life eternal.*"[88]

On the other hand, Pemberton's understanding of the ministry was decidedly traditional. He saw the pulpit as the focus of the pastor's office, and the sermon—above all, the evangelistic sermon—as the quintessence of his labors: "[I]t is the great duty of the *Ministers* of the gospel *to compel sinners to come in*, and accept of the blessings of the Gospel. . . . [I]t is the duty of the ministers of the *present* day, to use the . . . methods of compassion and friendly violence. . . . We must diligently endeavour to convince the understandings, engage the affections, and direct the practice of our hearers."[89] "Be exhorted, to increase *the gift that is in you*, by diligent study, and fervent prayer. . . . Make it your business to spread the saving knowledge of the blessed Jesus in the world. . . . Endeavour with a holy violence, to pluck sinners as brands out of the fire."[90] "That is the most useful method of preaching, which enters into the hearts of Men, and gives them a lively discovery of their guilt and danger. . . . [Listeners] can sit contented while they are only exhorted to some outward reformation, and reproved for those enormous vices, that are detestable in the eyes of the world, and a public scandal to human nature: But . . . [w]hen the hypocrisy of their hearts is defeated, and their secret iniquities are brought to light; . . . then they are offended and enraged, and perhaps stigmatise the preacher, as a dreaming visionary, and despise his doctrine as enthusiasm and folly."[91]

Though pastors owed their flocks such harrowing evangelistic homilies, in exchange their flocks owed them the greatest respect and deepest obedience. This note had been sounded at Pemberton's own ordination by Benjamin Colman himself: "[W]e should be very *thankful* to [God] for those whom he has . . . sent forth, . . . esteeming them highly in love for their work's sake, improving and profiting by them. . . . These are *Gifts* of Christ to us, to be highly esteemed by us, and whom we ought to *bless* God for, and to accompany with our prayers and *blessings*."[92]

Like Colman, Pemberton warmly embraced the clericalist perspective: "It is an effect of admirable grace, that [God] hath not sent messengers of wrath, to

---

88. Pemberton, *Knowlege of Christ Recommended*, 19.

89. Ebenezer Pemberton[, Jr.], *A Sermon Preach'd in New-Ark, June 12, 1744, at the Ordination of Mr. David Brainerd, a Missionary among the Indians upon the Borders of the Provinces of New-York, New-Jersey, and Pennsylvania* (Boston: Rogers and Fowle, 1744), 9–10.

90. Ebenezer Pemberton[, Jr.], *A Sermon Preach'd at the Ordination of Reverend Mr. Walter Wilmot at Jamaica on Long-Island, April 12, 1738* (Boston: J. Draper, 1738), 17–18.

91. Pemberton, *Practical Discourses*, 42–43.

92. Benjamin Colman, *Prayer to the Lord of the Harvest for the Mission of Labourers unto His Harvest* (Boston: Gamaliel Rogers, 1727), 13, 17.

execute his vengeance upon a guilty world; but heralds of peace, to proclaim the joyful news of a saviour. It is an instance of wonderful condescention, that he has appointed, for this blessed work, not the spotless angels of light; whose appearance would surprize and confound us; but men of the same nature with our selves, *formed out of the clay, whose terrors will not make us afraid.* These are the precious gifts of our ascended Lord, and should be highly esteem'd and reverenc'd for their work's sake.... [A]bove all, assist and encourage them by attending upon their ministry, with meek and teachable frames of spirit. Receive the word of truth into humble and obedient hearts."[93] "We rejoice, brethren, that ... God has not left you *as sheep without a shepherd*.... While we exhort you to receive this your new pastor with affection and joy, we must desire you with humility and reverence to attend his instructions from *the word of God*."[94]

Although Pemberton's ministry in New York City had been a great success, in Boston he was a failure.[95] It has been claimed that this was due to his outmoded style of preaching, that the very passion which drew crowds in the 1740s drove them away in the 1750s and 1760s.[96] But another important factor was his overdeveloped notion of the dignity of the clergy. Among the charges advanced even by members of his New York congregation were that he neglected pastoral visitation and treated parishioners with contempt; in Boston his sense of self-importance drew open ridicule.[97]

Plainly Pemberton conceived of the Great Awakening in terms of the clash of rival ideologies, evangelical and liberal, with revival hinging on the mere proclamation of the new birth in carefully honed evangelistic sermons. If this had been the case, Seventh Church would have been well situated for growth after his assumption of its pastorate in 1754. But such was not the congregation's experience. Statistics show early gains under the activist ministry of Waldron, subsequent stability and then a slow tailing off under the cool

---

93. Pemberton, *Ordination of Wilmot*, 18–19.

94. Ebenezer Pemberton[, Jr.], *A Sermon Preached at the Ordination of the Reverend Mr. Isaac Story, to the Pastoral Care of the Second Church in Marblehead, in Conjunction with the Reverend Mr. Simon Bradstreet, May 1, 1771* (Boston: Samuel Hall, 1771), 17.

95. For a discussion of Pemberton's success in New York and the flourishing condition of his congregation there, see Murray, *Jonathan Edwards*, 123.

96. Eliot asserts: "[I]n [Pemberton's] old age [he] grew unpopular in his delivery, though in former times he drew crowded assemblies by his manner" (*Dictionary*, 370). Similarly, McKenzie notes: "[I]n [Pemberton's] old age he did not retain his popularity" ("Provincial Period," 244).

97. Shipton observes that Pemberton's "idea of the dignity of the clergy did not help his popularity and caused even a little girl to poke fun at him" (*Sibley's Harvard Graduates*, 6: 539, 542).

Chapter 4: Nurturing New Vines 111

Chart 14: Seventh Church, first-time admissions to membership and baptisms

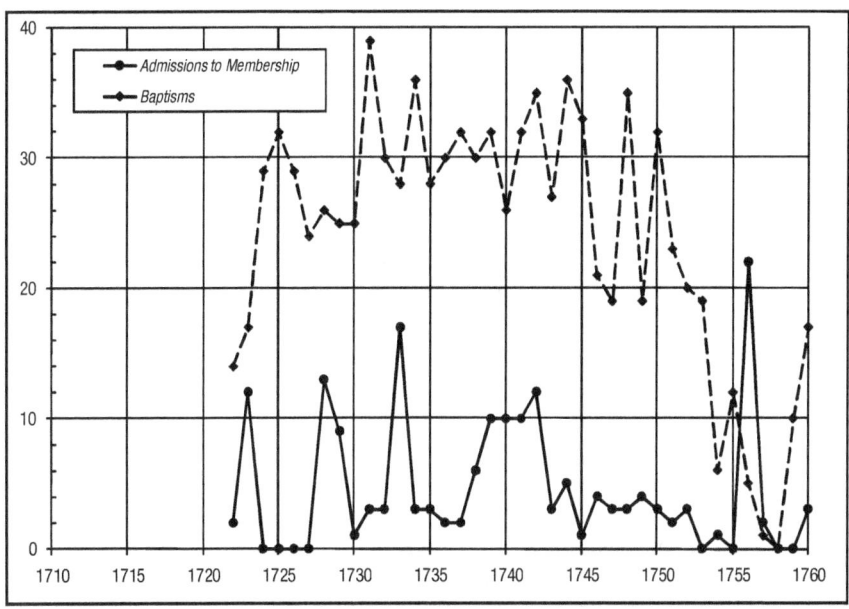

Chart 15: Seventh Church, covenant renewals

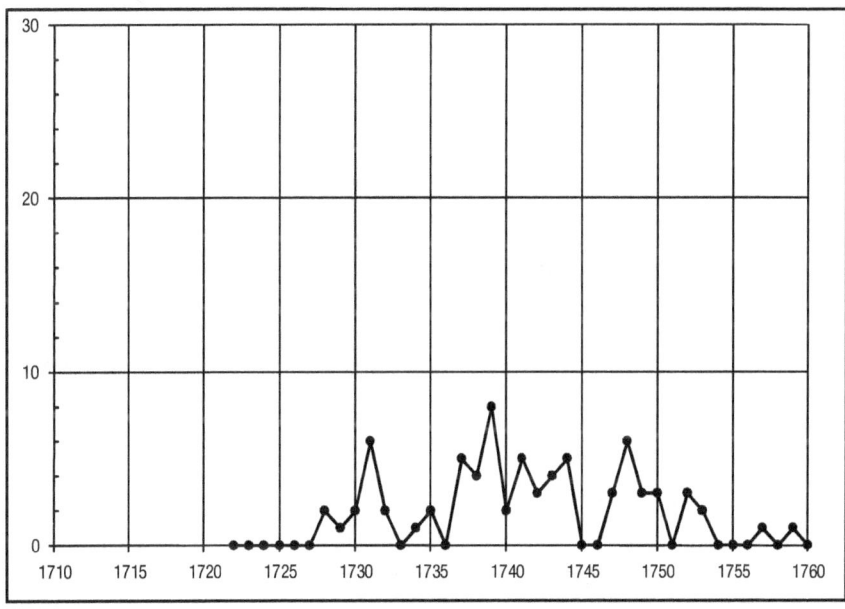

moderation of Welsteed and Gray, and a final, catastrophic collapse under Pemberton.[98] Within a few years of his arrival, the church had declined to the point that it was no longer able to support itself by voluntary collections and had to turn to the town for assistance.[99] Although he never formally resigned his position, in 1774 he gave up his salary and duties. Five years later, the rump of the congregation that remained was absorbed by Second Church.[100] Sermonizing was simply not sufficient.

Eighth ("Hollis Street") Church

Organized in 1732, this congregation was served by a single pastor, Mather Byles, throughout the interval under consideration.[101] Increase Mather's grandson and Cotton's nephew, Byles was a gifted poet and rhetorician.[102] Theologically he was a committed Calvinist all his life, as he reported his wife had remarked to him while she lay dying: "She said, . . . *I bless God that ever I saw you: The Doctrines of Grace* [i.e., the soteriological tenets of orthodox Calvinism], *in the comforts of which I die, have been more clearly explained and applied to my heart, under your preaching, and in your conversation, than ever they were by any one else.*"[103]

Some comment has already been made on Byles's early stance concerning conversion.[104] Here, too, he remained remarkably consistent over the coming years: "The Discourse between *Nicodemus* and our blessed Saviour in the Night, turned upon Repentance and Conversion. . . . It naturally, methinks, leads our

---

98. See Charts 14 and 15; and Appendix, Table 1, column 7, Table 3, column 5, and Table 5, column 7.

99. Shipton, *Sibley's Harvard Graduates*, 6: 542.

100. Ibid., 6: 543; McKenzie, "Provincial Period," 244.

101. McKenzie, "Provincial Period," 227; Weis, *Colonial Clergy*, 48, 242. For a comment on Eighth Church's meetinghouse and its location, see Whitehill, *Boston*, 38–40.

102. For short biographies of Byles, see Sprague, *Annals*, 1: 376–382; and Clifford K. Shipton, *Sibley's Harvard Graduates*, vol. 7: *Biographical Sketches of Those Who Attended Harvard College in the Classes 1722–1725* (Boston: Massachusetts Historical Society, 1945), 464–493. Shipton describes Byles as "the poet laureate and . . . official greeter of the province" (ibid., 468). For a longer account of Byles's life, see Arthur Wentworth Hamilton Eaton, *The Famous Mather Byles: The Noted Boston Tory Preacher, Poet, and Wit, 1707–1788* (Boston: W. A. Butterfield, 1914). Cotton Mather recorded his own resolution to "be much of a father" to his orphaned nephew (*Diary*, 2: 64, entry for April 17, 1711); Joshua Gee recorded the deathbed blessing that Cotton subsequently bestowed on Byles (*Israel's Mourning*, 29).

103. Mather Byles, *The Character and End of the Perfect Man* (Boston: B. Green, 1744), 34; this was Byles's funeral sermon for his wife. See also Shipton, *Sibley's Harvard Graduates*, 7: 474; and Eaton, *Mather Byles*, 78.

104. On this, see chapter 2 above.

Thoughts to this, that the most improper Season is still proper for our Concern about Repentance and the New-Birth. . . . But, my Brethren, if you refuse and rebel, at your own Peril be it. Better had you not come hither this Night, than going away, continue Strangers to CHRIST. The Golden Opportunities will become a Curse: and the higher your present Privileges are, the deeper will be your future Fall: Even from this Sermon you'll sink but the lower into Ruin."[105] "How foolish are those miserable Souls, who after so many Invitations to accept of the Rest of Heaven, go away unresolved whether to strive for it or no; refuse it, and despise it? Who can say but if you now think to put it off, and delay your Endeavours after it, an angry God may forever banish you from it. Are you sure you shall ever have another Opportunity to sue for Mercy? Nay, Death may strip you of all before To-morrow."[106]

Long after the Great Awakening had faded into memory, Byles continued to insist on conversion's centrality, especially for those aspiring to the pastorate: "[The minister] must be a Regenerated, *Holy Man*. . . . He must have gone through a Conversion to GOD. He must have an Experimental Acquaintance with the Doctrines of Repentance, Faith, Love to God, and Benevolence to Mankind. He must feel upon his own Soul, a deep Impression of those Truths which he preaches to others. Be sure he can never be a Perfect Minister, who is not so much as a good Christian."[107]

But the Awakening itself Byles resisted. In 1740 George Whitefield preached from a scaffolding erected in front of Eighth Church's meetinghouse, and Byles never published a direct attack on the revival such as made Charles Chauncy's name odious to New Lights. However, by the fall of 1741 his views were sufficiently hardened, and sufficiently well known, to draw the fire of the itinerant Eleazar Wheelock.[108] A passage from Wheelock's journal describes a sermon he delivered in Boston on November 9 of that year, before a large audience including many Harvard students, in which "I believe the children of God were very much refreshed. They told me afterwards, they believed that Mather Byles was never so lashed in his life."[109]

The motivation behind Byles's Old Light stance remains unclear. Implausibly, one historian has suggested that he may have been influenced by his uncle Cotton's handling of the witchcraft controversy in Salem.[110] It is much more

---

105. Byles, *Visit to Jesus*, 10–11, 22.
106. Mather Byles, *The Glorious Rest of Heaven* (Boston: B. Green, 1745), 31.
107. Mather Byles, *The Man of God Thoroughly Furnished to Every Good Work* (New London, Conn.: Nathanael Green and Timothy Green, Jr., 1758), 9–10.
108. Shipton, *Sibley's Harvard Graduates*, 7: 477; Eaton, *Mather Byles*, 82–83, 86–87.
109. Quoted in Tracy, *Great Awakening*, 203; and Kidd, *Great Awakening*, 115.
110. Shipton, *Sibley's Harvard Graduates*, 7: 477.

Chart 16: Eighth Church, first-time admissions to membership and baptisms

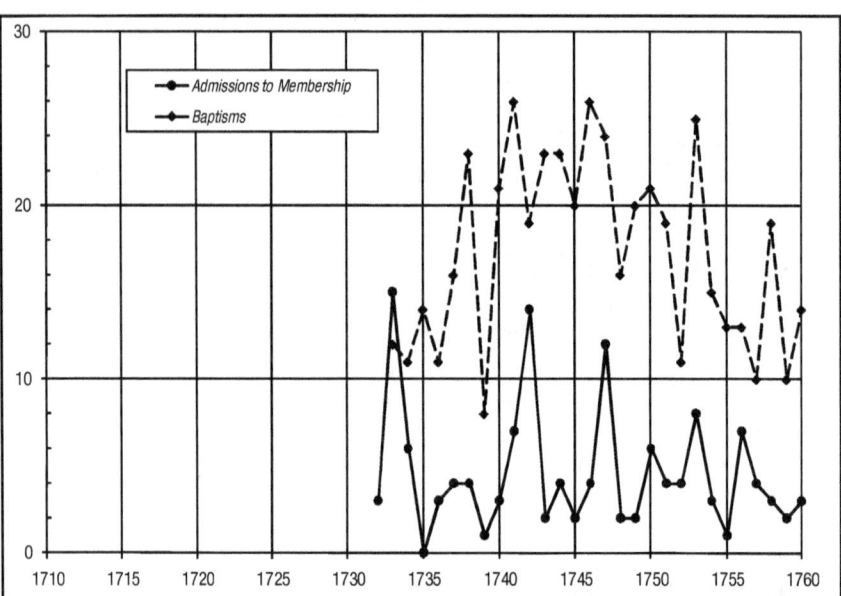

likely that the nascent Antinomianism of some radical itinerants simply grated on his own nascent moralism. As a pointer to his drift in that direction, compare his sermon, *The Flourish of the Annual Spring*, first delivered in 1739 and discussed in chapter 2 above, to his sermon, *God Glorious in the Scenes of Winter*, published only five years later. In spite of the overt thematic similarity of these two homilies, they are quite different in character; the former is aggressively evangelistic, while the latter restricts itself to a series of shallow, moralizing allegories without close application.[111]

Another credible and possibly complementary rationale is the fact that Byles's own perspective on the ministry was poles apart from the activist, pastorally-grounded paradigm embraced by many of the revivalists and their supporters. Preaching at his son's ordination to the ministry, he painted a picture of the ideal minister that was almost a caricature of the traditional clericalist image:

> That which might pass for Mirth and Humour in a common Man, would in [a minister] be Froth, and Levity, and Grimace: The Buffoon grafted on the Divine. No; he must be Grave, Temperate, Sober, Meek.... Natural *Good Sense*, *Learning*, and *Improvement of Mind*, enter into the idea of a finished Minister.... Paul was a Scholar, before he commenced a Divine.... He that

---

111. Byles, *Flourish of the Annual Spring*; idem, *God Glorious in the Scenes of Winter* (Boston: B. Green, 1744).

gives Light to others, had need have double Light himself. A Minister then, should be a Man of universal Knowledge. Especially, he should ... be a thorough Student in Divinity, in all its Branches and Connections.... He should understand the Controversies of the Polemical Systems.... He should have a Good Taste for Writing: And be truly Learned, without Pedantry; and truly Eloquent, without Stiffness and Affectation.... [H]e should be a Person of graceful Deportment, elegant Address, and fluent Utterance. He must study an easy Style, expressive Diction, and tuneful Cadences.... The next thing, to furnish the Man of GOD, and make him Perfect, is a talent at *entertaining and useful Conversation*.... In short, all the Excellencies of a superiour Mind, and a most elevated Christian, must conspire to render him Perfect and Compleat.[112]

This characterization had far more to do with eighteenth-century notions of upper-class gentility than with the ideal of pastoral activism articulated and exemplified by Byles's uncle Cotton.

It stands to reason that Byles himself, like his grandfather Increase, would identify the minister's study as the place of his greatest endeavors: "What mighty Labours attend him, invisible in his Closet, retired from Men? His neighbours perhaps fancy him pretty easy among his Books, when he is striving in Prayer.... The Study of the Minister is the Field of Battle: Here he plays the Hero; tries the Dangers of War, and repeats the Toils of Combat. How many massy Volumes must he go through, to enrich his Thought? What Pains must he take to compare, to digest, to understand, or to confute the various Pages of his Author? How often must he watch while others sleep? and his solitary Candle burn, when the Midnight-Darkness covers the Windows of the Neighbourhood?"[113] For all his eloquence about the minister's "mighty Labours," it is striking that he had absolutely nothing to say here about such laborious aspects of pastoral care as visitation and catechesis. He was finally discharged by Eighth Church in 1776. Though this was largely a reaction to his Loyalist political sentiments, one of the most telling rationales offered by members of the congregation was that he had "neglect[ed] to visit his people in their distress."[114]

The church's statistics for the era in question are much as one would expect of such a traditionalist pastorate, demonstrating little vitality under Byles's ministry. The record of admissions to membership peaks at fifteen the year after the congregation's organization and declines almost uniformly thereafter, broken only by brief upticks associated with episodes such as the Awakening's first blush and the earthquake of 1755.[115] The record of baptisms shows a steady

---

112. Byles, *Man of God*, 10–11, 13–14. Note the irony in this categorical rejection of "Mirth and Humour" by one known above all for his wit.

113. Ibid., 14.

114. McKenzie, "Provincial Period," 227; Shipton, *Sibley's Harvard Graduates*, 7: 483.

115. See Chart 16; and Appendix, Table 1, column 8.

increase through the congregation's first decade, then begins a decline which steepens after 1750.[116] That Eighth Church profited nothing from the Awakening and its aftermath is clear enough.[117] That this was as much due to Byles's clericalist understanding of the pastorate as to any theological scruples he may have had concerning the revivalists' message—indeed, that Byles's clericalist understanding of the pastorate was a major factor motivating his rejection of that message—seems clear as well.

Ninth ("West" or "Lynde Street") Church

This congregation was organized in 1737 to serve Boston's burgeoning West End.[118] Its pastors during the era under examination were William Hooper (1737–1746) and Jonathan Mayhew (1747–1766).[119] Hooper, a Scot and an alumnus of the University of Edinburgh, was a rationalist of the first water who actually dared to invoke "Pascal's Wager" against the unbeliever: "What is it that assures thee, thou Infidel, that there is no Day of Judgment, no future State? 'Tis not Reason, for Reason tells us, that there is in Man a Principle superior to Matter, and which in all Probability will never die.... If there is no Day of Judgment, no future State, the good Man loses the Pleasure of being wicked, and of following his criminal, base, and brutish Passions, which afford but a poor Pleasure at best. But if there is a Day of Judgment, profane and vicious Man, what dost thou loose [lose]! We dare not describe thy Misery."[120]

Hooper was a moralistic Arminian who invoked the Day of Judgment, not to elicit conversion as in the sermons of most of his clerical contemporaries, but to motivate obedience to divinely sanctioned law: "Is JESUS CHRIST to appear at the End of the World, and to call all Mankind to his Judgment Seat? *What manner of Persons ought we to be in all holy Conversation and Godliness....* Even the Light of Nature teaches us, that a future State of Rewards and Punishments is highly probable; but Scripture demonstrates this Point.... Whether you think of it or not, this Day will come.... Think then of the Day of the Lord, and think of it in such a manner as to prepare thy self for it. Leave all thy wicked

---

116. See Chart 16; and Appendix, Table 5, column 8.
117. Shipton, *Sibley's Harvard Graduates*, 7: 477.
118. McKenzie, "Provincial Period," 229.
119. Weis, *Colonial Clergy*, 110, 138, 242.
120. William Hooper, *Christ the Life of True Believers, and Their Appearance with Him in Glory* (Boston: D. Fowle, 1741), 13–14. For biographical sketches of Hooper, see C. A. Bartol, "Discourse on William Hooper," in *The West Church and Its Ministers* (Boston: Crosby, Nichols and Co., 1856), 61–78; and James Grant Wilson and John Fiske, eds., *Appleton's Cyclopaedia of American Biography*, 6 vols. (New York: D. Appleton and Co., 1900), 3: 252–253.

Thoughts and Practices; court the Favour of him that is to be thy Judge, submit to his Scepter, pay a willing Obedience to his Laws."[121]

Such a sermon, delivered at the height of the Awakening in Boston, plainly demonstrated Hooper's antipathy to New Light Calvinism. Evidently he saw the revival's partisans as at best Antinomian and at worst unregenerate: "Many think to be saved by a dead Faith, by a bare relying upon the Righteousness of JESUS CHRIST, without being at any pains to acquire Sanctity of Heart and Uprightness of Conduct. . . . Others [trust] to a Warmth of Fancy or Heat of Imagination, especially when they are engaged in the Worship of GOD. . . . You flatter your selves with the Hopes of being loved by GOD, and that you are in the Way to Heaven. But for all your Profession, whilst your Hearts are unsanctified, you are hated by GOD, and in the way to everlasting Misery. *Without Holiness, no Man shall see the LORD.*"[122]

Underscoring this point was Hooper's no-holds-barred attack on "enthusiasm": "Many Persons from the Conceits of a warmed or over-weening Brain, perswade themselves that they are the particular Favourites of Heaven, and that every vain Notion that settles strongly in their Fancies, is the Effect of divine Inspiration. . . . [A man] professes so much Truth and Sanctity, speaks with so great Zeal and Confidence, pretends so much Freedom and Familiarity with GOD, and looks with so much Emotion and Fire, that the Multitudes amazed at his extraordinary Air and Manner of Talking, are melted down before him, implicitly receive his Notions and Impressions, and become molded into what Form he pleases. . . . The *Apostles* were men of another Character."[123]

What sort of men were Hooper's Apostles? Philosopher-saints, it would seem: "Let us consider the great Regard which the Apostles had for Reason, and the Perfection to which they carried it. Enthusiasts are remarkable for their Hatred and Enmity to the Exercise of Religion and Understanding. There is very little of it to be seen, or heard in their Talk and Writings. . . . But this is not the Language, nor agreeable to the Practice of the Apostles. So far were they from despising, or even neglecting Reason, that on the contrary they made continual Use of it; they recommended it strongly to Christians, and earnestly exhorted them to examine the Doctrines which were taught them, by the Rules of Reason; they improved this divine Faculty, and carried it to a greater Degree of Perfection, than otherwise it could have arrived to."[124]

In Hooper's account, the Holy Spirit became little more than the human intellect writ large: "I acknowledge that Spirit of GOD resides in every true Chris-

---

121. Ibid., 24–25.
122. William Hooper, *Jesus Christ the Only Way to the Father* (Boston: D. Fowle, 1742), 21.
123. William Hooper, *The Apostles Neither Impostors nor Enthusiasts* (Boston: Rogers and Fowle, 1742), 21–23.
124. Ibid., 35, 37.

tian.... He enlightens our Minds, he renews our Wills, he causes us to believe in GOD, to love him and to obey his Laws: but he does these Things, by discovering to us Religion and Vertue, and propounding the Arguments, or Evidence, that perswade us to embrace them ... by enlarging our Knowledge, and strengthening our Reason in spiritual Things.... And these Things he generally, if not always performs in so calm and gentle a Manner, as that we cannot distinguish the Operation of the Spirit of GOD within us, from the Workings of our own Minds."[125]

In Hooper's eyes, revivalists who threw off reason's restraint posed a threat not just to the church but to society itself: "They are remarkable for fighting human Laws.... At first they seem to be innocent and inoffensive: But when the *Infatuation* prevails, and Numbers are added to them, they openly break the Laws, they despise Magistrates, and are for erecting a Government according to their own vain Imaginations.... The Church of the *Apostles* is so opposite to this, that it would be an Affront to their Memory to take much Pains to illustrate and prove it.... [T]he Apostles were subject to Magistrates, and to others in Authority; and they peremptorily commanded all Christians inviolably to observe the same Conduct."[126]

In short, for Hooper, the sort of religion being promulgated by the Awakeners was little to be preferred over the rankest unbelief: "*My dear Brethren*, suffer the Word of Exhortation. Be on your Guard against *Infidelity* and *Enthusiasm*. I know not which of these is the greatest Enemy to true Religion."[127] His own iconoclasm could hardly have escaped the notice of his colleagues. For example, on at least one occasion Benjamin Colman tangled with him over his sermonic slurs against Calvinist tenets concerning divine sovereignty.[128] Given his social and ecclesiastical elitism, it comes as no surprise that in 1746 he suddenly resigned his position at Ninth Church and entered the Church of England. After sailing for the mother country, where he took episcopal orders, he returned the following year to assume the rectorate of Trinity Church, Boston's third Anglican parish.[129]

Hooper's successor was Jonathan Mayhew.[130] If Boston's Congregational clergy had viewed with skepticism the arrival of the former, that of the latter

---

125. Ibid., 43–44.
126. Ibid., 33, 35.
127. Ibid., 46.
128. Bartol, "William Hooper," 64–67, 72–77; Chapman, "Benjamin Colman," 195–197.
129. McKenzie, "Provincial Period," 229; Bartol, "William Hooper," 63.
130. For biographical sketches of Mayhew, see Sprague, *Annals*, 8: 22–29; Shipton, *Sibley's Harvard Graduates*, 11: 440–472; and Jones, *Shattered Synthesis*, 143–164. For a book-length treatment, see Charles W. Akers, *Called unto Liberty: A Life of Jonathan Mayhew, 1720–1766* (Cambridge: Harvard University Press, 1964).

Chapter 4: Nurturing New Vines

they contemplated with downright dread. While a student at Harvard, Mayhew had been briefly but powerfully drawn to the Awakening, until the dissuasive efforts of his father and the college's faculty had steered him in the opposite direction, to the point that he even acquired a reputation as something of a heretic.[131] When Ninth Church called him to its pastorate, it took account of this by extending invitations to participate in his ordination council to the clergy of only two Boston churches, First and Fourth. Even these declined, and when he was finally ordained, his council of eleven clerics numbered in its ranks not a single representative of a Boston congregation.[132]

In a sense, Mayhew's pastorate simply carried forward and elaborated themes already sounded by Hooper. For example, there was the same rejection of revivalism as not just wrong but dangerous: "[A]ll *enthusiastic* notions . . . stand in opposition to Christian sobriety; and ought to be guarded against. . . . Superstition and enthusiasm . . . are real and great vices of the mind. . . . For they strongly imply a criminal misuse of the understanding, and of the word of God. . . . A person that makes such use of his reason, and of the holy scriptures, as he ought to make, never did, never will, never can fall into the errors of a raving, wild enthusiasm. . . . Enthusiasm has, perhaps, been productive of as much evil in the world, as the most flagrant and acknowledged immoralities: Yea, it leads naturally and directly to such immoralities."[133]

Moreover, there was the same tendency to reduce religion to morality, and, flowing from this, the same fondness for telescoping and even equating regeneration and sanctification:

> Upon the whole . . . Christianity appears to be a practical science; the art of living piously and virtuously. . . . The Gospel informs us, that in order to our salvation, it is necessary that we should be *born again*; *born of God*; born of the *spirit*. . . . Now I would ask, What is the meaning of all these phrases? . . . Is it not manifestly, this, that sinners must, by the gospel, and the co-operation of the spirit and grace of God therewith, be turned from sin to righteousness? . . .

---

131. Shipton, *Sibley's Harvard Graduates*, 11: 441–442; Jones, *Shattered Synthesis*, 143; Robert J. Wilson III, *The Benevolent Deity: Ebenezer Gay and the Rise of Rational Religion in New England, 1696–1787* (Philadelphia: University of Pennsylvania Press, 1984), 87.

132. Akers, *Called unto Liberty*, 47–53; Wilson, *Benevolent Deity*, 138–140; Shipton, *Sibley's Harvard Graduates*, 11: 442–443. Benjamin Colman stated his own grave reservations concerning Mayhew's ordination in a letter to Thomas Foxcroft dated May 15, 1747, now held in the Massachusetts Historical Society Archives, Boston.

133. Jonathan Mayhew, *Christian Sobriety* (Boston: Richard and Samuel Draper, 1763), 206, 209–210. It is striking that this collection of eight sermons, described on its title page as originally intended for the benefit of "the Young Men usually Attending the Public Worship at the West Church in Boston," eschewed any endorsement of or even reference to the religious societies that earlier generations of pastors had relied on to provide their young people with spiritual support and nurture.

> This is manifestly that *new birth*, or *regeneration*; that *putting off the old man with his deeds*, and *putting on the new man*, of which the scriptures speak: And the thing is in itself very plain and intelligible, how great a *mystery* soever, either the ancient or modern *Nicodemus's* and *masters in Israel*, have made of it.... I am sensible, that some persons have invented another sort of *regeneration*, which leaves the subject of it much as it found him, ... and which a man may *experience*, without being really any better than he was before; any more like God; any more observant of his laws. Yea, I wish there was not reason to say, that that which many have taken to be their *regeneration*, and a being *filled with the spirit*, might be more properly called a *Possession*.... According to their notion of regeneration, I acknowledge that a person may be born again, and yet not become a *doer of the word*. But the scriptures know of no regeneration, besides that which consists in a real change of heart and manners, from sin and unrighteousness to holiness; a regeneration, from which obedience to the laws of Christianity is inseparable; and with weak, habitual sinning is absolutely inconsistent.... [T]o say that it is necessary we should be born again, is, in effect to say neither more nor less than this, that it is necessary we should become holy in heart and conversation, by God's assistance and grace; which is the same thing, in other words, with ... yielding a practical obedience to the gospel of Christ.[134]

There was the same elevation of God's benevolence over the other attributes of deity, and, as a corollary, the same tendency to look askance at the Calvinist concept of election:

> The superintendency of divine providence, if conceived of in a right manner, is one of the most pleasurable and delightful considerations that can enter into the mind of a reasonable creature.... Indeed, if instead of a wise and infinitely gracious Being, one whose kind regards are extended to all his intellectual creatures; and one who governs the world with a view at promoting the moral rectitude, and so of advancing the happiness of his creatures and offspring; I say, if instead of such a Being as this, we, in our imaginations, place, at the head of the universe, a capricious, humoursome and tyrannical Being; one who loves and hates at random, and has no uniform, consistent, and benevolent design; we form a scheme of principles, more destructive of rational happiness than that of *Atheism* itself. For any man had rather be left to the mercy of *atoms*, and *fate*, and *chance*, or any other *chimerical Deity*, than be subjected to the pleasure of such a monster, as an all-knowing, infinitely powerful Being, destitute of a steady, uniform principle of justice and goodness; delighting himself in the exercise of a wanton, licentious omnipotence—But whatever schemes of religion have been propagated, in which the supreme ruler of the universe is represented in such a gloomy and formidable dress as this, they are equally inconsistent with the religion of nature, and the religion of Jesus Christ.[135]

---

134. Jonathan Mayhew, *Sermons* (Boston: Richard Draper, 1755), 83, 85–87.
135. Jonathan Mayhew, *Seven Sermons* (Boston: Rogers and Fowle, 1749), 109–110. See Shipton, *Sibley's Harvard Graduates*, 11: 448.

Chapter 4: Nurturing New Vines

However, Mayhew went farther than Hooper in that he turned his rhetorical guns not just against John Calvin and New Light Calvinism but against Martin Luther and the whole corpus of Reformation Protestantism:

> [T]ho' faith alone justifies us in this world, and *intitles* us to salvation in the world to come; yet obedience to the gospel is necessary in order to our being justified at Christ's tribunal hereafter, and so, in order to our actually being saved at last.... So much for the pretended *"Article of a standing, or a falling Church"*! It is really surprising that such a doctrine should ever be believed by any: It is still more wonderful, that it should ever be embraced by any *worthy, good* men: But what is most astonishing of all, is, that such an irrational, unscriptural doctrine; a doctrine of so pernicious a tendency with regard to the lives and manners of men, should be *insisted* upon with peculiar *warmth* and *zeal*, as a most important and fundamental article of the Christian Faith![136]

He went much farther than Hooper in that he even came to deny the deity of Christ. First airing his rejection of the doctrine of the Trinity in 1755, he went on to become a "father of American Unitarianism."[137]

Mayhew's sarcastic, scattergun approach to theological debate guaranteed his exclusion from Boston's clerical establishment.[138] Never even accepted into the local association of Congregational ministers, and consequently denied a place in the rotation of speakers for the regular Thursday lectures, he responded by organizing his own lecture series, a forum that drew listeners from across the community and in certain circles added a measure of luster to his reputation.[139] However, his preparation for these presentations, together with the two-sermons-per-Sunday workload imposed by the refusal of almost all his clerical peers to practice pulpit exchange with him, presumably meant that practically all of his time was spent simply getting ready to preach.[140]

---

136. Mayhew, *Sermons*, 252, 255.

137. Shipton, *Sibley's Harvard Graduates*, 11: 440, 449. Wilson, in *Benevolent Deity*, 129, notes Mayhew's admiration for the English anti-Trinitarian Samuel Clarke. See also Sydney E. Ahlstrom and Jonathan S. Carey, eds., *An American Reformation: A Documentary History of Unitarian Christianity* (Middletown, Conn.: Wesleyan University Press, 1985), 323.

138. Wilson observes: "Mayhew wasted no time in alienating most of the Boston clergy" (*Benevolent Deity*, 139).

139. Akers, *Called to Liberty*, 67–68; Shipton, *Sibley's Harvard Graduates*, 11: 445–446.

140. Although by this time many of Boston's clergy, influenced by Whitefield's example, had begun to discard full manuscripts in favor of outlines and extempore preaching, Mayhew persisted in writing out his sermon texts; see Shipton, *Sibley's Harvard Graduates*, 11: 445. Akers, in *Called unto Liberty*, 55, admits the arduous labor that must have gone into preparing three such manuscripts every week, but two pages later makes the unsupported assertion that Mayhew nevertheless at some unspecified time "spent

122 *Chapter 4: Nurturing New Vines*

This is admittedly inferential; the evidence is not sufficient to allow the sort of categorical statements about pastoral practice that are possible with other churches and their ministers. However, it is significant that of the four sermons on his death that were published, not one has anything to say about his day-to-day work as a pastor. Without exception, these sermons praise his character and especially his ministry as a preacher and teacher, but they are utterly silent on matters such as catechesis and visitation. Were there only one or two such sermons, this might be passed off as a mere oversight, but it seems unlikely that four of them would remain silent on the same topic if there were anything of substance to be said about it that might be made to flatter the deceased.[141] Mayhew's social elitism likely provided the same sort of rationale for his pastoral disengagement that it plainly did for Chauncy and other Old Lights.[142]

Certainly Ninth Church's records do not reflect any great impact on what was then a rapidly growing, prestigious neighborhood.[143] Throughout the era under examination, the congregation seems to have remained small in numbers, relatively homogeneous, and quite affluent, drawing people from an unusually wide area.[144] Although it enjoyed at least a measure of success under Hooper, with Mayhew there followed a period of precipitous decline. After his early death, Ebenezer Gay lamented: "During his painful labours among you, were there not numbers born to Christ in this church, as the fruit of his travelling [travailing], as it were in birth, to see Christ formed in you, and in your children? And were ye

---

many hours calling on his parishioners." It is hard to see how he could have managed this at any point during his tenure at Ninth Church.

141. John Browne, *A Discourse Delivered at the West Church in Boston, August 24, 1776, Six Weeks after the Death of the Reverend Dr. Mayhew* (Boston: R. and S. Draper, 1766); Charles Chauncy, *A Discourse Occasioned by the Death of the Reverend Jonathan Mayhew, D.D., Late Pastor of the West-Church in Boston* (Boston: R. and S. Draper, 1766); Ebenezer Gay, *A Beloved Disciple of Jesus Characterized* (Boston: R. and S. Draper, T. and J. Fleet, and Edes and Gill, 1766); and idem, *St. John's Vision of the Woman Cloathed with the Sun* (Boston: R. and S. Draper, Edes and Gill, and T. and J. Fleet, 1766). Compare Mayhew's situation with that of William Waldron, whose four published funeral sermons go into considerable detail on his pastoral ministry at Seventh Church, as noted above, in spite of his abbreviated tenure there.

142. Wilson, *Benevolent Deity*, 180; Corrigan, *Hidden Balance*, 86–107.

143. See Charts 17 and 18; and Appendix, Table 1, column 9, Table 3, column 6, and Table 5, column 9. On the affluence of Ninth Church's neighborhood and membership, see Corrigan, *Hidden Balance*, 97–98.

144. Browne refers to those who came "from the uttermost parts of the town to hear the wisdom of your late pastor, and may now be ready to think that [they] may with propriety worship elsewhere" (*West Church*, 17). Shipton comments that Mayhew "attracted to the West Church liberal members of all of the other congregations of the town" (*Sibley's Harvard Graduates*, 11: 445). See also Akers, *Called unto Liberty*, 56.

Chart 17: Ninth Church, first-time admissions to membership and baptisms

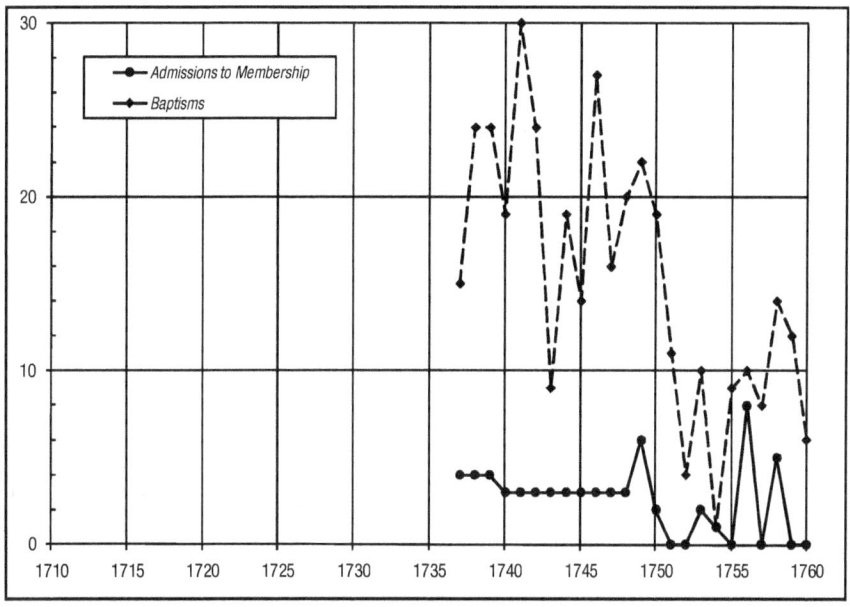

Chart 18: Ninth Church, covenant renewals

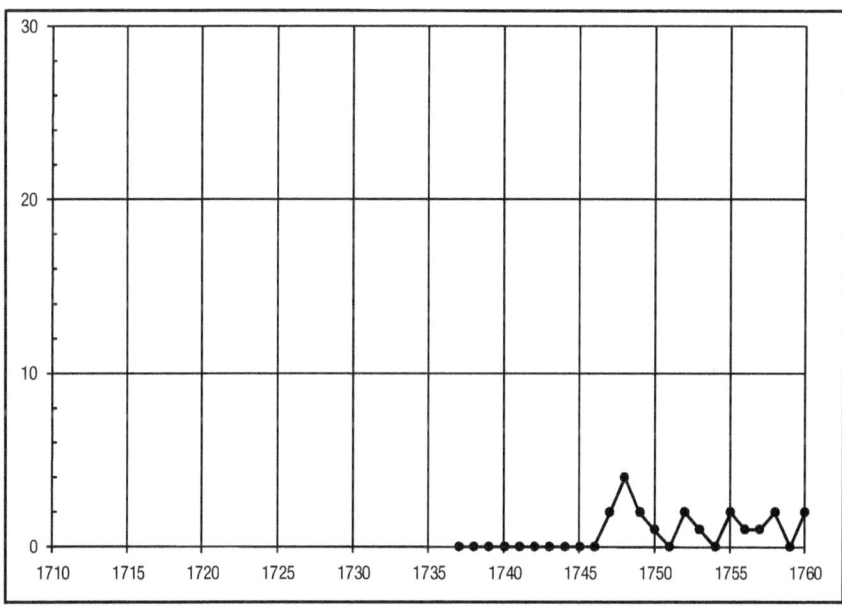

not, by the blessing of God on a faithful and fruitful ministry, increasing with the increase of God?"[145] The inescapable answer to this rhetorical question, say the statistics, is no.

Tenth ("Bennet Street") Church

This congregation was organized in 1742 by a group of Old Light dissidents who had withdrawn from Second Church in reaction to that congregation's dismissal of Samuel Mather.[146] The new congregation immediately called Mather to its pastorate, a position which he held until his death.[147] Some comment has already been made on his elitism and traditionalist approach to the ministry.[148] It should be noted that tradition figured prominently in his theologizing as well, so that he hewed much closer to New England's Calvinist conventions than did either Chauncy or Mayhew. For example, when Chauncy published *Salvation for All Men Illustrated and Vindicated*, defending the then-novel concept of universal redemption, Mather responded with *All Men Will Not Be Saved Forever*, upholding the customary Reformed position in regard to the limited scope of Christ's atonement.[149]

However, Mather shared with Chauncy and Mayhew a shallow sense of sin that manifested itself in creeping moralism: "'Tis a plain Case . . . that *such a Perfection as is sinless is not here attainable*; nor yet *a Perfection with regard to the Degree of any Grace or Vertue*. But however we must assert and maintain, that *there is a Perfection which may be attained*: And, by *This*, we mean *Sincerity and Uprightness*, which is Evangelical Perfection. . . . And now all *Sincerely good Men are* thus *perfect*. . . . And besides, *Men may attain*, and some actually do arrive at, *an Eminence in Divine Knowledge and Vertue*. And so they may be said to be in a comparative Sense *Perfect*, as rising to a higher Degree of Perfection than others about Them."[150]

---

145. Ebenezer Gay, *St. John's Vision*, 37.
146. For a comment on Tenth Church's meetinghouse and its location, see Whitehill, *Boston*, 41.
147. Weis, *Colonial Clergy*, 137, 242. For biographical sketches of Mather, see Sprague, *Annals*, 1: 371–374; and Shipton, *Sibley's Harvard Graduates*, 6: 216–238.
148. On this, see chapter 2 above; see also Remer, "Old Lights," 571.
149. Charles Chauncy, *Salvation for All Men Illustrated and Vindicated as a Scripture Doctrine in Numerous Abstracts from a Variety of Pious and Learned Men, Who Have Purposely Writ upon the Subject* (Boston: T. and J. Fleet, 1782); Samuel Mather, *All Men Will Not Be Saved Forever* (Boston: Benjamin Edes and Sons, 1782). The appearance of the latter volume, together with several of similar thrust by other authors, finally drew from Chauncy the definitive statement of his views on universal redemption, *The Mystery Hid from Ages and Generations, Made Manifest by the Gospel-Revelation* (London: Charles Dilly, 1784).
150. Mather, *Walk of the Upright*, 10.

Mather also shared with Chauncy and Mayhew both an unswerving hostility to the Awakening and a fundamental incompetence in matters related to the pastorate. His preaching was widely ridiculed; politician Robert Treat Paine commented that the sound of a sermon by Mather had driven even Paine's dog to flee.[151] It might have been thought that his pastoral ministry would have been more effective, since, like his father, he had a deep interest in German Pietism, even going so far as to edit a Latin-language biography of August Hermann Francke.[152] Obviously, though, he never internalized the pastoral priorities embodied in Francke's ministry. Although very few records survive for Tenth Church, contemporary accounts attest to the congregation's steady numerical decline. Ninety-three members of Second Church had withdrawn from that congregation out of sympathy for him, but Tenth Church soon shrank to number no more than twenty or thirty.[153] "The small size of his congregation," observes one scholar, "became a joke."[154] After his death in 1785, most of its few remaining members reunited with Second Church.[155]

Eleventh Church

If the history of the Great Awakening in Boston were truly nothing more than the story of "the idea of the 'new birth,'" no one ought to have been a more effective pastor during the era under consideration than Andrew Croswell, and certainly no congregation ought to have been healthier than his upstart Eleventh Church.[156] But such was not the case. Indeed, after a promising start, Croswell's flock dwindled until it numbered no more than a handful of parishioners, finally dissolving shortly after his own demise. What might account for this outcome? Can it be reconciled with traditional perspectives on the Awakening? Might it instead serve as final confirmation of the thesis here being tested? Obviously, this congregation and its controversial pastor merit our closer examination.

A member of Harvard's class of 1728 and a recipient of the M.A. from that institution in 1731, Croswell spent the years leading up to the Great Awakening

---

151. Quoted in Shipton, *Sibley's Harvard Graduates*, 6: 227.
152. Samuel Mather, ed., *Vita B. Augusti Hermanni Franckii, S.S. Theologiae in Academia Fridericiana nuper Professoris Eximiis nec non V.D.M. apud Glaucham, etc. prope Hallam Magdeburgicam: Cui Adjecta Est, Narratio Rerum Memorabilium in Ecclesiis Evangelicis per GERMANIAM etc.* (Boston: Samuel Kneeland, 1733).
153. Robbins, *History*, 122.
154. Shipton, *Sibley's Harvard Graduates*, 6: 227.
155. Robbins, *History*, 123; Shipton, *Sibley's Harvard Graduates*, 6: 233; Sprague, *Annals*, 1: 373. Sprague notes the irony that Tenth Church's meetinghouse, on Bennet Street, was sold to a Universalist congregation.
156. Tracy, *Great Awakening*, ix; Weis, *Colonial Clergy*, 64, 242.

as pastor of the Second Church of Groton, Connecticut.[157] Having already come to assurance of his own salvation, in the Awakening's first flush he found as well the tongue and pen that were to win him notoriety.[158] In December of 1740, he lashed out against Anglican commissary Alexander Garden, one of Whitefield's early critics, as a *"Meritmonger"* who denied the Protestant doctrine of justification by faith alone.[159] With this complaint, Croswell first sounded the theme that was to be threaded through practically all of his public disputations, from the pulpit and in print, over the next four decades. Looking to the example of George Whitefield and James Davenport, he soon found his life's vocation as an itinerant evangelist; in 1742 he conducted tumultuous campaigns in Plymouth and Charlestown, Massachusetts.[160]

Seeking a base of operations in the Boston area, Croswell eventually came to be associated with a congregation of New Light radicals who had withdrawn from other Boston churches in frustration at their tempered embrace of revival, a congregation which those churches consequently refused to recognize as legitimate. In 1746 his longsuffering Groton parish finally gave him permission to take his leave, and that same year the Boston radicals offered him their pastorate, a position in which he had already shown interest.[161] Though he declined this call, citing as justification the group's evident separatist tendencies, he did offer to serve as pastor of a new group whose members would be drawn from the radicals' own ranks. A sizable element of the congregation rejected his proposal, claiming that it reflected the very separatist tendencies he supposedly decried.[162] Nevertheless, a large number accepted his terms, in 1748 organizing yet

---

157. For a biographical sketch of Croswell, see Clifford K. Shipton, *Sibley's Harvard Graduates*, vol. 8: *Biographical Sketches of Those Who Attended Harvard College in the Classes 1726–1730* (Boston: Massachusetts Historical Society, 1951), 386–407. An excellent study is Leigh Eric Schmidt's "'A Second and Glorious Reformation': The New Light Extremism of Andrew Croswell," *William and Mary Quarterly*, 3d series, vol. 43, no. 2 (April 1986): 214–244.

158. Kidd describes Croswell as "the most prolific writer among the radicals" (*Great Awakening*, 144).

159. Andrew Croswell, *An Answer to the Rev. Mr. Garden's Three First Letters to the Rev. Mr. Whitefield* (Boston: S. Kneeland and T. Green, 1741), 11; Schmidt, "'Second and Glorious Reformation,'" 216–217.

160. Goen, *Revivalism and Separatism*, 11, 113; Shipton, *Sibley's Harvard Graduates*, 8: 390; Schmidt, "'Second and Glorious Reformation,'" 218–221; Tracy, *Great Awakening*, 160–161; Kidd, *Great Awakening*, 138–139.

161. Shipton, *Sibley's Harvard Graduates*, 8: 396–397; Schmidt, "'Second and Glorious Reformation,'" 225–226; Kidd, *Great Awakening*, 150; Hill, *Old South Church*, 1: 589–592.

162. In spite of his record, Croswell insisted, "I scarce know one Calvinistical Minister, except Mr. *Whitefield*, who carries the Matter of Union among Protestants so far as I

another congregation, Eleventh Church, under articles and a covenant which he himself had composed. Within a few months he was formally installed as their pastor. He was finally dismissed by the Groton congregation that same year.[163]

Eleventh Church was slow to win a measure of acceptance from the local religious establishment. Since the new congregation held its services in the Huguenots' old meetinghouse—just around the corner from that of Third Church, where several of Eleventh Church's members had formerly worshiped—from the outset Croswell had to face the enmity of Joseph Sewall and Thomas Prince.[164] However, clashes with fellow clerics were nothing new to him. After his early encounter with Alexander Garden, for example, there had been skirmishes with Thomas Foxcroft, the Massachusetts Congregationalist Ebenezer Turell, and even the New Jersey Presbyterian Jonathan Dickinson—New Lights all, but every one of them, in Croswell's opinion, holding to views that undercut the doctrine of justification by faith alone.[165] Dissension was certainly common within the revivalist camp; after all, Davenport and even Whitefield had drawn their share of sniping from fellow New Lights. But while these trail-blazing itinerants had responded to criticism by confessing their errors and changing their ways, Croswell stood firm to the end, carrying on long after even Davenport had left the field of battle. In fact, he was so obsessed with the doctrine of justification by faith alone that many who were otherwise sympathetic to the cause of renewal voiced suspicions in regard to his alleged Antinomianism.[166]

---

do" (*A Narrative of the Founding and Settling the New-Gathered Congregational Church in Boston* [Boston: Rogers and Fowle, 1749], 6).

163. Shipton, *Sibley's Harvard Graduates*, 8: 397–398; Schmidt, "'Second and Glorious Reformation,'" 226; Hill, *Old South Church*, 1: 589–592; McKenzie, "Provincial Period," 236; Goen, *Revivalism and Separatism*, 312; Tracy, *Great Awakening*, 254. For the text of Eleventh Church's covenant and articles of government, see Croswell, *Narrative*, 3–6.

164. Shipton, *Sibley's Harvard Graduates*, 8: 397–399; Hill, *Old South Church*, 1: 591–594, 597; Goen, *Revivalism and Separatism*, 57. Peterson puts the number of transfers from Third Church to Eleventh Church at six or seven; see *Price of Redemption*, 225. For a reproduction of the hostile early correspondence between the pastors of Third Church and Eleventh Church, with Croswell's commentary, see his *Narrative*, 7–17.

165. Schmidt, "'Second and Glorious Reformation,'" 222–223; Kidd, *Great Awakening*, 140; Shipton, *Sibley's Harvard Graduates*, 8: 391–392, 394. Shipton observes that "Croswell plunged into every religious controversy of his Boston days" (ibid., 401), going on to lengthy quarrels with Joseph Bellamy and Alexander Cumming, for example, over nothing more than misunderstood theological terminology; see also Murray, *Jonathan Edwards*, 264; and Mark Valeri, *Law and Providence in Joseph Bellamy's New England: The Origins of the New Divinity in Revolutionary America* (New York: Oxford University Press, 1994), 43.

166. Schmidt, "'Second and Glorious Reformation,'" 224–225.

In evaluating Croswell's message, it is easy to sympathize with moderate Calvinists who harbored such doubts about him. After all, he saw their own moderation in the cause of revival as anything but a virtue: "It puts me in Mind of a Minister's Conduct in *Connecticut,* who is since an eminent Opposer [of the Awakening].—When he first began to discover himself, he faulted his Hearers for *overdoing* in Religion: He would have had them *eat more* and *sleep more* and *work more* and *do themselves no Harm*. In a Word, he would have had them *labour* less than they *did for the Meat which endureth to everlasting Life, and more for that which perisheth.*"[167] He even moved to appropriate the moderates' spiritual patrimony, citing himself as the true heir of the Protestant Reformers they so often invoked, "*Luther, Calvin, Melanchton, Beza, Bullinger, Bucer, Knox,* etc. . . . *Ursinus, Zanchius, Junius, Piscator, Rollock, Danaeus, Wendelinus,* etc."[168]

Croswell argued that his spiritual kinship to these giants was attested by his stress on their guiding principle, justification by faith alone, a doctrine he saw as drawing the opposition not just of Catholics but now even of many who considered themselves to be good Protestants: "[M]inisters should preach forgiveness of sins in a consistency with these words of our Text; *having nothing to pay he frankly forgave them both* [Luke 7:42]. This divinity is not only oppos'd at Rome: but too often in protestant countries. The law saith, *pay me what thou owest*: the preacher cries out zealously, *give the law its due*: so that between the law and the minister, the poor sinner is perpetually dunned for his spiritual debts."[169] This fixation on justification by faith had implications for his understanding of the process of conversion: "When I, feeling myself Miserable for the Breaches of God's Law, which *curseth* me, let go all other Refuges and Confidences, and *in my Heart* stand before God who is a *consuming Fire,* in the *Righteousness of Christ,* willing to perish, if that will not Justify me; leaning in *my Heart* and Soul on *this,* and *this alone*; I am *Justified,* and accounted *Righteous* by God: All that ever were brought to this are certainly Justified; there never was a Man, that in his *Heart* (the *Heart* is *purified* at the same Time) rely'd *only* on *this Foundation,* but was Justified of God."[170]

Croswell's understanding of conversion led him to adopt an approach to evangelism on which he remained remarkably consistent over the years: "*Ministers should compassionately and earnestly call upon those who are destroying themselves, not to do themselves any Harm.* You will be ready to ask who they

---

167. Andrew Croswell, *A Letter from the Rev^d Mr. Croswell, to the Rev^d Mr. Turell, in Answer to His Direction to His People* (Boston: Rogers and Fowle, 1742), 5.

168. Andrew Croswell, *The Heavenly Doctrine of Man's Justification Only by the Obedience of Jesus Christ* (Boston: Green and Russell, 1758), vi.

169. Andrew Croswell, *Free Forgiveness of Spiritual Debts* (Boston: W. McAlpine, 1766), 12–13.

170. Croswell, *Heavenly Doctrine,* 6.

are who are so *desperately wicked, as to destroy their own selves*. I answer, *Thou art the Man, thou* art the Woman, whosoever thou art, who art still in a Christless, unconverted State. For 'tis true of *all such*, that they are about murdering their precious and immortal Souls."[171] "The Exhortation now speaketh, to those who have no scriptural Ground to think they ever were made Righteous by the Obedience of Christ.... Can you bear the thought that others should be justify'd, and not you? Can you bear that others should be righteous before God, and have the Happiness of such as this, and especially in the coming World, ... [a]nd you be under a Sentence of Condemnation living and dying ... ? O I beseech you, do *yourselves no harm*.... Fly, fly for your Lives to Jesus Christ, who is the end of the Law for Righteousness."[172] "I would now address myself to those who have no reason to think themselves in a state of justification.... Believe the heavenly report: Go to God tho' sinners, tho' ungodly; and receive the pardon of your sins, and the justification of your persons, as a free gift for the sake of Jesus Christ. There are no conditions for you to fulfill to make you welcome; you need not trouble yourselves about coming up to any terms of the gospel; only *set to your seals that God is true*, and take him at his word."[173]

Croswell rejected the notion that saving faith might consist of nothing more than assent to Christian doctrine, arguing that such "general Faith" was not only "an Enemy to [a sinner's] *true* Repentance" but also likely to render that person "an Opposer of the *Power of Godliness* and *experimental* Religion in the Place where he lives, and as far as he hath any Influence."[174] In his view, saving faith, what he called "particular" faith, connoted an appropriation of Christ as well as creed. Indeed, he insisted that this was one of the hallmarks of the Reformation: "'[T]is Men's *taking God at his Word*, that Jesus Christ is *their* Saviour, which makes them *new Creatures*.... I have sometime wonder'd, and believe I shall continue wondering as long as I live, how it should come to pass that in *so Protestant* a country as this, it should be a Disgrace to any Man to be a *true Protestant*. One must be a Stranger to the State of Religion in *New-England*, not to know that a *general* Faith is in Vogue, not only among *Arminians*, but among *Calvinists* also, especially of the Clergy; and that those who maintain a *particular* Faith are look'd upon to be *Enthusiasts* and *Antinomians* etc. And yet these few *Antinomians* and *Enthusiasts falsely so called*, are the only thorough Protestants in the Land."[175]

---

171. Andrew Croswell, *The Apostle's Advice to the Jaylor Improved* (Boston: Rogers and Fowle, 1744), 14.

172. Croswell, *Heavenly Doctrine*, 17.

173. Andrew Croswell, *Free Justification thro' Christ's Redemption* (Boston: T. and J. Fleet and Green and Russell, 1765), 20–21.

174. Andrew Croswell, *What Is Christ to Me, If He Is Not Mine?* (Boston: Rogers and Fowle, 1745), 33–34; see also Goen, *Revivalism and Separatism*, 149.

175. Ibid., 17, 10.

Inherent in saving faith as Croswell understood it was the believer's assurance of salvation: "[W]e learn to reject that divinity which saith there is not *such consolation in Christ. I mean the doctrine of doubting and darkness, which will not suffer us to know we are interested in that everlasting consolation. . . . They who have had much of the love of God shed abroad in their hearts by the holy Ghost, and have been habitually comforted under all their troubles, with a prospect of being *for ever with the Lord*, could hardly live under a deliberate doubt of their own Salvation. To take any assurance from us, is to take away our comfort; [']tis to take away a present heaven from us; and we may be assured that whatever idea of religion, makes the *consolations of God* to be *small*, ought for *that* reason to be rejected by us."[176]

This was a point on which the position of the Puritan mainstream had come to differ from that of Calvin.[177] Following Calvin, Croswell saw saving faith and assurance of salvation as so inseparable that he could summon the unregenerate to the latter almost as though he were calling them to the former: "Methinks I hear some poor Souls saying: 'If we had a Thousand Worlds, we would part with them all, for this *Assurance* of which you are speaking.['] I answer; I wish you were willing to have it *for Nothing*: Do but let go your own Righteousness, and I dare pawn my Soul, that you shall have it before I have done speaking with you. What is the Difficulty, what is the *Wall of Partition* that lies in the Way to your having *Assurance*? Is it that you are old Sinners, great Sinners, *Sinners against God exceedingly?*"[178]

Pastors who counseled their parishioners to seek assurance of salvation by looking not to Christ's sacrifice but to the fruits of their sanctification were directing them down a blind alley: "*We . . . testify, that those* Ministers putting

---

176. Andrew Croswell, *Comfort in Christ* (Boston: D. Kneeland and Kneeland and Adams, 1767), 18–20; see also Heimert, *American Mind*, 130.

177. See John Calvin, *Institutes of the Christian Religion*, ed. John T. McNeill, trans. Ford Lewis Battles, Library of Christian Classics (Philadelphia: Westminster Press, 1960), 3.2.15–16, 3.15.5, 3.24.7; William Ames, *The Marrow of Theology*, ed. and trans. John D. Eusden (Cleveland, Ohio: United Church Press, 1968; reprint, Durham, N.C.: Labyrinth Press, 1983), 167, 172; Heinrich Heppe, *Reformed Dogmatics Set Out and Illustrated from the Sources*, ed. Ernst Bizer, trans. G. T. Thomson (London: George Allen and Unwin, 1950), 585–589; R. T. Kendall, *Calvin and English Calvinism to 1649*, Oxford Theological Monographs (Oxford: Oxford University Press, 1979), 61–66, 107–109, 194–196; Paul Helm, *Calvin and the Calvinists* (Carlisle, Penn.: Banner of Truth Trust, 1982), 23–31; and Joel R. Beeke, *The Quest for Full Assurance: The Legacy of Calvin and His Successors* (Carlisle, Penn.: Banner of Truth Trust, 1999). For a helpful discussion of differences on this point among early New England Puritans, some of them following Ames and others following Richard Sibbes, see Janice Knight, *Orthodoxies in Massachusetts: Rereading American Puritanism* (Cambridge: Harvard University Press, 1994).

178. Croswell, *What Is Christ to Me*, 45.

Persons *upon finding out their* Justification *by their* Sanctification (*in such a Manner as they have done*) *hath a direct Tendency to make the many Thousands of strict* Pharisees *into whose Hands that Book may come, easy and quiet in their Minds, and so* speak Peace *to themselves while GOD hath no Peace for them.*"[179] This situation, Croswell felt, made for a stark contrast with that of the early church: "Those believers who have assurance of their justification, which was common in those early days, rejoice and triumph in Christ. . . . [B]ut alas! how few are there. . . . Most serious christians will own that their religion has not made them happy, yet they at best go on between hope and fear, and must be in bondage through fear of death. . . . We do not learn from the apostolick writings, that any consciencious christians were filled with horrors of conscience and fears of hell. . . . The first christians glorified Christ by their consciencious and joyful lives. What is the reason then, that many now-a-days, hang down their heads like bulrushes, and by their sorrowful countenances and sighings frighten away others from the joyful religion of Christ?"[180]

Croswell coupled this rejection of the typical Puritan reticence in regard to assurance with a repudiation of the time-honored preparationist approach to conversion. He called instead for the sinner's immediate response to the gospel message: "[N]ot to require [sinners] to come [to Christ] *immediately* would in Effect be to give them Liberty to despise Jesus Christ a little longer, which can't be imagin'd without Blasphemy. . . . To object that we must not call Sinners to come immediately, is more proper for *Arminian* Ministers than *Calvinists. Calvinistical* Ministers *always* bid Sinners do, what they know they can't do."[181] He pushed this to the point of ruling out even the preacher's offer of counsel to the inquiring penitent: "[W]hen Ministers give their Hearers a long Train of Directions, this naturally causes them to imagine that if they observe them carefully, God will thereby be inclin'd to save them, and this Imagination will lessen their Conviction, and lighten their Burden: And for Ministers to lighten the Burden of Sinners, is in Truth only to stop them from coming to Christ. . . . Telling *how* to come, however specious it may look is indeed and in Truth, stopping Sinners from coming at all. . . . 'Tis this Way of Preaching, I make no Doubt which hath been a great Cause why Multitudes in Years past, who were under strong Con-

---

179. Andrew Croswell, *Mr. Croswell's Reply to a Book Lately Publish'd, Entitled, "A Display of God's Special Grace," Attested by the Seven Following Ministers of Boston, viz Dr. Colman, Dr. Sewall, Mr. Prince, Mr. Webb, Mr. Cooper, Mr. Foxcroft, and Mr. Gee* (Boston: Rogers and Fowle, 1742), 2. This volume is an attack on a work by Jonathan Dickinson; the quotation is from Croswell's preface, bearing his own signature as well as those of three other men.

180. Andrew Croswell, *A Discourse, from the First Epistle of Thessalonians* (Boston: E. Russell, 1784), 40–42.

181. Croswell, *Reply*, 6.

victions, never were converted, but turn'd out *Pharisees* instead of true Christians."[182]

Croswell had no patience for theologians who described conversion as a long-drawn-out ordeal: "Perhaps [someone] may say with himself, I am afraid I have not been under convictions long enough; 'tis but a few days, or perhaps a less space, that I have been in earnest about religion; surely I am not yet prepared for justification. Conviction of sin is needful. . . . But how long a time were those thousands under convictions, who were wrought upon by Peter's preaching? . . . A man may go into a christian assembly stupid and unconcerned about the one thing needful, and yet go home to his house justify'd, and an heir of heaven."[183] In his view, though, preaching aimed at eliciting such an immediate decision for Christ had become rare indeed: "And should not the *Watchmen*, the Ministers of Christ, *who watch for Souls as those that must give an Account*; earnestly and vehemently call upon them not to do themselves *any Harm*? Oh, we should! . . . Our Hearts are harder than the nether Millstone, if we can see our Hearers going in the *broad Way*, without giving them *frequent and fervent Warnings* to get into the *City of Refuge* before the *Avenger of Blood overtakes them*. I know that this kind of preaching is everywhere *spoken against*. . . . We say little to [unregenerate listeners] about that *dreadful Hell* to which they are *going*, or else speak in *such a Manner* as if it were not a *dreadful Thing* to go to *Hell*."[184]

It should be clear from the preceding chapters that Croswell's complaints concerning his fellow Congregational clergy, at least in Boston, were largely unwarranted; their hostile response was therefore predictable. As noted above, one charge they repeatedly advanced against him, responding to his monomania in regard to justification by faith alone, was that he was an Antinomian. He noted that this accusation put him in good company: "I freely own I have had great Fears, lest *Antinomians* and *Libertines* who are always too plenty, and who shew themselves after a Day of *great Grace*, should like *vile Spiders* . . . suck Poison out of the *Flower of the Gospel*, and pervert what I have written to their *own Destruction*. But this I know, the Doctrine I advance is *essentially* different from theirs: (Tho' *Luther* and *Calvin*, and St. *Paul* were tho't *Antinomians* for holding it: perhaps never any one preached *pure Gospel* without being *honour'd* with the reproachful Name of an *Antinomian*:)."[185]

The Old Lights advanced the same charge against even moderate New Lights, of course, and the moderates' defense converged with his own—though, ironically, in taking this tack he introduced many of the same distinctions he had

---

182. Ibid., 7.
183. Croswell, *Free Justification*, 22–23. This obviously anticipated the position later taken by Charles G. Finney in his landmark *Lectures on Revivals of Religion* (1835).
184. Croswell, *Apostle's Advice*, 18–20.
185. Croswell, *What Is Christ to Me*, 7.

decried as heretical when the moderates introduced them. Good works, for example, which he had so ostentatiously cast out by the front door, he now smuggled back in by the rear: "[T]*ruly good Works*, such as are acceptable to God, are a *certain* Sign of the *Life* and *Health* of the Soul, and that 'tis not in Danger of being *hurt by the second Death*. . . . It matters not, what Experiences any of you imagine you have had, or, what joyful Discoveries of the Mercies of God: Nay, though you have in Pretence a *full Assurance* of *going to Heaven*, you will certainly go to *Hell*, if your *Lives are among the Unclean*, if you are not cleansed *from all Filthiness of Flesh and Spirit*."[186]

Though Croswell's overarching concern was to telescope the conversion experience, calling for the sinner's immediate response to the gospel, he was forced to admit that this necessarily involved at least a minimal preparatory prelude, with a protracted period of holy living that would surely follow in its wake: "The *Antinomians* don't hold it material, that there should be a *Work of Conviction* before, and a Work of *Sanctification* after Faith, whereas *we* maintain that no Man can *truly* believe *his* Sins are *freely* forgiven, till he sees himself *slain by the Law*; and that whosoever believes that he is *cleansed* in the *Blood of Christ*, will be *constrained* by the *Love of Christ* to *cleanse himself from all Filthiness of Flesh and Spirit, and to perfect Holiness in the Fear of God*: So that if *our* Faith is grounded (as it *always* should be) with a Work of *Conviction before*, and a Work of *Sanctification behind*, *Antinomians* and *Libertines* have nothing to do with it; instead of speaking Comfort to *such*, it condemns them all to the Flames of Hell."[187] "[A]*nother essential* Difference between the Doctrine of Faith which I maintain, and that of the *Antinomians*[, is that] I hold a Work of *Conviction before* Faith, and a Work of *Sanctification after* Faith. . . . The Faith that I preach . . . is always preceded with a *pricking at the Heart*, and followed with an holy Heart and Life."[188]

Even the spiritual uncertainty which Croswell was generally so concerned to minimize turned out to be useful in dealing with complacency: "If we are justified freely by God's grace, then let us live holy and godly lives. Shall we sin because grace abounds? God forbid! Yea, rather let the abounding of grace be the killing of sin in us. Let us be jealous over ourselves with a godly jealousy: Blessed is the man who feareth always. The soul is never safe but when afraid."[189] This was quite a concession, especially given his views on the "joyful religion of Christ." From such a vantage point, assurance became a matter of degrees: "Nor do we assert, as some have imagined, that a Man must have the *full Assurance* of Faith, or else not be on the List of true Believers. . . . [W]e don't mean that Doubting is inconsistent with a Man's being a Believer, but only

---

186. Ibid., 15, 21.
187. Ibid., 7.
188. Croswell, *Second Defence*, 9.
189. Croswell, *Free Justification*, 19.

that *the more Faith he hath, the less will he doubt.*"[190] Perhaps assurance might not even be as inseparable from saving faith as he generally insisted; in a concession that cut the ground from under his own argument, he posited that "Persuasion of our good Estate" was not essential to the possession of saving faith, but only to its exercise.[191]

This line of argument raises the question of how Croswell actually differed from the moderate New Lights. Where did the disparities really lie? How substantial were they? It seems clear that he and the moderates were separated, not by any great gulf of dogma, but merely by the way in which, while working within a common theological framework, each stressed points the other slighted and slighted points the other stressed. Croswell's moderate antagonists were certainly not Arminians, but neither was he an Antinomian. Evangelical style mattered more than Calvinist substance in setting apart Eleventh Church and its combative pastor.[192]

Certainly the congregation's articles of government and church covenant blazed few new trails, instead highlighting New England Puritanism's traditional ecclesiological distinctives while occasionally introducing an unusual emphasis.[193] For example, the covenant mixed references to familiar concepts like "the Duties of a Church-State" with novelties like a pledge to abstain from "spending Time idly at Taverns, Tippling-Houses, or elsewhere."[194] Moreover, at a time when most of Boston's mainstream congregations were backing away from the notion of the church as a collection of "visible saints" and consequently relaxing the requirement that applicants for communicant status give a public relation of their experience of conversion, Croswell's articles of government insisted on retaining the old ways—but then offered an escape clause much like that adopted by Fourth Church half a century earlier:

> Though we pretend not to know who are converted and who are not certainly, and beyond any Possibility of being mistaken, and abhor the Notion of a pure Church, which Man must purify with a pretended Spirit of Discerning, yet we look upon it as agreeable to Scripture, that those who are admitted as Members of our Church, should give an Account of a Work of the Law and of the Gospel

---

190. Croswell, *Heavenly Doctrine*, ix.

191. See the tedious elaboration of this unhelpful distinction in Croswell, *Reply*, 11–23.

192. Schmidt's assertion that Croswell's theological stance "led him to break with his Puritan forebears and his contemporaries on several theological points" ("'Second and Glorious Reformation,'" 229) seems to overstate the case, missing the convergences noted above.

193. A manuscript copy of Eleventh Church's articles of government and church covenant is preserved in the archives of the Massachusetts Historical Society, Boston. These documents are reproduced in Croswell, *Narrative*, 3–6.

194. Ibid., 5–6.

on their Souls ... [and t]hat such Persons having given an Account of such a Work to the Minister, shall be propounded at least a Fortnight before their Admission, that so all the Members of the Church may have an Opportunity to acquaint themselves with those who offer to join in so near a Relation to them; during which Time, the Deacons or other Persons appointed by the Church shall make strict Inquiry into their moral Character, and if nothing material can be charged unto them, and they relate to the Church the Substance of what they before related to the Minister concerning a Work of the Law and of the Gospel on their Souls, *or assent to it as related by the Minister* [italics added], they may be admitted as Members.[195]

On the other hand, Croswell's articles placed authority over the selection of the pastor in the hands, not of the parishioners, but of the communicant members alone: "We propose to have a Pastor or Pastors and Deacons, who shall appear to be Persons who have Scripture-Qualifications for their respective Offices, and shall be chosen and appointed by the *Church*."[196] Eleventh Church's articles of government featured a clause reflecting the common New Light abhorrence of an unregenerate ministry: "[T]ogether with Ministerial Qualifications, we think it necessary, and for God's Glory, that the Person or Persons who may be set over us in the Lord, should give the Church a regular Account of God's Dealings with their Souls, and declare themselves living Instances of the Grace of God. This we do to prevent as much as in us lies, any unconverted Minister being ever concerned with this Church."[197]

Beyond the usual educational and spiritual qualifications, Croswell's articles plainly anticipated that any minister to serve Eleventh Church would have highly developed pastoral skills: "[W]e look upon it as a main Part of the ministerial Work, besides preaching and praying publickly, administering the Ordinances, etc. [for the pastor] to know the State of the Flock, and for this End frequently to visit the Poor as well as the Rich, and to talk with them about the State of their Souls, that so he may more privately as well as publickly pull down the Kingdom of Satan, and build up the Kingdom of Christ in the Souls of his Hearers."[198] Furthermore, in Croswell's scheme, the congregation reserved the right to remove a minister who refused to conform to such stipulations: "[I]f notwithstanding our great Care and Caution any Minister of this Church walk contrary to God's Word and the tenor of these Articles, and be incorrigible, after all

---

195. Ibid., 3–4. On the relaxation of standards in other Congregational churches across New England, see Holifield, *Covenant Sealed*, 186, 206–220.

196. Croswell, *Narrative*, 3. The adoption of the same principle by Boston's Park Street Church at its founding in 1809 has sometimes been cited, erroneously, as setting a local precedent; see H. Crosby Englizian, *Brimstone Corner: Park Street Church, Boston* (Chicago: Moody Press, 1968), 36–38.

197. Croswell, *Narrative*, 4.

198. Ibid.

Christian Methods have been used to reclaim him, this Church hath full Power to take from him that Power over them which they gave to him."[199]

Yet Croswell himself was evidently inadequate to the very demands of pastoral ministry that he chose to highlight. In spite of his words about the importance of a systematic program of house-to-house visitation, which surely would have necessitated a settled parish ministry, he himself continued to itinerate widely in the years after 1748, and Eleventh Church's own pulpit became a haven for his fellow itinerants.[200] Further complicating matters for Croswell was the fact that he was never admitted into the local association of Congregational ministers. Sharing the plight, though not the theology, of Jonathan Mayhew, he could practice pulpit exchange only infrequently; this meant that when he was not itinerating, he was forced to devote a greater than usual proportion of his time to sermon preparation.[201]

Finally, it is worth noting that, in spite of Croswell's eloquence in regard to pastoral visitation in Eleventh Church's articles of government, his published sermons show a total disregard of this and related matters, focusing instead almost exclusively on polemics in regard to justification, assurance, and conversion itself. It is difficult to avoid the conclusion that visitation and other related aspects of pastoral ministry must have had a relatively low priority in the allotment of his time. Certainly Eleventh Church evidenced little of the vitality that a systematic program of visitation, for example, might have fostered. Although the congregation's records have not survived, contemporary accounts paint a grim picture, with the group having originally numbered as many as 500 but by 1785, the year of Croswell's death, counting as members only seven men and an unspecified number of women.[202]

Even before matters reached this extremity, Croswell had lost control of the congregation. For example, he was scathing in his denunciation of Universalist itinerants like John Murray: "The Preachers of Universal Salvation are great comforters . . . [but t]hey preach no terror. . . . They are never in their element, but when they are preaching comfort; in this they have an advantage over other

---

199. Ibid.

200. Schmidt, "'Second and Glorious Reformation,'" 225. Croswell noted that the need for such a haven was one of the rationales advanced by members of Eleventh Church to justify their withdrawal from other local Congregational churches: "[B]eing professed Friends of the present Reformation, [we desired that we] might have a Pulpit open to receive Mr. *Whitefield*, and others whom we look upon to be the zealous and faithful Ministers of Jesus Christ, who are so commonly shut out of other Pulpits" (*Narrative*, 13).

201. Schmidt, "'Second and Glorious Reformation,'" 226. On Mayhew's difficulties in this regard, see above.

202. The former is Timothy Cutler's estimate, cited in Goen, *Revivalism and Separatism*, 97; the latter is offered by Shipton in *Sibley's Harvard Graduates*, 8: 405.

Ministers, though not *an honorable one.* . . . Such blasphemous contempt of the truth and holiness of GOD ought to be shocking to all Christians."[203] Yet Murray himself, hailed by some New Lights as a second Whitefield, frequently occupied Eleventh Church's pulpit during 1773 and 1774.[204] Obviously Croswell and his parishioners had come to very different perspectives on this subject, and likely on others as well.

It seems probable that Croswell's evangelistic prowess, and certainly his penchant for diatribe, far outstripped his proficiency as a pastor. His deficiencies in regard to the latter, overriding his strengths in regard to the former, doomed Eleventh Church to an early demise. If the Great Awakening had marked nothing more than the reclamation of Reformation teaching in regard to justification and, based on this, the rediscovery of Reformation patterns of evangelism, as he certainly believed, no pastor ought to have been better equipped to reap a bountiful harvest of souls than he, and no congregation ought to have been better situated to grow and thrive than his own. That such was not this congregation's experience—that, indeed, far from thriving, Eleventh Church barely managed to outlive its first and only pastor—demonstrates the inadequacy of conventional perspectives on the Awakening and further corroborates the thesis here being advanced.

---

203. Croswell, *First Epistle of Thessalonians*, 24–25, 27.
204. Shipton, *Sibley's Harvard Graduates*, 8: 403; Marini, *Radical Sects*, 69.

Conclusion:
A People So Favored of God

> In this year 1741, the very face of the town seemed to be strangely altered. Some, who had not been here since the fall before, have told me their great surprise at the change in the general look and carriage of people.... [T]hus successfully did this divine work ... go on in town ... for above a year and a half after Mr. Whitefield left us.[1]

Now that the vicissitudes of Boston's eleven oldest Congregational churches have been considered individually, it remains to consider the overall health of the spiritual community comprising these churches and their associated parishes. This was certainly not a closed community; especially after 1689, other ecclesiastical options were open to a Bostonian with the inclination to wander. Still, relatively few were so inclined during the era under consideration. Anglicans, Baptists, and even Quakers offered the Congregationalists a measure of competition, the Anglicans wielding influence out of proportion to their numbers, but for all such alternative communions the numbers remained small. This implies that fluctuations in the aggregate statistics for Boston's Congregational churches can even be taken as a rough gauge of the fluctuating spiritual climate of the city as a whole.

Even a cursory examination of those statistics brings one point immediately to the fore. In spite of the Great Awakening's ubiquity and even notoriety in the literature of and about that era, it had an absolute numerical impact on the local religious community perceptibly smaller than that of the largely forgotten earthquake of 1727.[2] One scholar has even suggested that the 1727 earthquake may have lessened the Awakening's impact by stimulating the conversion of many young adults who would otherwise have enlarged the pool of potential converts fifteen years later.[3] In light of this, it is worth considering whether the role of earthquakes, fires, and other such "acts of God" in triggering periodic episodes of revival has received sufficient attention in the historiography of colonial reli-

---

1. Thomas Prince, quoted in Tracy, *Great Awakening*, 120; see also Kidd, *Great Awakening*, 100.
2. See Chart 19; and Appendix, column 10 of Tables 1 and 5.
3. Seeman, *Pious Persuasions*, 238 n. 9.

Chart 19: Aggregate first-time admissions to membership and baptisms

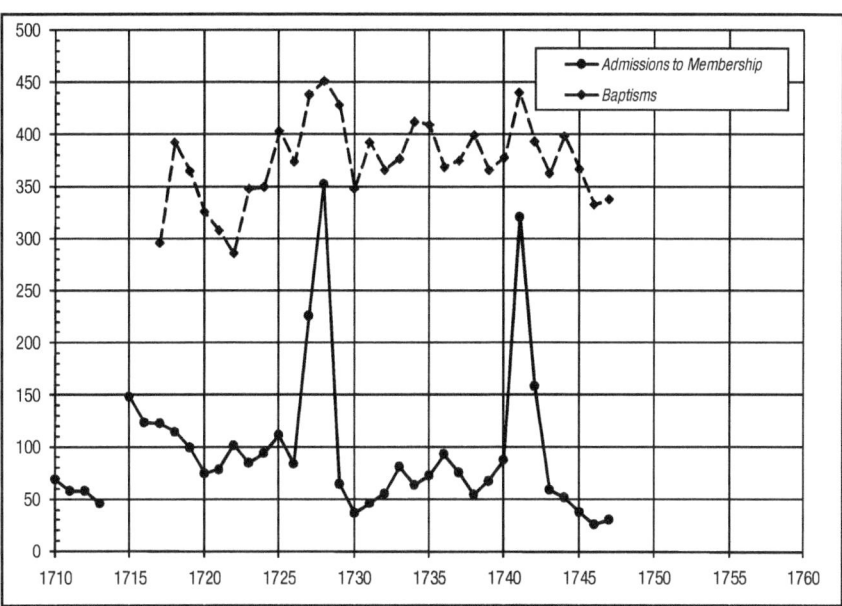

gion.[4] Of course the spiritual consequences of such catastrophes were well known to those of that era. Consider Thomas Prince's remarks on the 1727 earthquake:

> The People are thereby thrown into the utmost Consternation. And so mightily are many awakened with the Sense of their Danger and the Divine Displeasure, as has produced a wonderful Reformation. Profaneness, Drunkenness and other Vices abandoned; the earnest Pursuits of the World discarded; the Places of Publick Worship vastly thronged; the Worship of GOD set up in Prayerless Families; and great Numbers continually added to the flourishing Churches. Twenty, *Thirty*, or *Forty* on a Sabbath have offered either to make or renew their Dedication to the Blessed GOD: In our Assembly above *One Hundred and Fifty* in Three Weeks' time; and of these about *Fourscore* in one Day. What a Joy is There, even as the Joy of Harvest. . . . What an happy Effusion of the HOLY SPIRIT![5]

---

4. On the impact of the earthquake of 1727 on individual churches, see chapters 3 and 4 above. That not all communities were equally affected by this earthquake is noted by Cowing in "Sex and Preaching," 626–627.

5. Thomas Prince, *Earthquakes the Works of God, and Tokens of His Just Displeasure* (Boston: D. Henchman, 1727), 48. For a discussion of the eschatological framework in which Prince, Joseph Sewall, and others viewed this earthquake, a framework that even

Another matter which must be addressed is the possibility that the significance of the Awakening itself has been greatly exaggerated. This thesis has been advanced most forcefully by Jon Butler in several publications. Butler summarizes his position in the broadest of terms: "On reflection, [the Awakening] might better be thought of as . . . an American equivalent of the Roman Empire's Donation of Constantine, the medieval forgery that the papacy used to justify its subsequent claims to political authority."[6] On the face of it, this assertion would appear to have considerable merit. After all, what is there about the raw data for reception of new members into Boston's Congregational churches during the early 1740s which would lead anyone to suspect that those churches were caught up in a major revival, let alone a "Great Awakening"? However, a closer examination of the data in light of Boston's shifting demographics leads to the surprising conclusion that this was indeed the case.

Such an examination requires a measure of subtlety. Population estimates for both Boston and Massachusetts during the interval under consideration are just that.[7] Indeed, records of live births are quite unreliable, with those recorded

---

led them to hope for imminent revival, see Kidd, *Protestant Interest*, 162–164; and idem, *Great Awakening*, 10–12. After the 1755 earthquake, Prince published two treatises. The first of these, *Earthquakes the Works of God, and Tokens of His Just Displeasure* (Boston: D. Fowle, 1755), was quite different from his essay of 1727, in spite of the shared title, and in spite of Alan Heimert's claim to the contrary in *American Mind*, 69. The second, *An Improvement of the Doctrine of Earthquakes, Being the Works of God, and Tokens of His Just Displeasure* (Boston: D. Fowle, 1755), was an examination of the latest theories as to the mechanism underlying these tremors that in no way took such putative "second causes" as inconsistent with the moralizing he derived from God's role as universal "first cause." Other published sermons on earthquakes by Boston clergy of that era included Mather Byles, *Divine Power and Anger Displayed in Earthquakes* (Boston: S. Kneeland, 1755); Charles Chauncy, *Earthquakes a Token of the Righteous Anger of God* (Boston: Edes and Gill, 1755); idem, *The Earth Delivered from the Curse to Which It Is, at Present, Subjected* (Boston: Edes and Gill, 1756); Jonathan Mayhew, *The Expected Dissolution of All Things, a Motive to Universal Holiness* (Boston: Edes and Gill, 1755); Joseph Sewall, *The Duty of a People to Stand in Aw of God, and Not Sin, When under His Terrible Judgments* (Boston: D. Henchman, 1727); and idem, *Repentance the Sure Way to Escape Destruction*. See also Hill, *Old South Church*, 2: 21.

6. Jon Butler, *Awash in a Sea of Faith: Christianizing the American People* (Cambridge: Harvard University Press, 1990), 165. See also idem, "Enthusiasm Described and Decried," 307–308; and see chapter 2 above.

7. See Charts 20 and 21; and Appendix, Table 6. Figures for Boston's population and death rate are from John Blake, *Public Health in the Town of Boston, 1630–1822* (Cambridge: Harvard University Press, 1959), 247–249; Massachusetts population figures are from Evarts B. Greene and Virginia D. Harrington, *American Population before the Federal Census of 1790* (New York: Columbia University Press, 1932), 14–16. Note that the latter are somewhat speculative, as no provincial census was conducted before 1764; see Robert V. Wells, *The Population of the British Colonies in America before*

often totaling no more than half to two-thirds of the infants known to have been baptized in a given year.[8] This makes a direct calculation of the local birth rate impossible, and it makes even estimates of the birth rate somewhat dubious. Still, fairly close estimates at least of Boston's death rate have been made. Evidently mortality slowly declined from 1710 to about 1735, gradually increased from that point to around 1750, and then turned downward once again. This broad underlying pattern was broken by surges associated with smallpox epidemics in 1721–1722, 1730, and 1751–1752.[9] Projections of the populations of Boston and Massachusetts suggest that for both communities a long period of steady growth ended in about 1740, with Massachusetts as well as Boston then entering an era of equilibrium.

What might account for this pattern? In light of the steadily increasing threat posed by French and Native Americans along New England's frontier after the 1730s, it seems unlikely that such a plateau might be attributed mainly to emigration, especially since most emigrants from the Boston area would have remained within Massachusetts, whose population had also reached a plateau.[10] More suggestive is the observation that stability arrived about twenty years after the 1721–1722 smallpox epidemic, the first such outbreak Boston had seen in

---

1776: A Survey of Census Data (Princeton, N.J.: Princeton University Press, 1975), 78–79.

8. This assertion is based on my own examination of town records stored in the City Clerk's Archives, City Hall, Boston. Blake, in *Public Health*, 106, 213, notes that although the Commonwealth's legal code required the recording of such information after 1639, prior to 1810 this was not generally enforced.

9. Alison Franks, "Epidemics in US, 1628–1918," available from http://www.bjhughes.org/epidemic.html, Internet, accessed 24 June 2003; John D. Burton, "'The Awful Judgments of God upon the Land': Smallpox in Colonial Cambridge, Massachusetts," *New England Quarterly*, vol. 74, no. 3 (September 2001): 495–506; G. B. Warden, *Boston: 1689–1776* (Boston: Little, Brown and Co., 1970), 81, 100; Carl Bridenbaugh, *Cities in Revolt: Urban Life in America, 1743–1776* (New York: Alfred A. Knopf, 1955), 129; John Duffy, *Epidemics in Colonial America* (Baton Rouge, La.: Louisiana State University Press, 1953); Blake, *Public Health*, 74–98; Winslow, *Destroying Angel*, 44–58; Miller, *From Colony to Province*, 345–366.

10. On the clash of Britain and France over their North American colonies, see John A. Garraty, "Colonial Wars," in *The Reader's Companion to American History*, ed. John A. Garraty and Eric Foner (Boston: Houghton Mifflin, 1991), 205–207; Howard H. Peckham, *The Colonial Wars, 1689–1762* (Chicago: University of Chicago Press, 1964); Francis Jennings, *Empire of Fortune: Crown, Colonies, and Tribes in the Seven Years' War in America* (New York: W. W. Norton, 1988); and Fred Anderson, *Crucible of War: The Seven Years' War and the Fate of Empire in British North America, 1754–1766* (Alfred A. Knopf, 2000).

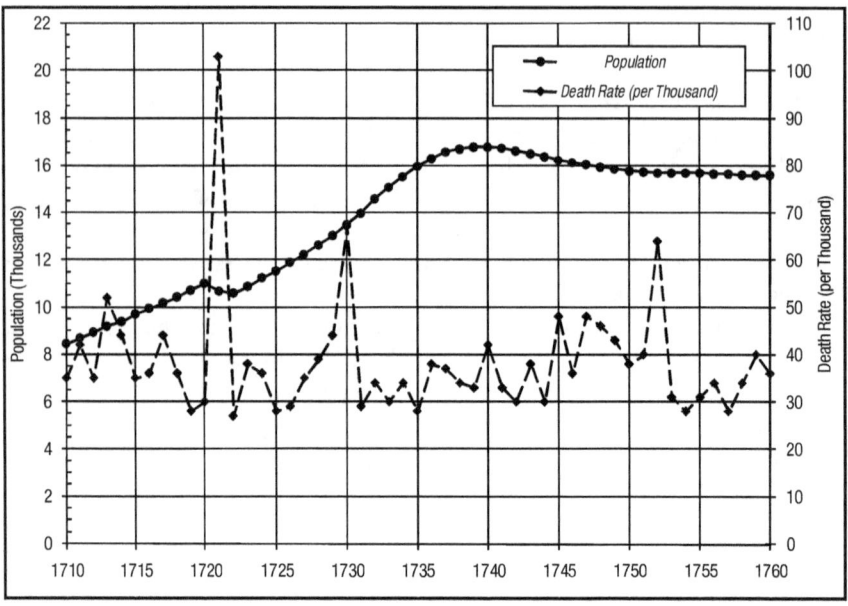

Chart 20: Boston population and death rate

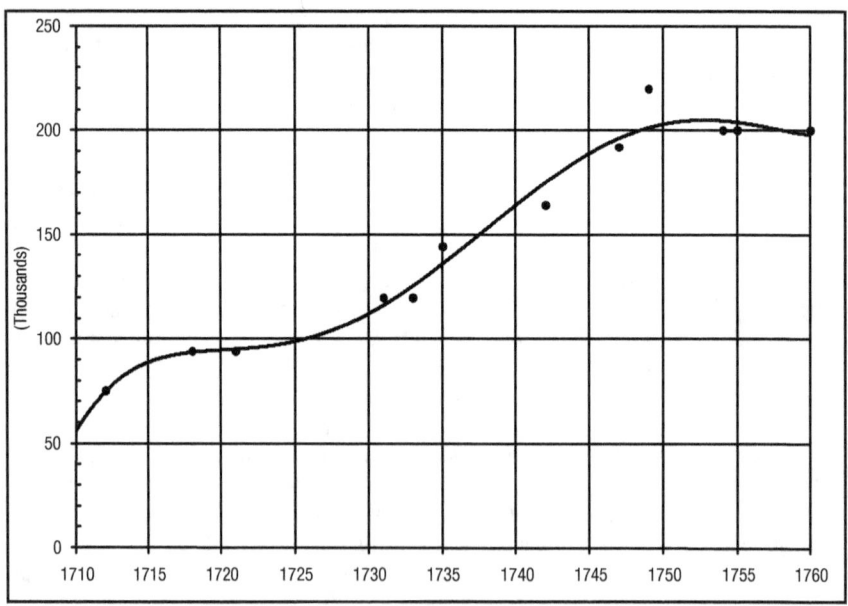

Chart 21: Massachusetts population

some decades. The impact of this disease would have been felt disproportionately by the weakest and least prepared; since many of the adult population would already have been exposed and developed an immunity, these would have been the very young and the very old.[11] Therefore it seems quite likely that this epidemic would have had the effect of shifting the population's age distribution. Female infants who died in 1721–1722 would have been just beginning to reach childbearing years in the late 1730s. Their absence would have been reflected in the absolute decline in size of the community's pool of fertile women. Moreover, unlike the mid-Atlantic colonies, Massachusetts received few European immigrants who might have made up for these losses.[12] The result would have been a decrease in live births, and thus a downturn in the birth rate itself, after about 1740.[13] For this reason, G. B. Warden describes the 1721–1722 epidemic as "a calamity from which Boston never really recovered in the eighteenth century."[14]

Another factor working to the same end would have been the skewing of the ratio of males to females brought about by the wars that repeatedly ravaged the Massachusetts frontier until 1763 and the British annexation of France's holdings in North America.[15] For example, the 1745 expedition against Cape Breton Island cost the lives of about eight percent of all Massachusetts males over the age of sixteen, with Boston paying a price that was proportionately even heavier.[16] The long-term consequences of this extended period of conflict, "[t]his al-

---

11. On the special vulnerability of the young, see Blake, *Public Health*, 56. This accounts for the observation that as inoculation became available in early-eighteenth-century Boston, parents' first concern was that the procedure be performed on their children; see Mather, *Diary*, 2: 632, entry for July 18, 1721.

12. See the discussion of immigration in Bernard Bailyn, *Voyagers to the West: A Passage in the Peopling of America on the Eve of the Revolution* (New York: Alfred A. Knopf, 1986), esp. 205–206; by Bailyn's estimate, less than one percent of those sailing for America in the 1760s and 1770s were bound for New England. See also Oscar Handlin, *Boston's Immigrants: A Study in Acculturation*, rev. ed. (Cambridge: Harvard University Press, 1959), 25.

13. For a further discussion of Massachusetts fertility and mortality rates, see Richard W. Wilkie and Jack Tager, eds., *Historical Atlas of Massachusetts* (Amherst: University of Massachusetts Press, 1991), 98–100.

14. Warden, *Boston*, 81.

15. The best discussion of these wars' devastating local demographic and economic impact is in Nash, *Urban Crucible*, 161–197, a chapter tellingly titled, "The Renewal of War and the Decline of Boston." See also Thomas Wentworth Higginson, "French and Indian Wars," in *The Memorial History of Boston, Including Suffolk County, Massachusetts*, vol. 2: *The Provincial Period*, ed. Justin Winsor (Boston: Ticknor and Co., 1881), 93–130; Carl Bridenbaugh, *Cities in the Wilderness: The First Century of Urban Life in America, 1625–1742* (New York: Ronald Press, 1938; reprint, New York: Alfred A. Knopf, 1955), 233; idem, *Cities in Revolt*, 47–49; and Warden, *Boston*, 127–128.

16. Nash, *Urban Crucible*, 172.

most biblical series of misfortunes," notes Gary B. Nash, were grim: "All of the data available indicates that the birthrate in Boston was lower than in the other northern ports, for the mid-century wars took a fearful toll on a generation of young males, leaving a surplus population of young women whose childbearing potential was cut short by the loss of a husband or who remained single and childless altogether for lack of marriageable men."[17] With smallpox skewing the average age of Boston's population and substantially decreasing the number of potential wives and mothers while warfare took a heavy toll on the number of potential husbands and fathers, the stabilization of the city's population after about 1740 should come as no surprise.

A birth rate in decline after 1740 helps to explain the downturn in the aggregate figures for Congregational baptisms beginning at about the same time. Simply put, there were fewer infants to whom the sacrament might have been administered. This may also help to explain the slump in aggregate admissions to membership after the mid-1740s. Crisis conversion is an event most commonly associated with the young; in an aging population, more and more people will either already have had this experience or be likely never to have it at all.[18] In fact, the rather modest scale of the declines in both baptisms and admissions to membership suggests that, on the whole, Boston's churches did better than might have been expected. That the totals over the latter part of the interval under consideration, an era characterized by a stagnant population and a relatively low birth rate, were nonetheless broadly similar to those over the earlier part of the interval, a period characterized by a steadily increasing population and a relatively high birth rate, is probably the clearest indication of the Great Awakening's cumulative local impact.[19]

---

17. Ibid., 184, 195.

18. Bumsted notes that "[h]igh admissions tend[ed] to occur in communities which ... had a large number of young men [sic] coming of age" ("Religion, Finance, and Democracy," 830). That the average age of those received into church membership actually declined in several New England communities over the years bracketing the Awakening is documented in Philip J. Greven, Jr., "Youth, Maturity, and Religious Conversion: A Note on the Ages of Converts in Andover, Massachusetts, 1711–1749," *Essex Institute Historical Collections*, vol. 108, no. 2 (April 1972): 119–134; Gerald F. Moran, "Conditions of Religious Conversion in the First Society of Norwich, Connecticut, 1718–1744," *Journal of Social History*, vol. 5, no. 3 (Spring 1972): 331–343; and William F. Willingham, "Religious Conversion in the Second Society of Windham, Connecticut, 1723–43: A Case Study," *Societas*, vol. 6, no. 2 (Spring 1976): 109–119. On the other hand, Stephen R. Grossbart has argued, in "Seeking the Divine Favor: Conversion and Church Admission in Eastern Connecticut, 1711–1832," *William and Mary Quarterly*, 3d series, vol. 46, no. 4 (October 1989): 696–740, that this was a temporary phenomenon whose significance should not be overstated.

19. Bumsted and Van de Wetering, in *What Must I Do to Be Saved?*, 127–133, claim to have found unambiguous evidence for the Awakening's direct and decisive impact on

The stability of Boston's population in the years after 1740 accounts for at least some of the rough sledding experienced by individual congregations, especially the younger ones, beginning in the middle of that decade. The town's population, now no longer growing, was being distributed among an increasing number of churches. One consequence of this, presumably unintended, was the lapse of the tradition that, where possible, individual parishes employ two ministers, one of these dubbed the "pastor" and the other the "teacher."[20] In 1710, two of Boston's four Congregational parishes were served in this way; in 1720, five of six; in 1730, four of seven; in 1740, five of nine; in 1750, three of eleven; and in 1760, only one of the same eleven. Reflecting this, although new Congregational churches continued to be organized in Boston through the 1740s, the aggregate number of ministers employed by the city's Congregational churches held fairly constant during most of the interval under examination, totaling six in 1710, eleven in 1720, eleven in 1730, fourteen in 1740, fourteen in 1750, and twelve in 1760. Thus the ratio of pastors to parishioners held fairly constant as well.

All other things being equal, though, settling Boston's clergy in many small, single-minister parishes was a less efficient use of resources than placing them by pairs over congregations that would have been larger and fewer in number. The result of this was that several of the newer churches never had the chance to establish themselves and were soon rendered untenable; within a quarter-century, three of the eleven congregations established before 1760 had gone out of existence. This demonstrates the validity of the concern voiced by Joseph Sewall and Thomas Prince in a letter to the soon-to-be pastor of Eleventh Church, Andrew Croswell: "Though we would be very tender of the Rights of Conscience, yet inasmuch as there are other Congregational Churches in Town, who have pious and orthodox Ministers, where you might be conveniently accommodated,

---

admissions to church membership in southeastern Massachusetts and Connecticut, but their assertions are rendered problematic by the fact that the interval they examine spans only fourteen years, from 1733 to 1747. Patricia U. Bonomi and Peter R. Eisenstadt overstate things in the opposite direction: "Nor do we find that the churched population was more than temporarily increased by the Great Awakening.... [T]he Awakening's greatest impact may have fallen in a realm other than that of numbers. Perhaps the character of piety, or styles of religious discourse, or popular attitudes toward authority changed, but the proportion of regular church adherents appears to have remained about the same" ("Church Adherence in the Eighteenth-Century British American Colonies," *William and Mary Quarterly*, 3d series, vol. 39, no. 2 [April 1982]: 275).

20. Hall, *Faithful Shepherd*, 11, 95–96. For the Reformed background of this distinction, see John Calvin, "Draft Ecclesiastical Ordinances," in *Calvin: Theological Treatises*, ed. and trans. J. K. S. Reid, Library of Christian Classics (Philadelphia: Westminster Press, 1954), 58, 62–63; idem, *Institutes of the Christian Religion*, 4.1.5; and Robert W. Henderson, *The Teaching Office in the Reformed Tradition: A History of the Doctoral Ministry* (Philadelphia: Westminster Press, 1962).

we cannot see any just reason for such a Multiplication of Churches; but judge it hath an unhappy Tendency to crumble them into small Societies, and hinder their Christian Union and Communion."[21] This was a problem not just in Boston but across eighteenth-century New England; the number of organized churches was increasing at a rate considerably faster than that of the region's population, so that the size of the average parish was necessarily declining.[22]

Far from undercutting the observations on specific churches already made, these remarks on aggregate figures simply bring them into sharper focus. For example, they help to account for the otherwise perplexing observation that even in the healthiest of congregations there seems to have been a gradual decline in the number of baptisms and admissions to membership after the early 1740s. Scholars need not grope for rationalizations or appeal to a mysterious decline in spiritual vigor in the aftermath of the Awakening's collapse. These observations also make the contrast between individual congregations—between Second Church and Fifth Church, for example—all the more suggestive. If a declining birth rate and a stagnant population help to account for the overall contour of events, differences between individual ministers' approaches to the ministry still offer the key to understanding the Awakening's divergent outcomes in different congregations.[23]

Peterson rightly warns against a reductionist approach to this material: "Much has been made of the significance of the Puritan minister as scholar, as theologian, and as preacher by twentieth-century historians. Each of these roles was important.... However, this emphasis underestimates the importance of pastoral prayer and counseling to the religion of early New England."[24] To assert that the Great Awakening's course in Boston can be described entirely in terms of the clash of opposed conceptions of pastoral ministry would be to engage in nothing more than a sort of reverse reductionism. It is true that after the early 1740s, theological considerations came increasingly to the forefront of the debate between Old Lights and New Lights. Yet it is also true that in its initial phase, the controversy surrounding the Awakening centered on its perceived threat to the traditional clericalist pastoral paradigm embodied in the ministries of men like Charles Chauncy and Samuel Mather, and its elevation instead of an activist pastoral paradigm promoted by Cotton Mather in word and deed and pursued in the next generation by men like Joseph Sewall and William Cooper.

---

21. Their letter is reproduced in Croswell, *Narrative*, 7.
22. Schmotter, "Clerical Professionalism," 162.
23. Kidd observes that while five of sixteen Boston-area churches—Boston's Third, Fourth, and Fifth as well as the First Church of Cambridge and the First Church of Charlestown—"showed signs of major revival in the months following Whitefield's fall [1740] tour," such results were "widespread, but not universal, . . . in eastern Massachusetts" (*Great Awakening*, 96).
24. Peterson, *Price of Redemption*, 125.

It has been shown that congregations served by clergy who were consistent in their opposition not only to the Great Awakening but to any deviation from the traditional understanding of the ministry had no reason to expect anything but decline; Eighth Church, Ninth Church, and Tenth Church represent this category. Congregations served by clergy who were equally consistent in their embrace both of the Awakening and of an activist approach to pastoral care were ideally situated to see new growth and vitality; Third Church, Fifth Church, and Sixth Church represent this category. Congregations served by clergy united in their support for the Awakening but divided in their understanding of the ecclesiological implications of this commitment faced a somewhat more problematic situation; Fourth Church represents this category. Congregations served by clergy divided over the fundamental question of the Awakening itself confronted the likelihood of controversy and even schism; First Church and Second Church represent this category. Congregations served by clergy who embraced the Awakening but embraced as well their traditional prerogatives could expect little in the way of growth, and might well see just the opposite; Seventh Church and Eleventh Church represent this category. The point is that the Awakening was at first primarily a crisis of praxis and only subsequently one of doctrine.

Critics to the contrary notwithstanding, Joseph Tracy was correct in designating the religious movement associated with the ministries of George Whitefield, Gilbert Tennent, Jonathan Edwards, and their spiritual progeny as a single complex but cohesive event, a genuine "Great Awakening" that first sounded themes to be amplified and elaborated in the awakenings of the nineteenth and twentieth centuries. Where Tracy was wrong was in his overly narrow conception of the identity of those themes. Conrad Wright has argued that the religious wars of the 1740s shattered the overarching theological synthesis that had prevailed across New England since the Puritans' first arrival, leaving in its place a spectrum of stratified alternatives: at one extreme, the moralistic Arminianism that was to evolve into Unitarianism; at the other, the Edwardsian "New Divinity" from which developed a panoply of efforts aimed at accommodating Calvinism to America's distinctive spirituality; and in the middle, the moderate Calvinism whose adherents tended eventually to align themselves with one or the other of these opposing soteriological poles.[25] In short, the Awakening set in motion a realignment of New England's doctrinal orientation from a monopolar to a bipolar pattern.

---

25. This is the central argument of Wright's treatise, *The Beginnings of Unitarianism in America.* See also Mark A. Noll, Nathan O. Hatch, George M. Marsden, David F. Wells, and John D. Woodbridge, eds., *Eerdmans' Handbook to Christianity in America* (Grand Rapids, Mich.: William B. Eerdmans, 1983), 116–117, 120; Murray, *Jonathan Edwards,* 281; Harlan, *The Clergy and the Great Awakening,* 49–96; Bumsted and Van de Wetering, *What Must I Do to Be Saved?,* 96–126; and Bushman, *From Puritan to Yankee,* 209–220.

It has been argued here that proceeding in parallel with this transformation, and even in advance of it, was a similar shift in the sphere of ecclesiology, with an older, pulpit-oriented consensus replaced by two alternative paradigms, one almost a caricature of the traditional clericalism, the other focusing instead on pastoral ministry and pragmatic tools such as systematic visitation and the religious society.[26] J. William T. Youngs, Jr., notes the role of revival in advancing this ecclesiastical revolution: "In the early eighteenth century, the ministers' status had been based in part upon their professional dignity and in part upon the effectiveness of their ministerial work. The Great Awakening forced [sic] the Congregational clergymen to place a new emphasis upon the more mundane, but more stable, source of their power, their ability to work with laymen."[27] Christopher Jedrey argues that the activist paradigm—"reformed orthodoxy, lay participation, evangelical-style ministry"—"came, in time, to dominate rural New England."[28] However, in urban Boston the story was considerably more complex.

Although ecclesiological rupture and realignment preceded and even to some extent drove the dramatic theological clashes that followed across New England, it has been noted that in Boston the correlation between particular ministers' theological views and their understanding of the pastoral office was far from perfect.[29] That is, even though all local opponents of the Awakening defended traditional notions of the ministry, and even though many of its supporters embraced the activist alternative, there remained a group of New Light clergy who nevertheless, whether by choice or out of necessity, proceeded with their day-to-day affairs much as did the Old Lights. Corroborating assertions of the primacy of the Awakening's pastoral dimension, an examination of congregational records has shown that churches whose pastors fell into this latter category—"ecclesiological Old Lights," they might almost be termed—suffered the same unhappy fate, by and large, as churches whose pastors were Old Lights plain and

---

26. On the use of religious societies by Jonathan Edwards, George Whitefield, Howell Harris, Daniel Rowland, Benjamin Ingham, and other revivalists of that era, see Noll, *Rise of Evangelicalism*, 77, 81, 86, 89, 92, and 101; and Kidd, "'Vital Breath of Christianity,'" 22–23.

27. Youngs, *God's Messengers*, 136.

28. Jedrey, *John Cleaveland*, 56. On the lay activism and social egalitarianism that similarly came to dominate revivalism in the Middle Colonies, as well as the antecedents for this in Scottish Presbyterianism, see Leigh Eric Schmidt, *Holy Fairs: Scotland and the Making of American Revivalism*, 2d ed. (Grand Rapids, Mich.: William B. Eerdmans, 2001), 104–107.

29. See Cooper's comments on "the complexity of [this] relationship" in *Tenacious of Their Liberties*, 202–203.

simple.³⁰ Only congregations led by New Light clergy who recognized the crisis of the Awakening for what it was and took up tools appropriate to the task before them saw growth and vitality. Cedric B. Cowing puts it nicely, though without noting the distinction between New Light activists and traditionalists: "[E]vangelical Calvinism was essential in revitalizing the male laity and restoring a measure of historic congregationalism. Without it, ministers dominated or churches languished."³¹

Yet the primacy of the Awakening's pastoral dimension was not at all apparent to many of the participants. James W. Schmotter observes: "Most ministers recognized the revival as a professional crisis, but did not realize that their own professionalism had helped bring about these difficulties."³² One such minister was Jonathan Edwards, theologian to the movement. For all of Edwards's undoubted effectiveness as a preacher and teacher, he was nonetheless an ineffective pastor whose failings in this regard helped to pave the way for his dismissal from the pastorate of the Congregational church in Northampton.³³ Moreover, his New Divinity disciples made a virtue of his deficiencies, showing a strange reverence for this least attractive aspect of his ministry even as they went about recasting his theological legacy.³⁴ Joseph A. Conforti describes the ironic process by which they came to embrace an understanding of the ministry

---

30. For a discussion of the Awakening's disastrous consequences in another parish led by an ineffective New Light pastor, see Stout and Onuf, "Great Awakening in New London."

31. Cowing, "Sex and Preaching," 644.

32. Schmotter, "Clerical Professionalism," 168.

33. On Edwards's ineffectiveness in this regard, see Murray, *Jonathan Edwards*, 342–344. Marsden, in *Jonathan Edwards*, 362, notes that Edwards himself came to have reservations about his pastoral ability. See also Elisabeth D. Dodds, *Marriage to a Difficult Man: The "Uncommon Union" of Jonathan and Sarah Edwards* (Philadelphia: Westminster Press, 1971), 71–72; Perry Miller, *Jonathan Edwards*, American Men of Letters Series (New York: William Sloane Associates, 1949), 128; Ola Elizabeth Winslow, *Jonathan Edwards, 1703–1758* (New York: Macmillan, 1940; reprint, New York: Collier Books, 1961), 120–122; and Henry Bamford Parkes, *Jonathan Edwards: The Fiery Puritan* (New York: Minton, Balch and Co., 1930), 124–137. On Edwards's pronounced clericalist streak, see Tracy, *Jonathan Edwards*, 144–145. Tracy's comment is to the point: "In spite of his broad and sensitive view of the revival and the good it entailed, Edwards focused on anti-clericalism as the major sign that evil was mixed in with the good" (ibid., 145).

34. Murray, in *Jonathan Edwards*, 342–343, attempts to minimize the importance of this point, arguing that systematic pastoral visitation was seldom practiced in colonial New England, and that Edwards's inadequacy in this area was passed over without criticism, and even with praise, by disciples such as Samuel Hopkins. But it seems odd to be forced to appeal to alleged tradition in defense of this least traditional of thinkers, and the recognition that his followers shared his failings is no defense at all.

150   *Conclusion: A People So Favored of God*

that was every bit as study- and pulpit-bound as that defended by Charles Chauncy and the Old Lights: "After the Awakening, doctrinal preparation for the ministry became more rigorous, particularly in New Divinity schools of the prophets where grounding in systematic divinity was stressed at the expense of training in the practical tasks of the ministry.... Bellamy and other New Divinity men ... emphasized the role of the minister as a theologian—a role for which Jonathan Edwards furnished a model."[35] This coin had another side, as Stephen Foster notes: "Practical divinity was a blind spot in Edwards and in Edwardseans generally until the end of the century."[36]

Perhaps most perplexing of all is the observation that New Light pastors who took the point, who responded to the spiritual crisis confronting their generation by developing exemplary ministries, too often failed to communicate to clergy of the next generation the sense of priorities motivating their activism. Even fathers failed to persuade their sons of this point. During the interval under consideration here, four local pastors were joined or followed in the ministry by offspring who also assumed positions in Boston: Cotton Mather, at Second Church, was followed by Samuel Mather, at Second Church and then Tenth Church; Ebenezer Pemberton, Sr., at Third Church, was followed by Ebenezer Pemberton, Jr., at Seventh Church; William Cooper, at Fourth Church, was followed by Samuel Cooper, also at Fourth Church; and Samuel Checkley, Sr., at Sixth Church, was joined by Samuel Checkley, Jr., at Second Church. As has been shown, at least three of the older generation—Cotton Mather, William Cooper, and Samuel Checkley, Sr.—were very effective pastors, but not one of the younger generation could be so characterized. Even more dramatically, and most ironically, while Cotton's closest ministerial protégés were all staunch New Lights, his closest ministerial relatives, not only his son Samuel but also his nephew Mather Byles, took precisely the opposite tack. What can this mean?

What it means is that there is nothing hereditary about the pastoral calling. What it illustrates is the more general tendency among clergy of the younger generation to revert to comfortable patterns of clerical elitism, even in churches that had once been New Light nerve centers.[37] Of the fourteen ministers serving

---

35. Joseph A. Conforti, *Samuel Hopkins and the New Divinity Movement: Calvinism, the Congregational Ministry, and Reform in New England between the Great Awakenings* (Grand Rapids, Mich.: Christian University Press and William B. Eerdmans, 1981), 36. See also Allen C. Guelzo, "Jonathan Edwards and the New Divinity: Change and Continuity in New England Calvinism, 1758–1858," in *Pressing toward the Mark: Essays Commemorating the Fiftieth Anniversary of the Orthodox Presbyterian Church*, ed. Charles Dennison and Richard Gamble (Philadelphia: Orthodox Presbyterian Church, 1986), 154.

36. Foster, *Long Argument*, 300.

37. Thus I question Youngs's identification of three stages in the evolution of colonial New England's structures of ecclesiastical authority, with ministers initially "the admired

Boston's nine Congregational churches in 1740, five—36%—might be described as strong pastors; of the fifteen serving eleven Congregational churches in 1750, four—27%—might be so described; of the twelve serving eleven Congregational churches in 1760, only two—17%—could be characterized thus. One long-term consequence was the weakening of these churches and ultimately the breaching of Trinitarian orthodoxy's dike by the rising tide of rationalist Unitarianism. The steady numerical decline experienced by many local Congregational churches meant that their associated parishes—those individuals who worshiped with them, likely even rented pews among them, but were unable or simply unwilling to apply for communicant status—would wield steadily increasing power in the selection of a pastor. Such parishes generally, and understandably, preferred ministers of a more liberal theological bent.[38]

How did it come to pass that so many of Boston's Congregational churches embraced Unitarianism in the decades after the American Revolution? Some scholars have pointed to the intellectual temper of the times, the pervasive climate of supernatural rationalism that saw religion's value mainly in its role as a buttress for morality.[39] Others have invoked Federalist America's political optimism, arguing that with their dogmatic disavowal of all dogma, Unitarians manifested the primitivist impulse as strikingly as did Alexander Campbell's "Disciples" or Barton Stone's "Christians."[40]

Though both of these perspectives offer important insights, it should be noted as well that the only one of Boston's eleven Congregational churches founded before 1809 to remain Trinitarian in its theological orientation was Third Church, which had so richly profited from the painstaking pastoral care of Joseph Sewall and Thomas Prince and even in the age of Jefferson was still borne along by the spiritual momentum they had imparted decades earlier. In the words of a historian of an earlier day, "[I]t was the impulse received at [the time of the Great Awakening], probably, which saved [Third] Church from going

---

religious leaders of a relatively harmonious society," then, beginning in the late seventeenth century, seeking "to establish a quasi-aristocratic control over a society of competing factions," and finally, after the Great Awakening, once again "bas[ing] their leadership upon a principle of consent" (*God's Messengers*, 138). Attractive though this simple schematization may be, at least in Boston it does not accord with reality.

38. Miller, *From Colony to Province*, 467.

39. See, for example, Wright, *Beginnings of Unitarianism*, 135–136, 246–248, and passim.

40. See, for example, Butler, *Sea of Faith*, 220–221; Thomas H. Olbricht, "Biblical Primitivism in American Biblical Scholarship, 1630–1870," in *The American Quest for the Primitive Church*, ed. Richard T. Hughes (Urbana: University of Illinois Press, 1988), 89–90; and Mark A. Noll's comment in response to Olbricht, describing the Unitarians as "[t]he biblical primitivists of early America" ("Primitivism in Fundamentalism and American Biblical Scholarship: A Response," in ibid., 124).

down, half a century later, when so many churches around it were falling away from their foundations. It yet stands, a striking illustration of the fact, that any Church which would preserve its doctrinal purity, and vigor of spiritual life, must hail the advent of revivals, and joyfully put itself in the way of their influence."[41]

Perhaps the most profound of the Awakening's legacies for religion in Boston was that it enabled Trinitarian Congregationalism to retain at least this institutional toehold in the lair of liberal Christianity. With the founding of Park Street Church and the advent of Lyman Beecher, that toehold was to become a beachhead.[42]

---

41. J. M. Manning, "Thomas Prince: A Biographical Sketch," *The Congregational Quarterly*, vol. 1, no. 1 (January 1859): 16.

42. That even as late as 1809 Trinitarians were to be found not only at Third Church but also on the rolls of far more liberal congregations is demonstrated by Park Street Church's roster of charter members. Englizian, in *Brimstone Corner*, 29–30, notes that these twenty-six individuals included two from First Church, one from Second Church, four from Fourth Church, one from Sixth Church, and even two from Ninth Church, in addition to six from Third Church.

Appendix: Church Statistics and Community Demographics[1]

Table 1: First-time admissions to membership

Year	1st Church	2nd Church	3rd Church	4th Church	5th Church	6th Church	7th Church	8th Church	9th Church	Aggregate
1710	24	26	7	12						69
1711	23	6	22	7						58
1712	13	12	26	7						58
1713	18	10	10	8						46
1714	15	8	0	16	—					
1715	72	36	0	20	21					149
1716	38	25	0	24	37					124
1717	25	15	18	45	20					123
1718	30	30	16	21	18					115
1719	22	18	25	17	14	4				100
1720	23	5	12	17	12	6				75
1721	15	8	13	19	21	3				79
1722	25	16	16	18	22	3	2			102
1723	16	11	12	15	13	6	12			85
1724	21	11	10	24	24	4	0			94
1725	17	54	8	11	17	5	0			112
1726	12	9	11	11	28	13	0			84
1727	30	37	47	28	51	33	0			226
1728	38	49	72	87	78	16	13			353
1729	10	13	14	7	6	6	9			65

1. Until 1752 the Julian calendar was in use across New England, with the year starting on March 25, but for the sake of uniformity, I have converted all data presented here to the Gregorian system, with the year starting on January 1. For more on the subject of the early modern calendar and calendar reform, see Mark M. Smith, "Culture, Commerce, and Calendar Reform in Colonial America," *William and Mary Quarterly*, 3d series, vol. 55, no. 4 (October 1998): 557–584; and Malcolm Freiberg, "Going Gregorian, 1582–1752: A Summary View," *Catholic Historical Review*, vol. 86, no. 1 (January 2000): 1–19.

Year	1st Church	2nd Church	3rd Church	4th Church	5th Church	6th Church	7th Church	8th Church	9th Church	Aggregate
1730	8	8	8	6	5	1	1			37
1731	7	9	7	8	6	6	3			46
1732	5	9	7	14	8	7	3	3		56
1733	5	8	10	12	8	6	17	15		81
1734	4	6	13	16	11	5	3	6		64
1735	9	8	13	14	9	17	3	0		73
1736	5	5	24	30	11	13	2	3		93
1737	13	9	12	10	15	7	2	4	4	76
1738	4	5	9	13	5	5	6	4	4	55
1739	6	4	12	14	15	2	10	1	4	68
1740	6	4	9	23	15	15	10	3	3	88
1741	9	9	67	85	99	33	10	7	3	322
1742	12	7	28	42	36	5	12	14	3	159
1743	3	6	14	10	12	6	3	2	3	59
1744	3	1	4	13	15	4	5	4	3	52
1745	0	2	10	5	12	3	1	2	3	38
1746	1	0	3	5	6	0	4	4	3	26
1747	1	0	6	4	1	1	3	12	3	31
1748	5		0		4	4	3	2	3	
1749	1		7		10	1	4	2	6	
1750	0		6		4	2	3	6	2	
1751	1		8		3	4	2	4	0	
1752	3		5		4	2	3	4	0	
1753	2		5		2	0	0	8	2	
1754	2		6		6	2	1	3	1	
1755	1		13		6	4	0	1	0	
1756	17		41		35	19	22	7	8	
1757	8		1		12	2	2	4	0	
1758	5		2		6	3	0	3	5	
1759	3		3		11	2	0	2	0	
1760	2		8		4	0	3	3	0	

Appendix: Church Statistics and Community Demographics 155

Table 2: Admissions to membership by gender, selected churches

Year	1st Church men	1st Church women	1st Church total	3rd Church men	3rd Church women	3rd Church total	Year	1st Church men	1st Church women	1st Church total	3rd Church men	3rd Church women	3rd Church total
1710	8	16	24	0	7	7	1736	3	3	6	8	16	24
1711	9	14	23	5	17	22	1737	4	9	13	4	8	12
1712	6	10	16	10	17	27	1738	3	4	7	2	7	9
1713	7	12	19	6	5	11	1739	1	5	6	4	8	12
1714	2	14	16	0	0	0	1740	2	5	7	4	5	9
1715	26	47	73	0	0	0	1741	2	7	9	30	39	69
1716	12	27	39	0	0	0	1742	6	8	14	14	14	28
1717	12	15	27	7	12	19	1743	1	2	3	5	9	14
1718	12	18	30	7	12	19	1744	1	2	3	3	2	5
1719	11	11	22	10	16	26	1745	0	0	0	1	11	12
1720	7	18	25	4	9	13	1746	0	1	1	2	2	4
1721	5	10	15	4	9	13	1747	0	1	1	2	4	6
1722	8	20	28	3	15	18	1748	4	1	5	1	0	1
1723	5	11	16	6	7	13	1749	0	1	1	7	1	8
1724	8	13	21	2	8	10	1750	0	0	0	3	3	6
1725	5	12	17	7	2	9	1751	1	0	1	1	7	8
1726	5	7	12	5	6	11	1752	1	2	3	2	5	7
1727	8	23	31	16	31	47	1753	0	2	2	2	3	5
1728	12	25	37	21	54	75	1754	0	2	2	2	5	7
1729	3	8	11	7	10	17	1755	0	1	1	2	11	13
1730	5	3	8	10	6	16	1756	2	16	18	10	34	44
1731	4	3	7	4	4	8	1757	1	7	8	0	1	1
1732	1	4	5	4	3	7	1758	0	5	5	0	2	2
1733	0	5	5	2	8	10	1759	0	3	3	4	2	6
1734	1	3	4	7	11	18	1760	1	1	2	5	3	8
1735	2	7	9	6	8	14							

Table 3: Covenant renewals, selected churches

Year	2nd Church	3rd Church	5th Church	6th Church	7th Church	9th Church	Year	2nd Church	3rd Church	5th Church	6th Church	7th Church	9th Church
1710	16						1736	6	9	9	3	0	
1711	19						1737	4	3	5	3	5	0
1712	29						1738	5	5	5	2	4	0
1713	27						1739	3	2	8	8	8	0
1714	26		8				1740	4	6	9	5	2	0
1715	20		6				1741	1	22	9	3	5	0
1716	17		6				1742	1	14	5	2	3	0
1717	12	4	6				1743	2	4	7	1	4	0
1718	14	11	15				1744	0	2	8	6	5	0
1719	12	7	8	6			1745	2	4	11	4	0	0
1720	11	5	4	6			1746	2	2	4	2	0	0
1721	9	12	4	2			1747	2	8	8	2	3	2
1722	4	4	4	3	0		1748		2	9	3	6	4
1723	6	6	7	10	0		1749		5	7	8	3	2
1724	7	4	4	5	0		1750		9	10	5	3	1
1725	8	11	10	6	0		1751		3	11	8	0	0
1726	7	10	9	4	0		1752		4	7	2	3	2
1727	6	17	11	11	0		1753		4	18	9	2	1
1728	8	9	4	11	2		1754		2	12	9	0	0
1729	3	5	7	11	1		1755		2	16	8	0	2
1730	3	9	4	3	2		1756		11	13	9	0	1
1731	6	4	1	5	6		1757		4	6	4	1	1
1732	1	2	0	5	2		1758		3	13	6	0	2
1733	9	6	7	3	0		1759		2	15	3	1	0
1734	4	3	3	3	1		1760		3	8	7	0	2
1735	6	5	4	3	2								

Table 4: Covenant renewals by gender, Third Church, 1669–1760

Year	3rd Church men	3rd Church women	3rd Church total	Year	3rd Church men	3rd Church women	3rd Church total	Year	3rd Church men	3rd Church women	3rd Church total
1669	1	5	6	1700	3	7	10	1731	2	2	4
1670	1	0	1	1701	11	10	21	1732	1	1	2
1671	3	0	3	1702	8	11	19	1733	5	1	6
1672	0	0	0	1703	3	10	13	1734	1	2	3
1673	0	0	0	1704	9	14	23	1735	4	1	5
1674	5	1	6	1705	4	9	13	1736	5	4	9
1675	3	3	6	1706	1	3	4	1737	1	2	3
1676	2	2	4	1707				1738	3	2	5
1677	5	9	14	1708				1739	0	2	2
1678	1	5	6	1709				1740	3	3	6
1679	3	3	6	1710				1741	15	7	22
1680	38	66	104	1711				1742	5	9	14
1681	3	5	8	1712				1743	3	1	4
1682	6	14	20	1713				1744	2	0	2
1683	3	10	13	1714				1745	2	2	4
1684	4	7	11	1715				1746	2	0	2
1685	5	11	16	1716				1747	5	3	8
1686	23	36	59	1717	2	2	4	1748	1	1	2
1687	18	19	37	1718	3	8	11	1749	4	1	5
1688	8	23	31	1719	6	1	7	1750	4	5	9
1689	9	12	21	1720	4	1	5	1751	1	2	3
1690	0	18	18	1721	9	3	12	1752	2	2	4
1691	5	22	27	1722	1	3	4	1753	1	3	4
1692	6	8	14	1723	1	5	6	1754	0	2	2
1693	9	10	19	1724	1	3	4	1755	1	1	2
1694	5	12	17	1725	9	2	11	1756	4	7	11
1695	7	10	17	1726	7	3	10	1757	2	2	4
1696	6	18	24	1727	6	11	17	1758	1	2	3
1697	4	11	15	1728	6	3	9	1759	0	2	2
1698	6	6	12	1729	2	3	5	1760	2	1	3
1699	8	7	15	1730	3	6	9				

Table 5: Baptisms

Year	1st Church	2nd Church	3rd Church	4th Church	5th Church	6th Church	7th Church	8th Church	9th Church	Aggregate
1710	34	84		38						
1711	47	138		48						
1712	54	118		68						
1713	32	122		67						
1714	43	114		59	12					
1715	49	115		78	42					
1716	48	105		66	64					
1717	47	87	59	60	43					296
1718	41	113	90	74	75					393
1719	51	81	74	76	65	18				365
1720	35	95	61	57	48	30				326
1721	46	70	57	63	57	15				308
1722	32	59	48	43	64	26	14			286
1723	48	67	68	59	61	28	17			348
1724	42	65	50	64	72	28	29			350
1725	44	79	74	72	68	35	32			404
1726	41	66	46	59	89	44	29			374
1727	50	76	81	71	88	49	24			439
1728	49	78	72	76	104	47	26			452
1729	38	55	67	75	108	61	25			429
1730	43	56	71	52	70	31	25			348
1731	49	53	65	59	84	44	39			393
1732	43	36	71	55	76	55	30			366
1733	41	53	59	56	80	48	28	12		377
1734	53	44	62	61	85	61	36	11		413
1735	49	49	66	59	95	50	28	14		410
1736	46	32	55	77	82	36	30	11		369
1737	45	51	39	56	67	54	32	16	15	375
1738	37	45	50	54	100	37	30	23	24	400
1739	41	31	50	57	77	46	32	8	24	366
1740	35	34	54	42	88	59	26	21	19	378
1741	37	27	62	72	111	44	32	26	30	441
1742	34	21	66	63	90	42	35	19	24	394
1743	29	22	57	56	102	38	27	23	9	363
1744	30	15	66	69	92	49	36	23	19	399
1745	34	23	58	64	84	37	33	20	14	367

Appendix: Church Statistics and Community Demographics 159

Year	1st Church	2nd Church	3rd Church	4th Church	5th Church	6th Church	7th Church	8th Church	9th Church	Aggregate
1746	24	13	50	46	88	38	21	26	27	**333**
1747	25	18	56	65	79	36	19	24	16	**338**
1748	16		58	45	83	40	35	16	20	
1749	27		43	26	93	36	19	20	22	
1750	18		63	35	90	41	32	21	19	
1751	23		42	—	79	36	23	19	11	
1752	13		30	30	62	29	20	11	4	
1753	13		35	34	87	28	19	25	10	
1754	13		38	6	76	37	6	15	1	
1755	13		31	38	80	37	12	13	9	
1756	14		40	—	77	39	5	13	10	
1757	13		41	57	79	33	1	10	8	
1758	21		35	34	83	35	0	19	14	
1759	19		32	36	69	26	10	10	12	
1760	15		35	41	77	28	17	14	6	

Table 6: Population and death rate

Year	Boston Population	Boston Death Rate	Massachusetts Population	Year	Boston Population	Boston Death Rate	Massachusetts Population
1710	8,450	35		1736	16,300	38	
1711	8,700	42		1737	16,600	37	
1712	8,950	35	75,102	1738	16,700	34	
1713	9,200	52		1739	16,800	33	
1714	9,400	44		1740	16,800	42	
1715	9,700	35		1741	16,750	33	
1716	9,950	36		1742	16,650	30	164,000
1717	10,200	44		1743	16,500	38	
1718	10,450	36	94,000	1744	16,400	30	
1719	10,750	28		1745	16,250	48	
1720	11,000	30		1746	16,150	36	
1721	10,700	103	94,000	1747	16,050	48	192,000
1722	10,600	27		1748	15,950	46	
1723	10,900	38		1749	15,850	43	220,000
1724	11,250	36		1750	15,800	38	
1725	11,550	28		1751	15,750	40	
1726	11,900	29		1752	15,700	64	
1727	12,250	35		1753	15,700	31	
1728	12,650	39		1754	15,700	28	200,000
1729	13,050	44		1755	15,700	31	200,000
1730	13,500	67		1756	15,650	34	
1731	14,000	29	120,000	1757	15,650	28	
1732	14,600	34		1758	15,600	34	
1733	15,100	30	120,000	1759	15,600	40	
1734	15,550	34		1760	15,600	36	200,000
1735	16,000	28	144,308				

Bibliography

Primary Sources

Ames, William. *The Marrow of Theology*. Edited and translated by John D. Eusden. Cleveland, Ohio: United Church Press, 1968. Reprint, Durham, N.C.: Labyrinth Press, 1983.

Baxter, Richard. *The Reformed Pastor*. Edited by William Brown. Introduction by J. I. Packer. Glasgow: William Collins, 1829. Reprint, Carlisle, Penn.: Banner of Truth Trust, 1974.

Birth Records. City Clerk's Archives, City Hall, Boston.

"The Boston Ministers: A Ballad." Massachusetts Historical Society Archives, Boston.

Browne, John. *A Discourse Delivered at the West Church in Boston, August 24, 1776, Six Weeks after the Death of the Reverend Dr. Mayhew*. Boston: R. and S. Draper, 1766.

Byles, Mather. *The Character and End of the Perfect Man*. Boston: B. Green, 1744

———. *Divine Power and Anger Displayed in Earthquakes*. Boston: S. Kneeland, 1755.

———. *The Flourish of the Annual Spring*. Boston: Rogers and Fowle, 1741.

———. *The Glorious Rest of Heaven*. Boston: B. Green, 1745.

———. *God Glorious in the Scenes of Winter*. Boston: B. Green, 1744.

———. *The Man of God Thoroughly Furnished to Every Good Work*. New London, Conn.: Nathanael Green and Timothy Green, Jr., 1758.

———. *The Nature and Necessity of Conversion*. Boston: S. Kneeland and T. Green, 1732.

———. *The Visit to Jesus by Night*. Boston: Rogers and Fowle, 1741.

Calvin, John. "Draft Ecclesiastical Ordinances." In *Calvin: Theological Treatises*, ed. and trans. J. K. S. Reid, 58–72. Library of Christian Classics. Philadelphia: Westminster Press, 1954.

———. *Institutes of the Christian Religion*. Edited by John T. McNeill; translated by Ford Lewis Battles. Library of Christian Classics. Philadelphia: Westminster Press, 1960.

Chauncy, Charles. *A Discourse Occasioned by the Death of the Reverend Dr. Joseph Sewall, Late Colleague Pastor of the South-Church in Boston*. Boston: Kneeland and Adams, 1769.

———. *A Discourse Occasioned by the Death of the Reverend Jonathan Mayhew, D. D., Late Pastor of the West-Church in Boston*. Boston: R. and S. Draper, 1766.

———. *A Discourse Occasioned by the Death of the Reverend Thomas Foxcroft, M.A., Late Colleague-Pastor of the First Church in Boston*. Boston: Daniel Kneeland, 1769.

———. *The Duty of Ministers to "Make Known the Mystery of the Gospel."* Boston: Edes and Gill, 1766.

———. *The Earth Delivered from the Curse to Which It Is, at Present, Subjected*. Boston: Edes and Gill, 1756.

———. *Earthquakes a Token of the Righteous Anger of God*. Boston: Edes and Gill, 1755.

———. *The Gifts of the Spirit to Ministers Consider'd in Their Diversity.* Boston: Rogers and Fowle, 1742.

———. *A Letter from a Gentleman in Boston, to Mr. George Wishart, One of the Ministers of Edinburgh, Concerning the State of Religion in New-England.* Edinburgh: n.p., 1742.

———. *Ministers Cautioned against the Occasions of Contempt.* Boston: Rogers and Fowle, 1744

———. *Ministers Exhorted, and Encouraged to Take Heed to Themselves, and to Their Doctrine.* Boston: Rogers and Fowle, 1744.

———. *The Mystery Hid from Ages and Generations, Made Manifest by the Gospel-Revelation.* London: Charles Dilly, 1784.

———. *The New Creature Describ'd.* Boston: G. Rogers, 1741.

———. *The Out-Pouring of the Holy Ghost.* Boston: T. Fleet, 1742.

———. *Salvation for All Men Illustrated and Vindicated as a Scripture Doctrine in Numerous Abstracts from a Variety of Pious and Learned Men, Who Have Purposely Writ upon the Subject.* Boston: T. and J. Fleet, 1782.

———. *A Sermon Delivered at the First Church in Boston, March 13th, 1785: Occasioned by the Return of the Society to Their House of Worship, after Long Absence, to Make Way for the Repairs That Were Necessary.* Boston: Greenleaf and Freeman, 1785.

———. *A Sermon Preached May 6, 1767, at the Ordination of the Reverend Simeon Howard, M.A., to the Pastoral Care of the West-Church in Boston.* Boston: R. Draper, Edes and Gill, and T. and J. Fleet, 1767.

Checkley, Samuel, Jr. *The Character and Hope of the Righteous Consider'd.* Boston: J. Draper, 1748.

———. *The Christian Triumphing over Death through Christ.* Boston: Kneeland and Adams, 1765.

Checkley, Samuel[, Sr.] *Little Children Brought to Jesus Christ.* Boston: Rogers and Fowle, 1741.

———. *Mercy with God for the Chief of Sinners.* Boston: T. Fleet, 1733.

Colman, Benjamin. *The Faithful Ministers of Christ Mindful of Their Own Death.* Boston: D. Henchman, 1729.

———. *Faithful Pastors Angels of the Churches.* Boston: J. Draper, 1739.

———. *The Great God Has Magnified His Word to the Children of Men.* Boston: T. Fleet, 1742.

———. *Jesus Weeping over His Dead Friend, and with His Friends in Their Mourning.* Boston: Rogers and Fowle, 1744.

———. *A Letter from the Reverend Dr. Colman of Boston, to the Reverend Mr. Williams of Lebanon, upon Reading the "Confessions" and "Retractations" of the Reverend Mr. James Davenport.* Boston: Rogers and Fowle, 1744.

———. Letter to Thomas Foxcroft, May 15, 1747. Massachusetts Historical Society Archives, Boston.

———. *The Merchandise of a People Holiness to the Lord.* Boston: J. Draper, 1736.

———. *Ministers and People under Special Obligations to Sanctity, Humility, and Gratitude; for the Great Grace Given Them in the Preached Gospel.* Boston: S. Kneeland and T. Green, 1732.

Bibliography 163

———. *One Chosen of God and Called to the Work of the Ministry, Willingly Offering Himself*. Boston: Rogers and Fowle, 1746.

———. *Prayer to the Lord of the Harvest for the Mission of Labourers unto His Harvest*. Boston: Gamaliel Rogers, 1727.

———. *Souls Flying to Jesus Christ Pleasant and Admirable to Behold*. Boston: G. Rogers and D. Fowle, 1740.

———. *The Wither'd Hand Stretched Forth at the Command of Christ, and Restored*. Boston: J. Draper, 1739.

Cooper, Samuel. *A Sermon Preach'd April 9, 1760, at the Ordination of the Reverend Mr. Joseph Jackson to the Pastoral Care of the Church in Brooklin* [sic]. Boston: John Draper, 1760.

Cooper, William. *Compendium Evangelicum*. Boston: T. Fleet, 1739.

———. *One Shall Be Taken, and Another Left*. Boston: T. Fleet, 1741.

———. *The Service of God Recommended to the Choice of Young People*. Boston: T. Fleet, 1726.

———. *The Sin and Danger of Quenching the Spirit*. Boston: G. Rogers, 1741.

———. *The Work of Ministers Represented under the Figure of Sowers*. Boston: J. Draper, 1736.

Croswell, Andrew. *An Answer to the Rev. Mr. Garden's Three First Letters to the Rev. Mr. Whitefield*. Boston: S. Kneeland and T. Green, 1741.

———. *The Apostle's Advice to the Jaylor Improved*. Boston: Rogers and Fowle, 1744.

———. *Comfort in Christ*. Boston: D. Kneeland and Kneeland and Adams, 1767.

———. *A Discourse, from the First Epistle of Thessalonians*. Boston: E. Russell, 1784.

———. *Free Forgiveness of Spiritual Debts*. Boston: W. McAlpine, 1766.

———. *Free Justification thro' Christ's Redemption*. Boston: T. and J. Fleet and Green and Russell, 1765.

———. *The Heavenly Doctrine of Man's Justification Only by the Obedience of Jesus Christ*. Boston: Green and Russell, 1758.

———. *A Letter from the Rev^d Mr. Croswell, to the Rev^d Mr. Turell, in Answer to His Direction to His People*. Boston: Rogers and Fowle, 1742.

———. *Mr. Croswell's Reply to a Book Lately Publish'd, Entitled, "A Display of God's Special Grace," Attested by the Seven Following Ministers of Boston, viz Dr. Colman, Dr. Sewall, Mr. Prince, Mr. Webb, Mr. Cooper, Mr. Foxcroft, and Mr. Gee*. Boston: Rogers and Fowle, 1742.

———. *A Narrative of the Founding and Settling the New-Gathered Congregational Church in Boston*. Boston: Rogers and Fowle, 1749.

———. *A Second Defence of the Old Protestant Doctrine of Justifying Faith*. Boston: Rogers and Fowle, 1747.

———. *What Is Christ to Me, If He Is Not Mine?* Boston: Rogers and Fowle, 1745.

Edwards, Jonathan. *The Sermons of Jonathan Edwards. A Reader*. Edited by Wilson H. Kimnach, Kenneth P. Minkema, and Douglas A. Sweeney. New Haven, Conn.: Yale University Press, 1999.

———. *The Works of Jonathan Edwards*. Edited by Perry Miller, John E. Smith, et al. 20 vols. to date. New Haven, Conn.: Yale University Press, 1957– .

Eighth (Congregational) Church. Records. City Clerk's Archives, City Hall, Boston.

Eleventh (Congregational) Church. Articles of Government and Church Covenant. Massachusetts Historical Society Archives, Boston.

Eliot, Andrew. *A Burning and Shining Light Extinguished*. Boston: Daniel Fowle, 1750.

———. *Christ's Promise to the Penitent Thief*. Boston: John Boyle, 1773.

———. *The Faithful Steward*. Boston: T. Fleet, 1742.

———. *A Sermon Preached at the Ordination of the Reverend Mr. Joseph Roberts, to the Pastoral Care of a Church in Leicester, October 23d 1754*. Boston: D. Fowle, 1754.

Fifth (Congregational) Church. Records. City Clerk's Archives, City Hall, Boston.

First Baptist Church. Records. City Clerk's Archives, City Hall, Boston.

First (Congregational) Church. Records. City Clerk's Archives, City Hall, Boston.

Fourth (Congregational) Church. Records. City Clerk's Archives, City Hall, Boston.

Foxcroft, Thomas. *An Apology in Behalf of the Rev^d Mr. Whitefield*. Boston: Rogers and Fowle, 1745.

———. *A Discourse Preparatory to the Choice of a Minister*. Boston: Gamaliel Rogers, 1727.

———. *Divine Providence Ador'd and Justify'd in the Early Death of God's Children and Servants*. Preface by William Cooper. Boston: S. Gerrish, S. Kneeland, N. Belknap, and B. Love, 1727.

———. *The Importance of Ministers Being Men in Christ*. Boston: D. Henchman, 1728.

———. *Ministers Spiritual Parents, or Fathers in the Church of God*. Boston: B. Green, 1726.

———. *Observations Historical and Practical on the Rise and Primitive State of New-England. With a Special Reference to the Old or First Gather'd Church in Boston*. Boston: S. Kneeland and T. Green, 1730.

———. *A Practical Discourse Relating to the Gospel-Ministry*. Boston: Nicholas Buttolph, 1718.

———. *A Seasonable Memento for New Year's Day*. Boston: S. Kneeland and T. Green, 1747.

———. *Some Seasonable Thoughts on Evangelic Preaching; Its Nature, Usefulness, and Obligation*. Boston: G. Rogers and D. Fowle, 1740.

Gay, Ebenezer. *A Beloved Disciple of Jesus Characterized*. Boston: R. and S. Draper, T. and J. Fleet, and Edes and Gill, 1766.

———. *St. John's Vision of the Woman Cloathed with the Sun*. Boston: R. and S. Draper, Edes and Gill, and T. and J. Fleet, 1766.

Gee, Joshua. *Israel's Mourning for Aaron's Death*. Boston: S. Gerrish and N. Belknap, 1728.

———. *A Letter to the Reverend Mr. Nathanael Eells, Moderator of the Late Convention of Pastors in Boston; Containing Some Remarks on Their Printed Testimony against Several Errors and Disorders in the Land*. Boston: J. Draper, 1743.

———. *The Strait Gate and the Narrow Way, Infinitely Preferable to the Wide Gate and the Broad Way*. Boston: D. Henchman, 1729.

Gray, Ellis. *The Design of the Institution of the Gospel-Ministry, Fidelity in the Discharge of It; and the Obligation upon the Ministers of the Gospel Thankfully to Acknowledge the Power and Grace of God towards Them*. Boston: G. Rogers, 1741.

———. *The Fidelity of Ministers to Themselves, and to the Flock of God, Consider'd and Enforc'd*. Boston: G. Rogers, 1742.

Hooper, William. *The Apostles Neither Impostors nor Enthusiasts*. Boston: Rogers and Fowle, 1742.

———. *Christ the Life of True Believers, and Their Appearance with Him in Glory.* Boston: D. Fowle, 1741.
———. *Jesus Christ the Only Way to the Father.* Boston: D. Fowle, 1742.
Mather, Cotton. *The A, B, C. of Religion.* Boston: T. Green, 1713.
———. *The Ambassadors Tears.* Boston: T. Fleet, 1721.
———. *Bonifacius: An Essay upon the Good.* Boston: S. Gerrish, 1710. Reprint, Cambridge: Harvard University Press, Belknap Press, 1966.
———. *A Brief Memorial, of Matters and Methods for Pastoral Visits.* Boston: n.p., 1723.
———. *Cares about the Nurseries.* Boston: T. Green, 1702.
———. "Cotton Mather's Book." Second (Congregational) Church. Records, vol. 2. Massachusetts Historical Society, Boston.
———. *The Diary of Cotton Mather.* Preface by Worthington Chauncey Ford. 2 vols. New York: Frederick Ungar, 1911.
———. *Early Religion.* Boston: Benjamin Harris, 1694.
———. *Family Religion Excited and Assisted.* Boston: n.p., 1705.
———. *A Family-Sacrifice.* Boston: B. Green and J. Allen, 1703.
———. *A Family Well-Ordered.* Boston: B. Green and J. Allen, 1699.
———. *Golgotha.* Boston: B. Green, 1713.
———. *The Heavenly Conversation.* Boston: B. Green, 1710.
———. *Hor-Hagidgad.* Boston: S. Gerrish, S. Kneeland, N. Belknap, and B. Love, 1727.
———. *Love Triumphant.* Boston: S. Kneeland, 1722.
———. *Magnalia Christi Americana.* 2 vols. Hartford, Conn.: Silas Andrus and Son, 1853. Reprint, Carlisle, Penn.: Banner of Truth Trust, 1979.
———. *Magnalia Christi Americana: Books I and II.* Edited by Kenneth B. Murdock and Elizabeth W. Miller. Introduction by Kenneth B. Murdock. Cambridge: Harvard University Press, Belknap Press, 1977.
———. *The Man of God Furnished: The Way of Truth Laid Out.* Boston: S. Phillips, 1708.
———. *Manuductio ad Ministerium: Directions for a Candidate of the Ministry.* Boston: T. Hancock, 1726. Reprint, New York: Columbia University Press, 1938.
———. *Methods and Motives for Societies to Suppress Disorders.* Boston: B. Green and J. Allen, 1703.
———. *A Midnight Cry.* Boston: S. Phillips, 1692.
———. *The Minister.* Boston: S. Kneeland, 1722.
———. *Much in a Little.* Boston: Benjamin Eliot, 1702.
———. *Pastoral Desires: A Short Catalogue of Excellent Things Which a Pastor Will Desire to See Approved and Practised and Abounding among His People; A Book Design'd to Be Lodg'd and Left in Their Hands by One Desirous to Be Such an One in His Pastoral Visits to the Houses of All His People.* Boston: T. Green, 1712.
———. *Pia Desideria.* Boston: S. Kneeland, 1722.
———. *Private Meetings Animated and Regulated.* Boston: T. Green, 1706.
———. *Ratio Disciplinae Fratrum Nov-Anglorum: A Faithful Account of the Discipline Professed and Practised in the Churches of New England.* Boston: S. Gerrish, 1726.
———. *Religious Societies: Proposals for the Revival of Dying Religion by Well Ordered Societies for That Purpose.* Boston: J. Phillips, 1724.
———. *Rules for the Society of Negroes.* Boston: B. Green, 1693.

———. *The Rules of a Visit: An Essay upon That Case, How the Visits of Christians to One Another, May Be So Managed, As to Answer the Noble Designs of Christianity.* Boston: T. Green, 1705.

———. *Selected Letters of Cotton Mather.* Edited by Kenneth Silverman. Baton Rouge: Louisiana State University Press, 1971.

———. *Small Offers towards the Service of the Tabernacle in the Wilderness.* Boston: R. Pierce, 1689.

———. *The Summ of the Matter.* Boston: n.p., 1709.

———. *The Young Man's Glory.* Boston: R. Pierce, 1690.

Mather, Increase. *Practical Truths, Plainly Delivered.* Boston: B. Green, 1718.

Mather, Samuel. *All Men Will Not Be Saved Forever.* Boston: Benjamin Edes and Sons, 1782.

———. *The Departure and Character of Elijah Considered and Improved.* Boston: G. Rogers, 1728.

———. *Of the Pastoral Care.* Boston: Thomas Fleet and John Fleet, 1762.

———. *The State of Religion in New England.* Glasgow: Robert Foulis, 1743.

———. *The Walk of the Upright, with Its Comfort.* Boston: Michael Dennis, 1753.

———, ed. *Vita B. Augusti Hermanni Franckii, S.S. Theologiae in Academia Fridericiana nuper Professoris Eximiis nec non V.D.M. apud Glaucham, etc. prope Hallam Magdeburgicam: Cui Adjecta Est, Narratio Rerum Memorabilium in Ecclesiis Evangelicis per GERMANIAM etc.* Boston: Samuel Kneeland, 1733.

Mayhew, Jonathan. *Christian Sobriety.* Boston: Richard and Samuel Draper, 1763.

———. *The Expected Dissolution of All Things, a Motive to Universal Holiness.* Boston: Edes and Gill, 1755.

———. *Sermons.* Boston: Richard Draper, 1755.

———. *Seven Sermons.* Boston: Rogers and Fowle, 1749.

Ninth (Congregational) Church. Records. City Clerk's Archives, City Hall, Boston.

Pemberton, Ebenezer[, Jr.] *All Power in Heaven, and in Earth Given unto Jesus Christ.* Boston: D. Fowle, 1756.

———. *Heaven the Residence of the Saints.* Boston: D. Kneeland, 1770.

———. *The Knowlege of Christ Recommended.* New London, Conn.: T. Green, 1741.

———. *Practical Discourses on Various Texts.* Boston: T. Fleet, 1741.

———. *A Sermon Preach'd at the Ordination of Reverend Mr. Walter Wilmot at Jamaica on Long-Island, April 12, 1738.* Boston: J. Draper, 1738.

———. *A Sermon Preached at the Ordination of the Reverend Mr. Isaac Story, to the Pastoral Care of the Second Church in Marblehead, in Conjunction with the Reverend Mr. Simon Bradstreet, May 1, 1771.* Boston: Samuel Hall, 1771.

———. *A Sermon Preach'd in New-Ark, June 12, 1744, at the Ordination of Mr. David Brainerd, a Missionary among the Indians upon the Borders of the Provinces of New-York, New-Jersey, and Pennsylvania.* Boston: Rogers and Fowle, 1744.

———. *Sermons on Several Subjects.* Boston: T. Fleet, 1738.

Pierce, Richard D., ed. *The Records of the First Church in Boston, 1630–1868.* 2 vols. Boston: Colonial Society of Massachusetts, 1961.

The Prince Library: A Catalogue of the Collection of Books and Manuscripts Which Formerly Belonged to the Reverend Thomas Prince, and Was by Him Bequeathed to the Old South Church, and Is Now Deposited in the Public Library of the City of Boston. Boston: Alfred Mudge and Son, 1870.

Bibliography

Prince, Thomas. *An Account of the Revival of Religion in Boston, in the Years 1740–1–2–3.* N.p., n.d. Reprint, Boston: Samuel Armstrong, 1823.

———. *The Christian History, Containing Accounts of the Revival and Propagation of Religion in Great-Britain and America for the Year 1743.* Boston: S. Kneeland and T. Green, 1744.

———. *A Chronological History of New-England, in the Form of Annals.* Boston: Kneeland and Green, 1736.

———. *The Departure of Elijah Lamented.* Boston: D. Henchman, 1728.

———. "Diary of the Rev. Thomas Prince, 1737." Edited by Albert Matthews. In *Publications of the Colonial Society of Massachusetts*, vol. 19, Transactions, 1916–1917, 331–364. Boston: Colonial Society of Massachusetts, 1918.

———. *The Dying Prayer of Christ, for His People's Preservation and Unity.* Boston: S. Kneeland and T. Green, 1732.

———. *Earthquakes the Works of God, and Tokens of His Just Displeasure.* Boston: D. Henchman, 1727.

———. *Earthquakes the Works of God, and Tokens of His Just Displeasure.* Boston: D. Fowle, 1755.

———. *An Improvement of the Doctrine of Earthquakes, Being the Works of God, and Tokens of His Just Displeasure.* Boston: D. Fowle, 1755.

———. *Morning Health No Security against Sudden Arrest of Death before Night.* Boston: D. Henchman, 1727.

———. *A Sermon Delivered by Thomas Prince, M.A., on Wednesday, October 1, 1718, at His Ordination to the Pastoral Charge of the South-Church in Boston, N.E. in Conjunction with the Reverend Mr. Joseph Sewall.* Boston: J. Franklin, 1718.

———. *The Sovereign God Acknowledged and Blessed, Both in Giving and in Taking Away.* Boston: Rogers and Fowle, 1744.

Second (Congregational) Church. Records. City Clerk's Archives, City Hall, Boston.

Seventh (Congregational) Church. Records. City Clerk's Archives, City Hall, Boston.

Sewall, Joseph. *All Flesh Is as Grass, but the Word of the Lord Endureth Forever.* Boston: S. Kneeland and T. Green, 1741.

———. *The Certainty and Suddenness of Christ's Coming to Judgment, Improved as a Motive to Diligence in Preparing for It.* Boston: B. Green, 1716.

———. *The Character and Reward of the Faithful Ministers of Christ.* Boston: S. Kneeland, 1763.

———. *Desires That Joshua's Resolution May Be Revived: Or, Excitations to the Constant and Diligent Exercise of Family-Religion.* Boston: B. Green, 1716.

———. "Diary, November 15, 1711 – July 30, 1716." Massachusetts Historical Society Archives, Boston.

———. *The Duty, Character, and Reward of Christ's Faithful Servants.* Boston: S. Kneeland, 1758.

———. *The Duty of a People to Stand in Aw of God, and Not Sin, When under His Terrible Judgments.* Boston: D. Henchman, 1727.

———. *The Duty of Every Man to Be Always Ready to Die.* Boston: B. Green, 1727.

———. *God's People Must Enquire of Him to Bestow the Blessings Promised in His Word.* Boston: D. Fowle, 1742.

———. *The Holy Spirit Convincing the World of Sin, of Righteousness, and of Judgment.* Boston: J. Draper, 1741.

———. *The Holy Spirit the Gift of God Our Heavenly Father, to Them That Ask Him.* Boston: D. Henchman, 1728.

———. *Precious Treasures in Earthen Vessels.* Boston: B. Green, 1717.

———. *Repentance the Sure Way to Escape Destruction.* Boston, D. Henchman, 1727.

———. *The Thirsty Invited to Come, and Take the Waters of Life Freely.* Boston: Rogers and Fowle, 1742.

Sewall, Samuel. *The Diary of Samuel Sewall, 1674–1729.* Edited by M. Halsey Thomas. 2 vols. New York: Farrar, Straus and Giroux, 1973.

Sixth (Congregational) Church. Records. City Clerk's Archives, City Hall, Boston.

Stiles, Ezra. *Extracts from the "Itineraries" and Other Miscellanies of Ezra Stiles, D. D., LL.D., 1755–1794, with a Selection from His Correspondence.* Edited by Franklin Bowditch Dexter. New Haven, Conn.: Yale University Press, 1916.

Tennent, Gilbert. *The Danger of an Unconverted Ministry.* Philadelphia: Benjamin Franklin, 1740.

———. *The Necessity of Holding Fast the Truth.* Preface by Joshua Gee et al. Boston: S. Kneeland and T. Green, 1743.

The Testimony and Advice of an Assembly of Pastors of Churches in New-England, at a Meeting in Boston July 7, 1743. Boston: S. Kneeland and T. Green, 1743.

The Testimony and Advice of a Number of Laymen Respecting Religion, and the Teachers of It, Address'd to the Pastors of New-England. Boston: n.p., 1743.

The Testimony of the Pastors of the Churches in the Province of the Massachusetts-Bay in New-England, at Their Annual Convention in Boston, May 25, 1743. Boston: Rogers and Fowle, 1743.

Thacher, Peter. *Man's Frailty Practically Exhibited in His Life and Death.* Boston: S. Kneeland and T. Green, 1730.

Third (Congregational) Church. Records. City Clerk's Archives, City Hall, Boston.

Webb, John. *The Believer's Redemption in the Precious Blood of Christ.* Newport, R.I.: J. Franklin, 1728.

———. *Christ's Suit to the Sinner, While He Stands and Knocks at the Door.* Boston: S. Kneeland and T. Green, 1741.

———. *The Duty of a Degenerate People to Pray for the Reviving of God's Work.* Boston: S. Kneeland and T. Green, 1734.

———. *The Duty of Ministers to Work the Works of Him That Sent Them, While It Is Day.* Boston: S. Gerrish, 1727.

———. *The Duty of Survivors to Remember and to Follow the Faith of Their Godly Deceased Pastors.* Boston: J. Draper, 1739.

———. *The Young-Man['] s Duty, Explained and Pressed upon Him.* Boston: S. Kneeland, 1718.

Welsteed, William. *The Dignity and Duty of the Civil Magistrate.* Boston: S. Kneeland, 1751.

Whitefield, George. *Journals.* Carlisle, Penn.: Banner of Truth Trust, 1960.

Willard, Samuel. *Brief Directions to a Young Scholar Designing the Ministry.* Boston: J. Draper, 1735.

———. *A Compleat Body of Divinity in Two Hundred and Fifty Expository Lectures on the Assembly's Shorter Catechism.* Boston: B. Green and S. Kneeland, 1726.

Secondary Sources

Adams, Brooks. *The Emancipation of Massachusetts: The Dream and the Reality.* Rev. ed. Boston: Houghton Mifflin, 1919.

Adams, Charles Francis. *Massachusetts: Its Historians and Its History.* Boston: Houghton Mifflin, 1893.

Ahlstrom, Sydney E., and Carey, Jonathan S., eds. *An American Reformation: A Documentary History of Unitarian Christianity.* Middletown, Conn.: Wesleyan University Press, 1985.

Akers, Charles W. *Called unto Liberty: A Life of Jonathan Mayhew, 1720–1766.* Cambridge: Harvard University Press, 1964.

―――. *The Divine Politician: Samuel Cooper and the American Revolution.* Boston: Northeastern University Press, 1982.

Alden, John. "The Reverend Thomas Prince Recollected; or, The Early Libraries of the Old South Church Reviewed." Typewritten ms. Congregational Library, Boston.

Anderson, Fred. *Crucible of War: The Seven Years' War and the Fate of Empire in British North America, 1754–1766.* New York: Alfred A. Knopf, 2000.

Askew, Thomas A., and Spellman, Peter W. *The Churches and the American Experience: Ideals and Institutions.* Grand Rapids, Mich.: Baker Book House, 1984.

Bacon, Leonard Woolsey. *A History of American Christianity.* American Church History Series, vol. 12. New York: Christian Literature Co., 1897. Reprint, New York: Charles Scribner's Sons, 1921.

Bailyn, Bernard. *Voyagers to the West: A Passage in the Peopling of America on the Eve of the Revolution.* New York: Alfred A. Knopf, 1986.

Bartol, C. A. "Discourse on William Hooper." In *The West Church and Its Ministers.* Boston: Crosby, Nichols and Co., 1856.

Battis, Emery. *Saints and Sectaries: Anne Hutchinson and the Antinomian Controversy in the Massachusetts Bay Colony.* Chapel Hill, N.C.: University of North Carolina Press, 1962.

Beales, Ross W., Jr. "The Half-Way Covenant and Religious Scrupulosity: The First Church of Dorchester, Massachusetts, as a Test Case." *William and Mary Quarterly*, 3d series, vol. 31, no. 3 (July 1974): 465–480.

Beall, Otho T., Jr., and Shryock, Richard H. *Cotton Mather: First Significant Figure in American Medicine.* Baltimore, Md.: Johns Hopkins University Press, 1954.

Beeke, Joel R. *The Quest for Full Assurance: The Legacy of Calvin and His Successors.* Carlisle, Penn.: Banner of Truth Trust, 1999.

Bercovitch, Sacvan. *The Puritan Origins of the American Self.* New Haven, Conn.: Yale University Press, 1975.

Bernhard, Virginia. "Cotton Mather's 'Most Unhappy Wife': Reflections on the Uses of Historical Evidence." *New England Quarterly*, vol. 60, no. 3 (September 1987): 341–362.

Black, J. William. "From Martin Bucer to Richard Baxter: 'Discipline' and Reformation in Sixteenth- and Seventeenth-Century England." *Church History*, vol. 70, no. 4 (December 2001): 644–673.

Blake, Francis Everett. *History of the Town of Princeton in the County of Worcester and Commonwealth of Massachusetts.* 2 vols. Princeton, Mass.: By the Town, 1915.

Blake, John. *Public Health in the Town of Boston, 1630–1822*. Cambridge: Harvard University Press, 1959.
Boas, Ralph, and Boas, Louise. *Cotton Mather: Keeper of the Puritan Conscience*. Hamden, Conn.: Archon Books, 1964.
Bonomi, Patricia U. *Under the Cope of Heaven: Religion, Society, and Politics in Colonial America*. New York: Oxford University Press, 1986.
——— and Eisenstadt, Peter R. "Church Adherence in the Eighteenth-Century British American Colonies." *William and Mary Quarterly*, 3d series, vol. 39, no. 2 (April 1982): 245–286.
Breen, Timothy H., and Foster, Stephen. "The Puritans' Greatest Achievement: A Study of Social Cohesion in Seventeenth-Century Massachusetts." *Journal of American History*, vol. 60, no. 1 (June 1973): 5–22.
Bridenbaugh, Carl. *Cities in Revolt: Urban Life in America, 1743–1776*. New York: Alfred A. Knopf, 1955.
———. *Cities in the Wilderness: The First Century of Urban Life in America, 1625–1742*. New York: Ronald Press, 1938. Reprint, New York: Alfred A. Knopf, 1955.
Bumsted, J. M. "Religion, Finance, and Democracy in Massachusetts: The Town of Norton as a Case Study." *Journal of American History*, vol. 57, no. 4 (March 1971): 817–831.
———. "Revivalism and Separatism in New England: The First Society of Norwich, Connecticut, as a Case Study." *William and Mary Quarterly*, 3d series, vol. 24, no. 4 (October 1967): 588–612.
——— and Van de Wetering, John E. *What Must I Do to Be Saved? The Great Awakening in Colonial America*. Berkshire Studies in History. Hinsdale, Ill.: Dryden Press, 1976.
Burnett, Amy Nelson. "Confirmation and Christian Fellowship: Martin Bucer on Commitment to the Church." *Church History*, vol. 64, no. 2 (June 1995): 202–217.
———. *The Yoke of Christ: Martin Bucer and Christian Discipline*. Sixteenth Century Essays and Studies, vol. 26. Kirksville, Mo.: Sixteenth Century Journal Publishers, 1994.
Burton, John D. "'The Awful Judgments of God upon the Land': Smallpox in Colonial Cambridge, Massachusetts." *New England Quarterly*, vol. 74, no. 3 (September 2001): 495–506.
Bushman, Richard L. *From Puritan to Yankee: Character and the Social Order in Connecticut, 1690–1765*. Cambridge: Harvard University Press, 1967. Reprint, New York: W. W. Norton, Norton Library, 1970.
Butler, Jon. *Awash in a Sea of Faith: Christianizing the American People*. Cambridge: Harvard University Press, 1990.
———. "Enthusiasm Described and Decried: The Great Awakening as Interpretative Fiction." *Journal of American History*, vol. 69, no. 2 (September 1982): 305–325.
Carpenter, John B. "New England's Puritan Century: Three Generations of Continuity in the City upon a Hill." *Fides et Historia*, vol. 35, no. 1 (Winter-Spring 2003): 41–58.
Chapman, Clayton Harding. "Benjamin Colman's Daughters." *New England Quarterly*, vol. 26, no. 2 (June 1953): 169–192.
———. "Life and Influence of Rev. Benjamin Colman, D.D." Th.D. dissertation, Boston University, 1947.

Clark, Joseph S. *A Historical Sketch of the Congregational Churches in Massachusetts from 1620 to 1858*. Boston: Congregational Board of Publication, 1858.

Coffman, Ralph J. *Solomon Stoddard*. Twayne's United States Authors. Boston: G. K. Hall and Co., Twayne Publishers, 1978.

Cohen, Charles Lloyd. *God's Caress: The Psychology of Puritan Religious Experience*. New York: Oxford University Press, 1986.

Conforti, Joseph A. *Samuel Hopkins and the New Divinity Movement: Calvinism, the Congregational Ministry, and Reform in New England between the Great Awakenings*. Grand Rapids, Mich.: Christian University Press and William B. Eerdmans, 1981.

Cooper, James F., Jr. *Tenacious of Their Liberties: The Congregationalists in Colonial Massachusetts*. New York: Oxford University Press, 1999.

Cornman, Thomas H. L. *Caterpillars and Newfangled Religion: The Struggle for the Soul of Colonial American Presbyterianism*. Lanham, Md.: University Press of America, 2003.

Corrigan, John. "Catholick Congregational Clergy and Public Piety." *Church History*, vol. 60, no. 2 (June 1991): 210–222.

———. *The Hidden Balance: Religion and the Social Theories of Charles Chauncy and Jonathan Mayhew*. Cambridge: Cambridge University Press, 1987.

———. *The Prism of Piety: Catholick Congregational Clergy at the Beginning of the Enlightenment*. New York: Oxford University Press, 1991.

Cowing, Cedric B. *The Great Awakening and the American Revolution: Colonial Thought in the Eighteenth Century*. Chicago: Rand McNally, 1971.

———. "Sex and Preaching in the Great Awakening." *American Quarterly*, vol. 20, no. 3 (Fall 1968): 624–644.

Crawford, Michael J. "New England and the Scottish Religious Revivals of 1742." *American Presbyterians: Journal of Presbyterian History*, vol. 69, no. 1 (Spring 1991): 23–32.

———. *Seasons of Grace: Colonial New England's Revival Tradition in Its British Context*. New York: Oxford University Press, 1991.

Dallimore, Arnold. *George Whitefield: The Life and Times of the Great Evangelist of the Eighteenth-Century Revival*. 2 vols. Carlisle, Penn.: Banner of Truth Trust, 1970.

Dexter, Henry M. "Joseph Sewall." *Congregational Quarterly*, vol. 5, no. 3 (July 1863): 201–205.

Dodds, Elisabeth D. *Marriage to a Difficult Man: The "Uncommon Union" of Jonathan and Sarah Edwards*. Philadelphia: Westminster Press, 1971.

Duffy, John. *Epidemics in Colonial America*. Baton Rouge, La.: Louisiana State University Press, 1953.

Eaton, Arthur Wentworth Hamilton. *The Famous Mather Byles: The Noted Boston Tory Preacher, Poet, and Wit, 1707–1788*. Boston: W. A. Butterfield, 1914.

Eliot, John. *A Biographical Dictionary, Containing a Brief Account of the First Settlers, and Other Eminent Characters among the Magistrates, Ministers, Literary and Worthy Men, in New-England*. Boston: Edward Oliver, 1809.

Elliott, Emory. *Power and the Pulpit in Puritan New England*. Princeton, N.J.: Princeton University Press, 1975.

Ellis, Arthur B. *History of the First Church in Boston, 1630–1880*. Boston: Hall and Whiting, 1881.

Emerson, William. *An Historical Sketch of the First Church in Boston, from Its Foundation to the Present Period.* Boston: Munroe and Francis, 1812.

Englizian, H. Crosby. *Brimstone Corner: Park Street Church, Boston.* Chicago: Moody Press, 1968.

Foster, Stephen. *The Long Argument: English Puritanism and the Shaping of New England Culture, 1570–1700.* Chapel Hill, N.C.: University of North Carolina Press, 1991.

———. "New England and the Challenge of Heresy, 1630 to 1660: The Puritan Crisis in Transatlantic Perspective." *William and Mary Quarterly*, 3d series, vol. 38, no. 4 (October 1981): 624–660.

Franks, Alison. "Epidemics in US, 1628–1918." Available from http://www.bjhughes.org/epidemic.html; Internet; accessed 24 June 2003.

Freiberg, Malcolm. "Going Gregorian, 1582–1752: A Summary View." *Catholic Historical Review*, vol. 86, no. 1 (January 2000): 1–19.

Garraty, John A. "Colonial Wars." In *The Reader's Companion to American History*, ed. John A. Garraty and Eric Foner, 205–207. Boston: Houghton Mifflin, 1991.

Gaustad, Edwin Scott. "Charles Chauncy and the Great Awakening: A Survey and Bibliography." *Papers of the Bibliographical Society of America*, vol. 45, no. 2 (Spring 1951): 125–135.

———. *The Great Awakening in New England.* New York: Harper and Row, 1957. Reprint, Gloucester, Mass.: Peter Smith, 1965.

———. "Society and the Great Awakening in New England." *William and Mary Quarterly*, 3d series, vol. 11, no. 4 (October 1954): 566–577.

Gay, Peter. *A Loss of Mastery: Puritan Historians in Colonial America.* Berkeley, Calif.: University of California Press, 1966. Reprint, New York: Random House, Vintage Books, 1968.

Goen, C. C. *Revivalism and Separatism in New England, 1740–1800: Strict Congregationalists and Separate Baptists in the Great Awakening.* New Haven, Conn.: Yale University Press, 1962.

Greene, Evarts B., and Harrington, Virginia D. *American Population before the Federal Census of 1790.* New York: Columbia University Press, 1932.

Greven, Philip J., Jr. *The Protestant Temperament: Patterns of Child-Rearing, Religious Experience, and the Self in Early America.* New York: Alfred A. Knopf, 1977.

———. "Youth, Maturity, and Religious Conversion: A Note on the Ages of Converts in Andover, Massachusetts, 1711–1749." *Essex Institute Historical Collections*, vol. 108, no. 2 (April 1972): 119–134.

Griffin, Edward M. *Old Brick: Charles Chauncy of Boston, 1705–1787.* Minneapolis: University of Minnesota Press, 1980.

Grossbart, Stephen R. "Seeking the Divine Favor: Conversion and Church Admission in Eastern Connecticut, 1711–1832." *William and Mary Quarterly*, 3d series, vol. 46, no. 4 (October 1989): 696–740.

Guelzo, Allen C. "Jonathan Edwards and the New Divinity: Change and Continuity in New England Calvinism, 1758–1858." In *Pressing toward the Mark: Essays Commemorating the Fiftieth Anniversary of the Orthodox Presbyterian Church*, ed. Charles Dennison and Richard Gamble, 147–167. Philadelphia: Orthodox Presbyterian Church, 1986.

Hall, David D. *The Faithful Shepherd: A History of the New England Ministry in the Seventeenth Century.* Chapel Hill, N.C.: University of North Carolina Press, 1972.

Bibliography

———. *Worlds of Wonder, Days of Judgment: Popular Religious Belief in Early New England*. New York: Alfred A. Knopf, 198.
Hall, Michael G. *The Last American Puritan: The Life of Increase Mather*. Middletown, Conn.: Wesleyan University Press, 1988.
Hambrick-Stowe, Charles E. *The Practice of Piety: Puritan Devotional Disciplines in Seventeenth-Century New England*. Chapel Hill, N.C.: University of North Carolina Press, 1982.
Hammann, Gottfried. "Ecclesiological Motifs behind the Creation of the 'Christlichen Gemeinschaften.'" Translated by D. F. Wright. In *Martin Bucer: Reforming Church and Community*, ed. D. F. Wright, 129–143. Cambridge: Cambridge University Press, 1994.
Handlin, Oscar. *Boston's Immigrants: A Study in Acculturation*. Rev. ed. Cambridge: Harvard University Press, 1959.
Hardman, Keith J. *The Spiritual Awakeners: American Revivalists from Solomon Stoddard to D. L. Moody*. Chicago: Moody Press, 1983.
Harlan, David. *The Clergy and the Great Awakening in New England*. Ann Arbor, Mich.: UMI Research Press, 1980.
———. "A People Blinded from Birth: American History According to Sacvan Bercovitch." *Journal of American History*, vol. 78, no. 3 (December 1991): 949–971.
Haroutunian, Joseph. *Piety versus Moralism: The Passing of the New England Theology*. New York: Henry Holt, 1932.
Harper, George W. "Clericalism and Revival: The Great Awakening in Boston as a Pastoral Phenomenon." *New England Quarterly*, vol. 57, no. 4 (December 1984): 554–566.
———. "*Manuductio ad Ministerium*: Cotton Mather as Pastoral Innovator." *Westminster Theological Journal*, vol. 54, no. 1 (Spring 1992): 79–97.
Hatch, Nathan O. *The Sacred Cause of Liberty: Republican Thought and the Millennium in Revolutionary New England*. New Haven, Conn.: Yale University Press, 1977.
Heimert, Alan. *Religion and the American Mind: From the Great Awakening to the Revolution*. Cambridge: Harvard University Press, 1966.
Helm, Paul. *Calvin and the Calvinists*. Carlisle, Penn.: Banner of Truth Trust, 1982.
Henderson, Robert W. *The Teaching Office in the Reformed Tradition: A History of the Doctoral Ministry*. Philadelphia: Westminster Press, 1962.
Henretta, James A. *The Evolution of American Society, 1700–1815: An Interdisciplinary Approach*. Lexington, Mass.: D. C. Heath, 1973.
Heppe, Heinrich. *Reformed Dogmatics Set Out and Illustrated from the Sources*. Edited by Ernst Bizer; translated by G. T. Thomson. London: George Allen and Unwin, 1950.
Higginson, Thomas Wentworth. "French and Indian Wars." In *The Memorial History of Boston, Including Suffolk County, Massachusetts*, ed. Justin Winsor, vol. 2, *The Provincial Period*, 93–130. Boston: Ticknor and Co., 1881.
Hill, Hamilton Andrews. *History of the Old South Church*. 2 vols. Boston: Houghton Mifflin, 1890.
———. *The Rev. Joseph Sewall: His Youth and Early Manhood*. Boston: David Clapp and Son, 1892.
Hofstadter, Richard. *Anti-Intellectualism in American Life*. New York: Alfred A. Knopf, 1963.

———. *America at 1750: A Social Portrait.* New York: Alfred A. Knopf, 1971. Reprint, New York: Random House, Vintage Books, 1973.

Holifield, E. Brooks. *The Covenant Sealed: The Development of Puritan Sacramental Theology in Old and New England, 1570–1720.* New Haven, Conn.: Yale University Press, 1974.

———. *A History of Pastoral Care in America: From Salvation to Self-Realization.* Nashville, Tenn.: Abingdon Press, 1983.

Holmes, Thomas James. *Cotton Mather: A Bibliography of His Works.* 3 vols. Newton, Mass.: Crofton Publishing Corp., 1974.

Hood, Edwin Paxton. *The Great Revival of the Eighteenth Century.* Philadelphia: American Sunday School Union, 1882.

Hudson, Winthrop S. *Religion in America.* New York: Charles Scribner's Sons, 1965.

Isaac, Rhys. "Evangelical Revolt: The Nature of the Baptists' Challenge to the Traditional Order in Virginia, 1765–1775." *William and Mary Quarterly*, 3d series, vol. 31, no. 3 (July 1974): 345–368.

———. *The Transformation of Virginia, 1740–1790.* Chapel Hill, N.C.: University of North Carolina Press, 1983.

Jedrey, Christopher M. *The World of John Cleaveland: Family and Community in Eighteenth-Century New England.* New York: W. W. Norton, 1979.

Jeffries, John W. "The Separation in the Canterbury Congregational Church: Religion, Family, and Politics in a Connecticut Town." *New England Quarterly*, vol. 52, no. 4 (December 1979): 522–549.

Jennings, Francis. *Empire of Fortune: Crown, Colonies, and Tribes in the Seven Years' War in America.* New York: W. W. Norton, 1988.

Jones, James W. *The Shattered Synthesis: New England Puritanism before the Great Awakening.* New Haven, Conn.: Yale University Press, 1973.

Kendall, R. T. *Calvin and English Calvinism to 1649.* Oxford Theological Monographs. Oxford: Oxford University Press, 1979.

Kidd, Thomas S. "Daniel Rogers' Egalitarian Great Awakening." *Journal of the Historical Society*, vol. 7, no. 1 (March 2007): 111–135.

———. *The Great Awakening: The Roots of Evangelical Christianity in Colonial America.* New Haven, Conn.: Yale University Press, 2007.

———. *The Protestant Interest: New England after Puritanism.* New Haven, Conn.: Yale University Press, 2004.

———. "'The Very Vital Breath of Christianity': Prayer and Revival in Provincial New England." *Fides et Historia*, vol. 36, no. 2 (Summer-Fall 2004): 19–33.

Kittelson, James. "Martin Bucer and the Ministry of the Church." In *Martin Bucer: Reforming Church and Community*, ed. D. F. Wright, 83–94. Cambridge: Cambridge University Press, 1994.

Knight, Janice. *Orthodoxies in Massachusetts: Rereading American Puritanism.* Cambridge: Harvard University Press, 1994.

Labaree, Benjamin W. *Colonial Massachusetts: A History.* Millwood, N.Y.: KTO Press, 1979.

Lambert, Frank. "The Great Awakening as Artifact: George Whitefield and the Construction of Intercolonial Revival, 1739–1745." *Church History*, vol. 60, no. 2 (June 1991): 223–246.

———. "'Pedlar in Divinity': George Whitefield and the Great Awakening, 1737–1745." *Journal of American History*, vol. 77, no. 3 (December 1990): 812–837.
———. *"Pedlar in Divinity": George Whitefield and the Transatlantic Revivals, 1737–1770*. Princeton, N.J.: Princeton University Press, 1994.
Levin, David. *Cotton Mather: The Young Life of the Lord's Remembrancer, 1663–1703*. Cambridge: Harvard University Press, 1978.
Lewis, A. J. *Zinzendorf the Ecumenical Pioneer: A Study in the Moravian Contribution to Christian Mission and Unity*. London: SCM Press, 1962.
Lippy, Charles H. *Seasonable Revolutionary: The Mind of Charles Chauncy*. Chicago: Nelson-Hall, 1981.
Lockridge, Kenneth A. *A New England Town: The First Hundred Years; Dedham, Massachusetts, 1636–1736*. Norton Essays in American History. New York: W. W. Norton, 1970.
Lothrop, Samuel Kirkland. *A History of the Church in Brattle Street, Boston*. Boston: William Crosby and H. P. Nichols, 1851.
———. *Memorial of the Church in Brattle Square*. Boston: John Wilson and Son, 1871.
Lovejoy, David S. *Religious Enthusiasm and the Great Awakening*. Englewood Cliffs, N.J.: Prentice-Hall, 1969.
———. *Religious Enthusiasm in the New World: Heresy to Revolution*. Cambridge: Harvard University Press, 1985.
———. "Shun Thy Father and All That: The Enthusiasts' Threat to the Family." *New England Quarterly*, vol. 60, no. 1 (March 1987): 71–85.
Lovelace, Richard F. *The American Pietism of Cotton Mather: Origins of American Evangelicalism*. Grand Rapids, Mich.: Christian University Press and William B. Eerdmans, 1979.
Lowrie, Ernest Benson. *The Shape of the Puritan Mind: The Thought of Samuel Willard*. New Haven, Conn.: Yale University Press, 1974.
Lucas, Paul R. "'An Appeal to the Learned': The Mind of Solomon Stoddard." *William and Mary Quarterly*, 3d series, vol. 30, no. 2 (April 1973): 257–292.
———. *Valley of Discord: Church and Society along the Connecticut River, 1636–1725*. Hanover, N.H.: University Press of New England, 1976.
McKenzie, Alexander. "The Religious History of the Provincial Period." In *The Memorial History of Boston, Including Suffolk County, Massachusetts*, ed. Justin Winsor, vol. 2, *The Provincial Period*, 187–248. Boston: Ticknor and Co., 1881.
McLoughlin, William G. *New England Dissent, 1630–1833: The Baptists and the Separation of Church and State*. 2 vols. Cambridge: Harvard University Press, 1971.
———. *Revivals, Awakenings, and Reform: An Essay on Religion and Social Change in America, 1607–1977*. Chicago History of American Religion. Chicago: University of Chicago Press, 1978.
McNeill, John T. *A History of the Cure of Souls*. New York: Harper and Row, 1951; Harper's Ministers Paperback Library, 1977.
Manning, J. M. "Thomas Prince: A Biographical Sketch." *The Congregational Quarterly*, vol. 1, no. 1 (January 1859): 15–16.
Marini, Stephen A. *Radical Sects of Revolutionary New England*. Cambridge: Harvard University Press, 1982.
Marsden, George M. *Jonathan Edwards: A Life*. New Haven, Conn.: Yale University Press, 2003.

Marty, Martin E. *Faith of Our Fathers*. Vol. 4, *Religion, Awakening, and Revolution*. Wilmington, N.C.: McGrath Publishing Co., 1977.
Middlekauff, Robert. *The Glorious Cause: The American Revolution, 1763–1789*. The Oxford History of the United States, vol. 2. New York: Oxford University Press, 1982.
———. *The Mathers: Three Generations of Puritan Intellectuals, 1596–1728*. New York: Oxford University Press, 1971.
Miller, John C. "Religion, Finance, and Democracy in Massachusetts." *New England Quarterly*, vol. 6, no. 1 (March 1933): 29–58.
Miller, Perry. "The Great Awakening from 1740 to 1750." In *Nature's Nation*. Cambridge: Harvard University Press, Belknap Press, 1967.
———. *Jonathan Edwards*. American Men of Letters Series. New York: William Sloane Associates, 1949.
———. "Jonathan Edwards and the Great Awakening." In *Errand into the Wilderness*. Cambridge: Harvard University Press, 1956. Reprint, New York: Harper and Row, Harper Torchbooks, 1964.
———. *The New England Mind: From Colony to Province*. Cambridge: Harvard University Press, 1953. Reprint, Boston: Beacon Press, 1961.
Minkema, Kenneth P. "Old Age and Religion in the Writings and Life of Jonathan Edwards." *Church History*, vol. 70, no. 4 (December 2001): 674–704.
Moran, Gerald F. "Conditions of Religious Conversion in the First Society of Norwich, Connecticut, 1718–1744." *Journal of Social History*, vol. 5, no. 3 (Spring 1972): 331–343.
Morgan, Edmund S. *The Puritan Family: Religion and Domestic Relations in Seventeenth-Century New England*. Rev. ed. New York: Harper and Row, Harper Torchbooks, 1966.
Morison, Samuel Eliot. *Builders of the Bay Colony*. Rev. ed. Boston: Houghton Mifflin, 1964.
———. *Harvard College in the Seventeenth Century*. 2 vols. Cambridge: Harvard University Press, 1936.
Murray, Iain H. *Jonathan Edwards: A New Biography*. Carlisle, Penn.: Banner of Truth Trust, 1987.
Nash, Gary B. *The Urban Crucible: Social Change, Political Consciousness, and the Origins of the American Revolution*. Cambridge: Harvard University Press, 1979.
Neal, Daniel. *The History of New-England, Containing an Impartial Account of the Civil and Ecclesiastical Affairs of the Country, to the Year of Our Lord, 1700*. 2d ed. 2 vols. London: J. Clarke, R. Ford, and R. Cruttenden, 1747.
Noll, Mark A. "Primitivism in Fundamentalism and American Biblical Scholarship: A Response." In *The American Quest for the Primitive Church*, ed. Richard T. Hughes, 120–128. Urbana: University of Illinois Press, 1988.
———. *The Rise of Evangelicalism: The Age of Edwards, Whitefield, and the Wesleys*, A History of Evangelicalism: People, Movements, and Ideas in the English-Speaking World, ed. David W. Bebbington and Mark A. Noll. Downers Grove, Ill.: InterVarsity Press, 2003.
———; Hatch, Nathan O.; Marsden, George M.; Wells, David F.; and Woodbridge, John D., eds. *Eerdmans' Handbook to Christianity in America*. Grand Rapids, Mich.: William B. Eerdmans, 1983.

Bibliography

O'Brien, Susan. "A Transatlantic Community of Saints: The Great Awakening and the First Evangelical Network, 1735–1755." *American Historical Review*, vol. 91, no. 4 (October 1986): 811–832.

Olbricht, Thomas H. "Biblical Primitivism in American Biblical Scholarship, 1630–1870." In *The American Quest for the Primitive Church*, ed. Richard T. Hughes, 81–98. Urbana: University of Illinois Press, 1988.

Onuf, Peter. "New Lights in New London: A Group Portrait of the Separatists." *William and Mary Quarterly*, 3d series, vol. 37, no. 4 (October 1980): 627–643.

Packer, J. I. "The Puritan View of Preaching the Gospel." In *Puritan Papers, Volume One: 1956–1959*, ed. D. Martyn Lloyd-Jones, 255–269. Phillipsburg, N.J.: P&R Publishing, 2000.

———. *A Quest for Godliness: The Puritan Vision of the Christian Life*. Wheaton, Ill.: Good News Publishers, Crossway Books, 1990.

Palfrey, John G. *A Sermon Preached to the Church in Brattle Square, in Two Parts, July 18, 1824*. Boston: Phelps and Farnham, 1825.

Parkes, Henry Bamford. *Jonathan Edwards: The Fiery Puritan*. New York: Minton, Balch and Co., 1930.

Parrington, Vernon L. *Main Currents in American Thought*. Vol. 1, *The Colonial Mind, 1620–1800*. New York: Harcourt, Brace and Co., 1927.

Peckham, Howard H. *The Colonial Wars, 1689–1762*. Chicago: University of Chicago Press, 1964.

Peterson, Mark A. *The Price of Redemption: The Spiritual Economy of Puritan New England*. Stanford, Calif.: Stanford University Press, 1997.

Pettit, Norman. *The Heart Prepared: Grace and Conversion in Puritan Spiritual Life*. New Haven, Conn.: Yale University Press, 1966.

Pope, Robert G. *The Half-Way Covenant: Church Membership in Puritan New England*. Princeton, N.J.: Princeton University Press, 1969.

Remer, Rosalind. "Old Lights and New Money: A Note on Religion, Economics, and the Social Order in 1740 Boston." *William and Mary Quarterly*, 3d series, vol. 47, no. 4 (October 1990): 566–573.

Robbins, Chandler. *A History of the Second Church, or Old North, in Boston, to Which Is Added a History of the New Brick Church*. Boston: John Wilson and Son, 1852.

Roeber, Anthony Gregg. "'Her Merchandize . . . Shall Be Holiness to the Lord': The Progress and Decline of Puritan Gentility at the Brattle Street Church, Boston, 1715–1745." *New England Historical and Genealogical Register*, vol. 131, no. 3 (July 1977): 175–194.

Savelle, Max, and Middlekauff, Robert. *A History of Colonial America*. Rev. ed. New York: Holt, Rinehart and Winston, 1964.

Schmidt, Leigh Eric. *Holy Fairs: Scotland and the Making of American Revivalism*. 2d ed. Grand Rapids, Mich.: William B. Eerdmans, 2001.

———. "'A Second and Glorious Reformation': The New Light Extremism of Andrew Croswell." *William and Mary Quarterly*, 3d series, vol. 43, no. 2 (April 1986): 214–244.

Schmotter, James W. "The Irony of Clerical Professionalism: New England's Congregational Ministers and the Great Awakening." *American Quarterly*, vol. 31, no. 2 (Summer 1979): 148–168.

———. "Ministerial Careers in Eighteenth-Century New England: The Social Context, 1700–1760." *Journal of Social History*, vol. 9, no. 2 (Winter 1975): 249–267.

Scott, Donald. *From Office to Profession: The New England Ministry, 1750–1850*. Philadelphia: University of Pennsylvania Press, 1978.

Seeman, Erik R. *Pious Persuasions: Laity and Clergy in Eighteenth-Century New England*. Baltimore, Md.: Johns Hopkins University Press, 1999.

Selement, George. *Keepers of the Vineyard: The Puritan Ministry and Collective Culture in Colonial New England*. Lanham, Md.: University Press of America, 1984.

———. "Publication and the Puritan Minister." *William and Mary Quarterly*, 3d series, vol. 37, no. 2 (April 1980): 219–241.

Shipton, Clifford K. *Sibley's Harvard Graduates*. 14 vols. Boston: Massachusetts Historical Society, 1933–1975.

Sibley, John Langdon. *Biographical Sketches of Graduates of Harvard University, in Cambridge, Massachusetts*. 3 vols. Cambridge: Harvard University Press, 1873–1885.

Silverman, Kenneth. *The Life and Times of Cotton Mather*. New York: Harper and Row, 1984.

Smith, Mark M. "Culture, Commerce, and Calendar Reform in Colonial America." *William and Mary Quarterly*, 3d series, vol. 55, no. 4 (October 1998): 557–584.

Sperry, Willard L. *Religion in America*. American Life and Institutions. New York: Macmillan, 1946.

Sprague, William B. *Annals of the American Pulpit*. 9 vols. New York: Robert Carter and Brothers, 1859–1869.

Stein, Stephen J. "Editor's Introduction." In *The Works of Jonathan Edwards*, ed. Perry Miller et al., vol. 5: *Apocalyptic Writings*, ed. Stephen J. Stein, 1–93. New Haven, Conn.: Yale University Press, 1977.

Stoeffler, F. Ernest, ed. *Continental Pietism and Early American Christianity*. Grand Rapids, Mich.: William B. Eerdmans, 1976.

Stout, Harry S. *The Divine Dramatist: George Whitefield and the Rise of Modern Evangelicalism*. Library of Religious Biography. Grand Rapids, Mich.: William B. Eerdmans, 1991.

———. "The Great Awakening in New England Reconsidered: The New England Clergy." *Journal of Social History*, vol. 8, no. 1 (Fall 1974): 21–47.

———. *The New England Soul: Preaching and Religious Culture in Colonial New England*. New York: Oxford University Press, 1986.

———. "Religion, Communication, and the Ideological Origins of the American Revolution." William and Mary Quarterly, 3d series, vol. 34, no. 4 (October 1977): 519–541.

——— and Onuf, Peter. "James Davenport and the Great Awakening in New London." *Journal of American History*, vol. 70, no. 3 (December 1983): 556–578.

Sweet, William Warren. *The Story of Religion in America*. 2d ed. New York: Harper and Brothers, 1950.

Toulouse, Teresa. *The Art of Prophesying: New England Sermons and the Shaping of Belief*. Athens: University of Georgia Press, 1987.

Tracy, Joseph. *The Great Awakening: A History of the Revival of Religion in the Time of Edwards and Whitefield*. Boston: Tappan and Dennet, 1842. Reprint, Carlisle, Penn.: Banner of Truth Trust, 1976.

Tracy, Patricia J. *Jonathan Edwards, Pastor: Religion and Society in Eighteenth-Century Northampton*. American Century Series. New York: Hill and Wang, 1979.

Trinterud, Leonard J. *The Forming of an American Tradition: A Re-Examination of Colonial Presbyterianism*. Philadelphia: Westminster Press, 1949.
Turell, Ebenezer. *The Life and Character of the Reverend Benjamin Colman, D.D.* Boston: Rogers and Fowle, 1749.
Valeri, Mark. *Law and Providence in Joseph Bellamy's New England: The Origins of the New Divinity in Revolutionary America*. New York: Oxford University Press, 1994.
Van de Wetering, Maxine. "A Reconsideration of the Inoculation Controversy." *New England Quarterly*, vol. 58, no. 1 (March 1985): 46–67.
Van Dyken, Seymour. *Samuel Willard, 1640–1707: Preacher of Orthodoxy in an Era of Change*. Grand Rapids, Mich.: William B. Eerdmans, 1972.
Walker, Williston. *The Creeds and Platforms of Congregationalism*. New York: Charles Scribner's Sons, 1893. Reprint, Philadelphia: Pilgrim Press, 1960.
———. *Ten New England Leaders*. New York: Silver Burdett, 1901.
Walsh, James. "The Great Awakening in the First Congregational Church of Woodbury, Connecticut." *William and Mary Quarterly*, 3d series, vol. 28, no. 4 (October 1971): 543–562.
Ward, W. R. *Christianity under the Ancien Régime, 1648–1789*. New Approaches to European History. Cambridge: Cambridge University Press, 1999.
———. *Early Evangelicalism: A Global Intellectual History, 1670–1789*. Cambridge: Cambridge University Press, 2006.
———. *The Protestant Evangelical Awakening*. Cambridge: Cambridge University Press, 1992.
Warden, G. B. *Boston: 1689–1776*. Boston: Little, Brown and Co., 1970.
Ware, Henry. *Two Discourses Containing the History of the Old North and New Brick Churches, United as the Second Church in Boston*. Boston: James W. Burditt, 1821.
Weis, Frederick Lewis. *The Colonial Clergy and the Colonial Churches of New England*. Lancaster, Mass.: Society of the Descendants of the Colonial Clergy, 1936. Reprint, Baltimore, Md.: Genealogical Publishing Co., 1977.
Wells, Robert V. *The Population of the British Colonies in America before 1776: A Survey of Census Data*. Princeton, N.J.: Princeton University Press, 1975.
Wendell, Barrett. *Cotton Mather: The Puritan Priest*. New York: Dodd, Mead and Co., 1891. Reprint, New York: Harcourt, Brace and World, 1963.
Westerkamp, Marilyn J. "Anne Hutchinson, Sectarian Mysticism, and the Puritan Order." *Church History*, vol. 59, no. 4 (December 1990): 482–496.
———. *Triumph of the Laity: Scots-Irish Piety and the Great Awakening, 1625–1760*. New York: Oxford University Press, 1988.
White, Eugene E. "Decline of the Great Awakening in New England: 1741 to 1746." *New England Quarterly*, vol. 24, no. 1 (March 1951): 35–52.
Whitehill, Walter Muir. *Boston: A Topographical History*. 2d ed. Cambridge: Harvard University Press, Belknap Press, 1968.
Wilkie, Richard W., and Tager, Jack, eds. *Historical Atlas of Massachusetts*. Amherst: University of Massachusetts Press, 1991.
Willingham, William F. "Religious Conversion in the Second Society of Windham, Connecticut, 1723–43: A Case Study." *Societas*, vol. 6, no. 2 (Spring 1976): 109–119.
Wilson, James Grant, and Fiske, John, eds. *Appleton's Cyclopaedia of American Biography*. 6 vols. New York: D. Appleton and Co., 1900.

Wilson, Robert J., III. *The Benevolent Deity: Ebenezer Gay and the Rise of Rational Religion in New England, 1696–1787*. Philadelphia: University of Pennsylvania Press, 1984.

Winship, Michael P. *Making Heretics: Militant Protestantism and Free Grace in Massachusetts, 1636–1641*. Princeton, N.J.: Princeton University Press, 2002.

———. "'The Most Glorious Church in the World': The Unity of the Godly in Boston, Massachusetts, in the 1630s." *Journal of British Studies*, vol. 39, no. 1 (January 2000): 71–98.

———. "Were There Any Puritans in New England?" *New England Quarterly*, vol. 74, no. 1 (March 2001): 118–138.

Winslow, Ola Elizabeth. *"And Plead for the Rights of All": Old South Church in Boston, 1669–1969*. Boston: Nimrod Press, 1970.

———. *A Destroying Angel: The Conquest of Smallpox in Colonial Boston*. Boston: Houghton Mifflin, 1974.

———. *Jonathan Edwards, 1703–1758*. New York: Macmillan, 1940. Reprint, New York: Collier Books, 1961.

———. *Meetinghouse Hill: 1630–1783*. New York: Macmillan, 1952. Reprint, New York: W. W. Norton, Norton Library, 1972.

Wisner, Benjamin B. *The History of the Old South Church in Boston*. Boston: Crocker and Brewster, 1830.

Wood, Nathan E. *The History of the First Baptist Church of Boston*. Philadelphia: American Baptist Publication Society, 1899.

Woodbridge, John D., Noll, Mark A., and Hatch, Nathan O. *The Gospel in America: Themes in the Story of America's Evangelicals*. Grand Rapids, Mich.: Zondervan, 1979.

Worthley, Harold Field. *An Inventory of the Records of the Particular (Congregational) Churches of Massachusetts Gathered 1620–1805*. Harvard Theological Studies, vol. 25. Cambridge: Harvard University Press, 1970.

———. "The Lay Offices of the Particular (Congregational) Churches of Massachusetts, 1620–1755: An Investigation of Practice and Theory." Th.D. dissertation, Harvard Divinity School, 1970.

Wright, Conrad. *The Beginnings of Unitarianism in America*. Boston: Starr King Press, 1955. Reprint, Hamden, Conn.: Archon Books, 1976.

Wright, David. "Sixteenth-Century Reformed Perspectives on the Minority Church." *Scottish Journal of Theology*, vol. 48, no. 4 (1995): 469–488.

Youngs, J. William T., Jr. *God's Messengers: Religious Leadership in Colonial New England*. Baltimore, Md.: Johns Hopkins University Press, 1976.

———. "Congregational Clericalism: New England Ordinations before the Great Awakening." *William and Mary Quarterly*, 3d series, vol. 31, no. 3 (July 1974): 481–492.

Ziff, Larzer. *Puritanism in America: New Culture in a New World*. New York: Viking Press, 1973.

Zuck, Lowell H. "Cotton Mather and German Pietism." *Historical Intelligencer*, vol. 2, no. 1 (Fall 1982): 11–16.

Index

Adams, Brooks, 1
Adams, Charles Francis, 1
Ahlstrom, Sydney E., 121
Akers, Charles W., 86, 87, 88, 118, 119, 121, 122
Alden, John, 71, 72
Ames, William, 20, 130
Anabaptists, 13
Anderson, Fred, 141
Anglicans, 45, 118, 138
Antinomianism, 4, 13, 21, 59, 114, 117, 127, 129, 132, 133, 134
Arianism, xv, 29, 108
Arminianism, xv, 36, 45, 99, 116, 129, 131, 134, 147
Arndt, Johann, 20
Askew, Thomas A., 27
assurance of salvation, 3, 126, 130–31, 133, 134, 136
atonement, 35, 91, 124
Bacon, Leonard Woolsey, 29
Bailyn, Bernard, 143
baptism, 4, 14, 31, 61, 63, 106
  records of, 16, 44–47, 63, 89, 97, 115–16, 141, 144, 146
Baptists, 43, 45, 138
Barnard, John, Jr., 91
  preparation of sermons, 8
Barnard, John, Sr., 19
Bartol, C. A., 116, 118
Baxter, Richard, x, 1, 8, 20, 21, 22–23, 72
Beales, Ross W., Jr., 45
Beall, Otho T., Jr., 2
Beecher, Lyman, x, 152
Beeke, Joel R., 130
Bellamy, Joseph, 127, 150
Bercovitch, Sacvan, 3
Bernhard, Virginia, 15
Black, J. William, 21
Blake, Francis Everett, 71

Blake, John, 140, 141, 143
Boas, Louise, 2
Boas, Ralph, 2
Boehm, Anthony William, 24
Bonomi, Patricia U., 18, 54, 145
Boston, Massachusetts, xi, xii, xvi, 2, 4, 5, 6, 7, 9, 20, 24, 25, 46, 47, 53, 56, 89, 97, 110, 113, 121, 126, 127, 134, 135, 138, 141, 151
  Anglican churches of, records of, 45
  Anglican clergy of, 118
  Baptist churches of, records of, 45
  birth rate, xi, 141, 143, 144, 146
  Congregational churches of, xi, xvi, 44–137
  Congregational churches of, records of, 44–47, 138–40, 141, 144
  Congregational clergy of, 49, 119, 121, 132, 150–51
  death rate, xi, 140, 141
  elite of, 65, 85, 122
  emigration, 141
  frontier warfare, demographic impact of, on, 143–44
  Great Awakening in, xvi, 26–43, 44, 46, 50–51, 58–60, 69–70, 74, 82–83, 93–94, 95–96, 101, 104, 106, 113, 117–18, 125, 140, 146, 148–49
  North End, 15, 18, 19, 91, 94, 97
  organization of new churches in, 90, 145–46
  population, 140, 141, 144, 145, 146
  religious societies in, 17, 22, 40
  smallpox epidemics in, 2, 24, 141, 143, 144
  South End, 18
  West End, 116, 122
Bowen, Penuel, 101
Bradstreet, Benjamin, 40, 41
Brainerd, David, 60, 106, 109

Breck, Robert, 83, 99
Breen, Timothy H., 5
Bridenbaugh, Carl, 141, 143
Bridgewater, Massachusetts, 41
Bucer, Martin, 20, 21, 128
Bumsted, J. M., 19, 23, 28, 144, 147
Burnett, Amy Nelson, 20
Burton, John D., 141
Bushman, Richard L., 25, 29, 33, 147
Butler, Jon, 28, 140, 151
Byles, Mather, 112–15, 140, 150
  clericalism of, 114–15, 116
  Cotton Mather and, 112, 113
  Great Awakening, rejection of, 113
  moralism of, 113
  on conversion, 31, 112–13
  on sermon preparation, 115
  on unregenerate clergy, 113
  pastoral visitation, neglect of, 115
  theology of, 30–31, 112–13
calendar reform, 153
Calvin, John, 67, 121, 128, 130, 132, 145
Calvinism, 29, 30, 31, 35, 45, 48, 56, 60, 67, 72, 75, 80, 83, 86, 91, 94, 99, 107, 112, 117, 118, 120, 121, 124, 126, 128, 129, 131, 134, 147, 149
Cambridge Platform, 7
Cambridge University, 20
Cambridge, Massachusetts, 6
Campbell, Alexander, 151
Canterbury, Connecticut, 41
Cape Breton Island, 143
Carey, Jonathan S., 121
Carpenter, John B., 25, 63, 80
catechesis, xv, 6, 7, 9, 10, 11, 12, 13, 23, 38, 39, 45, 53, 73, 95, 105, 115, 122
Chapman, Clayton Harding, 39, 79, 80, 82, 83, 84, 91, 93, 94, 118
Charlestown, Massachusetts, 45, 47, 126
Chauncy, Charles, xii, 31, 32, 33, 34, 35, 39, 42, 43, 47, 48, 51–53, 53, 54, 56, 59, 61, 81, 89, 102, 104, 113, 122, 124, 125, 140, 150

biographies of, 45
clericalism of, 33–34, 42, 52–53, 146
early theology of, 30
Great Awakening, rejection of, 29, 32
Jonathan Edwards and, 29
on Joshua Gee, 58
on preparation for conversion, 31–32
on Thomas Prince, 73
on unregenerate clergy, 51–52
religious societies, rejection of, 22
Samuel Mather and, 59
Thomas Foxcroft and, 52
universal redemption, defense of, 124
Checkley, Samuel, Jr., 60–61, 150
  Jonathan Edwards and, 60
  neglect of church records, 61
  theology of, 60–61
Checkley, Samuel, Sr., 99–101, 150
  concern for young people, 100–101
  Great Awakening, support for, 101
  pastoral activism of, 101
  theology of, 99
  William Waldron and, 104
Cheever, Samuel, 7
Christian History, The, 39, 40, 73, 74
church covenant, 4, 11, 45, 127, 134
church government, 4, 10, 79, 97, 127, 134, 135, 136, 145
church membership, admissions to, 4, 134
  gender and, 54–55, 75–77
  records of, 16, 44–47, 53–55, 61, 75–77, 89, 97, 115, 138, 140, 144, 146
church organization, 90, 145–46
Clark, Joseph S., 35, 37
Clarke, John, 56
Clarke, Samuel, 121
Cleaveland, John, xv
Clement of Alexandria, 12
clericalism, xv, 4, 5, 22, 25, 34, 35, 38, 39, 41, 42, 43, 47, 52–53, 65, 81, 86–88, 96–97, 104–5, 105–6, 109–10, 114, 146, 148, 149
Coffman, Ralph J., 25
Cohen, Charles Lloyd, 50
Colman, Benjamin, 3, 4, 38, 39, 47, 79–83, 83, 84, 86, 87, 88, 89, 109

Index 183

Barnard, John, Jr., and, 91
  clericalism of, 37, 38, 39, 46, 81, 109
  Cotton Mather and, 49, 79–80
  elitism of, 81, 87
  Gilbert Tennent and, 58
  Great Awakening, support for, 46, 82–83
  Jonathan Mayhew and, 119
  on evangelism, 80–81, 81–82
  on Great Awakening, 82, 83
  on unregenerate clergy, 81
  on William Cooper, 84–85
  preaching of, 83
  Samuel Mather and, 59
  theology of, 80
  William Cooper and, 39, 88
  William Hooper and, 118
Conforti, Joseph A., 149, 150
Congregationalists, Congregationalism, xi, xvi, 4, 30, 45, 46, 47, 53, 54, 77, 79, 90, 97, 135, 136, 138, 140, 145, 151, 152
Connecticut, 74, 82, 128
  Great Awakening in, 25, 145
Connecticut River Valley Revival, 54
conservatism, 1, 32, 35, 42, 48, 64, 80, 104
conversion, 9, 14, 30, 31, 32, 38, 41, 50, 51, 57, 58, 59, 68, 69, 80, 81, 84, 85, 99, 106, 108, 112, 113, 116, 128, 131, 132, 133, 136, 138, 144
conversion, narratives of, 4, 16, 77, 134
conviction of sin, 51, 58, 59, 69, 70, 84, 93, 96, 99, 105, 109, 131, 132, 133
Cooper, James F., Jr., 4, 59, 64, 65, 79, 94, 148
Cooper, Samuel, 39, 79, 86–88, 150
  clericalism of, 86–88
  theology of, 86
Cooper, William, xii, 79, 83–86, 86, 88, 89, 94, 95, 102, 103, 150
  Benjamin Colman and, 39, 88
  Benjamin Colman on, 84–85
  evangelism of, 87
  Gilbert Tennent and, 58
  Great Awakening, support for, 84
  itinerant evangelism of, 84

  Jonathan Edwards and, 72
  on Peter Thacher, 94–95
  on William Waldron, 102, 103
  pastoral activism of, 38–39, 42, 46, 84–85, 86, 89, 92, 146
  pastoral counseling of, 38–39, 84
  pastoral visitation, practice of, 87
  popularity of, 88
  preaching of, 83–84
  religious societies, use of, 85–86
  religious societies, writings on, 38, 85
  theology of, 83–84
  William Waldron and, 103, 104
Cornman, Thomas H. L., 107
Corrigan, John, 29, 35, 48, 49, 52, 79, 80, 91, 102, 122
Cotton, John, 3, 64
covenant renewal, 6, 63, 97
  gender and, 77
Cowing, Cedric B., 28, 29, 77, 139, 149
Crawford, Michael J., 20, 24, 28
Croswell, Andrew, 125, 126–36, 136, 137, 145
  Alexander Garden and, 126
  early ministry of, 125–26
  evangelism of, 128–29
  George Whitefield and, 126, 136
  pastoral priorities of, 136
  preparation for conversion, rejection of, 131–32
  relations with other Boston clergy, 132, 136, 145–46
  relations with other New Light clergy, 127
  theology of, 127–28, 129–34
Cumming, Alexander, 127
Cutler, Timothy, 136
Dallimore, Arnold, 82, 107
Davenport, James, 32, 44, 95, 96, 126, 127
Davenport, John, 8, 64
declension, 3, 104
depravity, 30, 31, 49, 68, 80, 99
Dexter, Henry M., 66
Dickinson, Jonathan, 127, 131
diphtheria, 27

Dodds, Elisabeth D., 149
Dorchester, Massachusetts, 4
Duffy, John, 141
Earthquake Revival, 53, 54, 61
earthquakes, 138, 140
   1727, xi, 53, 61, 75, 89, 97, 138, 139
   1755, 53, 54, 75, 97, 115, 140
Eaton, Arthur Wentworth Hamilton, 112, 113
ecclesiology, xv, 32, 34, 35, 77, 80, 86, 99, 104, 134, 148
Edinburgh, University of, 116
Edwards, Jonathan, x, xi, xv, 2, 27, 30, 32, 37, 41, 60, 72, 83, 106, 147, 148, 149
   Charles Chauncy and, 29
   clericalism of, 37–38, 149
   Great Awakening, support for, 29
   pastoral ministry of, 2
Edwardsians, 107, 147
   clericalism of, 149–50
Eells, Nathanael, 58
Eighth ("Hollis Street") Congregational Church, Boston, 90, 97, 112–16, 147
   pastorate of Mather Byles, 112–15
   records of, 115–16
Eisenstadt, Peter R., 145
election, 35, 83, 120
Eleventh Congregational Church, Boston, 45, 90, 125–37, 145, 147
   articles of government, 134–36
   pastorate of Andrew Croswell, 126–36
   records of, 136–37
Eliot, Andrew, 91, 93, 95–97, 97
   clericalism of, 96–97
   Ephraim Eliot on, 96–97
   evangelism of, 95
   Great Awakening, rejection of, 95–96
   on George Whitefield, 95
   on John Webb, 93–94, 97
   pastoral priorities of, 96
Eliot, Ephraim, 96
Eliot, John, 57, 59, 66, 68, 74, 79, 84, 86, 110

elitism, 33, 38, 41, 44, 46, 52, 61, 65, 79, 81, 87, 118, 122, 124, 150
Elliott, Emory, 25
Ellis, Arthur B., 47, 51, 52, 53, 56
Emerson, William, 48
Englizian, H. Crosby, 135, 152
evangelicalism, xi, 2, 64, 65, 110
evangelism, 6, 7, 30, 31, 50, 60, 68, 69, 70, 72, 80, 81, 84, 86, 87, 93, 95, 109, 110, 114, 128, 137
   itinerant, xv, 32, 36, 37, 44, 51, 74, 82, 84, 113, 114, 126, 127, 136
faith, 56, 60, 68, 73, 80, 99, 101, 107, 108, 113, 117, 121, 126, 127, 128, 129, 130, 132, 133, 134
family devotions, 11, 14, 67, 103, 104
Fifth ("New North") Congregational Church, Boston, 146
Fifth ("New North") Congregational Church, Boston, 38, 40, 63, 90, 91, 102, 146, 147
   lay leadership of, 97
   pastorate of Andrew Eliot, 95–97
   pastorate of John Webb, 91–94
   pastorate of Peter Thacher, 94–95
   records of, 97
Finney, Charles, x
Finney, Charles G., 132
First ("Old Brick") Congregational Church, Boston, 20, 22, 39, 40, 47, 59, 61, 63, 64, 65, 75, 89, 97, 119, 147, 152
   pastorate of Charles Chauncy, 51–53
   pastorate of Thomas Foxcroft, 47–51
   records of, 53
First Baptist Church, Boston, 45
First Congregational Church, Cambridge, 146
First Congregational Church, Charlestown, 146
Ford, Worthington Chauncey, 1
Foster, Stephen, 5, 6, 21, 64, 79, 150
Fourth ("Brattle Street") Congregational Church, Boston, 146
Fourth ("Brattle Street") Congregational Church, Boston, 3–

Index 185

  4, 4, 38, 39, 40, 45, 72, 79–89, 90,
     97, 119, 134, 147, 150, 152
  pastorate of Benjamin Colman, 79–
     83
  pastorate of Samuel Cooper, 86–88
  pastorate of William Cooper, 83–86
  records of, 88–89
  religious societies in, 85–86
Foxcroft, Thomas, 40, 47–51, 52, 53,
     65, 81, 89, 108, 119
  Andrew Croswell and, 127
  Charles Chauncy and, 52
  Cotton Mather and, 48–49
  distribution of books to parishioners,
     50
  ecclesiology of, 49–50
  Gilbert Tennent and, 58
  Great Awakening, support for, 50–51
  ill health of, 47, 48, 54, 61
  on evangelism, 50
  on George Whitefield, 50
  on unregenerate clergy, 48–49
  pastoral activism of, 39–40, 48
  religious societies, writings on, 40
  theology of, 47–48
  William Waldron and, 104
Francke, August Hermann, x, 1, 8, 23,
     72, 125
Franks, Alison, 141
Freiberg, Malcolm, 153
frontier warfare, 141, 143
funeral sermons, 1, 10, 12, 38, 39, 44,
     54, 57, 60, 66, 72, 73, 74, 81, 83,
     84, 93, 108, 112, 122
Garden, Alexander, 126, 127
Garraty, John A., 141
Gaustad, Edwin Scott, 27, 29, 33, 35,
     37, 44, 50, 51, 58, 73, 82, 104, 106
Gay, Ebenezer, 108, 122
Gay, Peter, 2
Gee, Joshua, 56–60, 60, 61, 63, 99, 112
  Charles Chauncy on, 58
  Cotton Mather and, 57
  Gilbert Tennent and, 58
  Great Awakening, support for, 58
  ill health of, 47, 57, 61–62
  Samuel Mather and, 59–60

  theology of, 56–57
  William Waldron and, 104
gender
  church membership and, 54–55, 75–
     77
  covenant renewal and, 77
Gloucester, Massachusetts, 40, 41
Goen, C. C., 43, 126, 127, 129, 136
good works, 14, 107, 120, 121, 133
gospel, 9, 34, 50, 60, 68, 69, 70, 71, 72,
     83, 86, 92, 95, 107, 108, 109, 119,
     129, 131, 132, 133, 134
Gray, Ellis, 34, 35, 102, 105–6, 107,
     112
  clericalism of, 105–6
  Great Awakening, neutrality toward,
     106
  Jonathan Edwards and, 106
  theology of, 105
Great Awakening, x, xi, xv, xvi, 7, 22,
     25, 26–43, 45, 48, 52, 58, 59, 63,
     69, 73, 74, 75, 82, 83, 84, 88, 92,
     93, 97, 104, 110, 113, 116, 119,
     125, 126, 128, 140, 144, 145, 146,
     147, 149, 150, 151
  Andrew Eliot on, 95–96
  Benjamin Colman on, 82, 83
  church membership, admissions to,
     during, 54, 75–77, 89, 97, 115, 138,
     140
  covenant renewal during, 77
  Ellis Gray on, 106
  historians' perspectives on, 26–29
  John Webb on, 92–93
  Joseph Sewall on, 69–70, 70
  long-term impact of, in Boston, 144,
     152
  Old Lights' perspectives on, 32–36
  pastoral ministry and, xv–xvi, 25,
     41–43, 44, 46–47, 63, 77, 99, 137,
     146–47, 148–49
  religious societies and, 40–41, 101
  Samuel Mather on, 59
  theological impact of, in New
     England, 147
  Thomas Foxcroft on, 51
  William Cooper on, 84

young people and, 40–41, 74, 84, 101
Greene, Evarts B., 140
Gregorian calendar, 153
Greven, Philip J., Jr., 33, 144
Griffin, Edward M., 45, 48, 51, 52, 59
Grossbart, Stephen R., 144
Groton, Connecticut, 126, 127
Guelzo, Allen C., 150
Halfway Covenant, 28, 61, 63, 64
Hall, David D., 4, 22, 44, 54, 63, 145
Hall, Michael G., 8, 45, 63, 91, 94
Halle, University of, 17, 23, 24
Hambrick-Stowe, Charles E., 21
Hammann, Gottfried, 20
Handlin, Oscar, 143
Hardman, Keith J., 25
Harlan, David, xv, 5, 147
Haroutunian, Joseph, 35
Harrington, Virginia D., 140
Harris, Howell, 148
Harvard College, 3, 47, 49, 56, 102, 106, 108, 113, 119, 125
  religious societies at, 18, 66, 71, 102
Hatch, Nathan O., 26, 27, 147
Hatfield, Massachusetts, 7
Haven, Elias, 41
Heimert, Alan, 26, 29, 130, 140
Helm, Paul, 130
Henderson, Robert W., 145
Henretta, James A., 27
Heppe, Heinrich, 130
Higginson, Thomas Wentworth, 143
Hill, Hamilton Andrews, 64, 66, 70, 73, 74, 75, 82, 126, 127, 140
Hofstadter, Richard, 1, 26, 33
Holifield, E. Brooks, 4, 5, 24, 79, 135
Hood, Edwin Paxton, 27
Hooper, William, 116–18, 118, 119, 121, 122
  Benjamin Colman and, 118
  Great Awakening, rejection of, 117, 118
  rationalism of, 116, 117–18
  theology of, 116–18
Hopkins, Samuel, 149
Hudson, Winthrop S., 29
Hutchinson, Anne, 21

immigration, 143
Ingham, Benjamin, 148
Isaac, Rhys, 27, 43
Jedrey, Christopher M., 97, 148
Jeffries, John W., 28
Jennings, Francis, 141
jeremiad, 3, 6
Jones, James W., 35, 48, 51, 80, 118, 119
Julian calendar, 153
justification, 29, 60, 68, 101, 121, 126, 127, 128, 129, 131, 132, 133, 136, 137
Keayne, Sarah, 22
Kendall, R. T., 130
Kidd, Thomas S., 17, 22, 35, 37, 43, 44, 50, 51, 58, 63, 70, 74, 77, 79, 82, 92, 93, 101, 113, 126, 127, 140, 146, 148
Kittelson, James, 20
Knight, Janice, 130
Labaree, Benjamin W., 27
Lambert, Frank, 13, 28
latitudinarianism, 48
lay exhorters, 37
Leverett, John, 49
Levin, David, 2, 15, 17, 18, 19, 45
Lewis, A. J., 17
liberalism, 35, 42, 59, 64, 65, 86, 99, 107, 110, 122, 151, 152
Lippy, Charles H., 45, 48, 51, 59
Lockridge, Kenneth A., 5
Lord's Supper, 11, 106
Lord's Supper, 85
Lothrop, Samuel Kirkland, 79, 81, 83, 86, 87, 88, 89
Lovejoy, David S., 29
Lovelace, Richard F., x, xi, xii, 2, 15, 19, 20, 23, 24
Lowrie, Ernest Benson, 65
Lucas, Paul R., 24
Luther, Martin, 121, 128, 132
Lyme, Connecticut, 41, 82
Manning, J. M., 152
Mansfield, Connecticut, 96
Marblehead, Massachusetts, 7, 8
Marini, Stephen A., 43, 137

Index

Marsden, George M., 72, 147, 149
Marty, Martin E., 27, 29
Massachusetts, 140
　frontier warfare in, 143
　Great Awakening in, 145
　immigration, 143
　population, 140, 141
　religious societies in, 40–41
Mather, Cotton, x, xii, 1–25, 49, 51, 56, 58, 61, 72, 73, 150
　as synthesist, 3, 20
　August Hermann Francke and, 23
　Benjamin Colman and, 49, 79–80
　biographies of, 2, 45
　catechesis, writings on, 12–15
　covenant renewal, use of, 63
　disciples, 25, 57, 66, 71–72, 85, 91, 102–3, 150
　distribution of books to parishioners, 9, 16, 50
　Ebenezer Pemberton, Sr., and, 49
　historians' perspectives on, 1–2
　Mather Byles and, 112, 113
　on William Waldron, 102, 103
　on William Welsteed, 105
　pastoral activism of, 8, 9, 42, 56, 57, 103, 115, 146
　pastoral ministry of, 3–24
　pastoral priorities of, 8, 10, 73
　pastoral visitation, practice of, 15–16, 73, 103
　pastoral visitation, writings on, 9–12
　Pietism and, 23–24
　preparation of sermons, 8
　reforming societies, use of, 19–20
　religious societies, participation in, 19
　religious societies, use of, 17, 18–19, 38, 66
　religious societies, writings on, 17–18, 40, 66, 71
　Richard Baxter and, 22–23
　theology of, 49, 56, 68
　Thomas Foxcroft and, 48–49
　witchcraft and, 113
Mather, Increase, 3, 6, 56, 58, 103, 112
　biographies of, 45
　covenant renewal, use of, 63
　John Barnard, Jr., and, 91
　love of privacy, 6
　pastoral priorities of, 5–6, 10, 34, 96, 115
　preparation of sermons, 8
Mather, Richard, 3, 4
Mather, Samuel, 12, 18, 34, 35, 52, 58, 59, 63, 104, 106, 124–25, 150
　Benjamin Colman and, 59
　Charles Chauncy and, 59
　clericalism of, 34, 35, 61, 124, 146
　Great Awakening, rejection of, 59, 125
　Joshua Gee and, 59–60
　preaching of, 125
　theology of, 124
　universal redemption, rejection of, 124
Mayhew, Jonathan, 86, 108, 116, 118–21, 122, 124, 125, 136, 140
　Benjamin Colman and, 119
　clericalism of, 122
　relations with other Boston clergy, 119, 121
　theology of, 119–21
McKenzie, Alexander, 59, 75, 79, 91, 94, 99, 110, 112, 115, 116, 118, 127
McLoughlin, William G., 26, 43
McNeill, John T., 9, 12
Messinger, Henry, 41
Middlekauff, Robert, 3, 20, 26, 29, 79
Miller, John C., 27
Miller, Perry, 2, 4, 6, 19, 20, 24, 25, 27, 63, 64, 79, 141, 149, 151
Minkema, Kenneth P., 41, 77
missionary outreach, 8
Mitchell, Jonathan, 6, 10
moralism, 31, 114, 116, 119, 124, 147
Moran, Gerald F., 144
Morgan, Edmund S., xi, 7
Morison, Samuel Eliot, 3, 4
Murdock, Kenneth B., 2, 3
Murray, Iain H., 72, 97, 110, 127, 147, 149
Murray, John, 136, 137
Nash, Gary B., 27, 143, 144

Neal, Daniel, 21
New Divinity, 147, 149, 150
New England, 4, 22, 44
 church membership, admissions to, gender and, 54
 clergy of, 7, 8
 early theological consensus, 1, 3, 6, 124
 frontier warfare in, 141
 Great Awakening in, 25
 later theological alternatives, 1, 29, 34–35, 147
 organization of new churches in, 90, 146
 pastoral ministry in, 4–8, 24–25, 42, 43, 47, 148
 population, 146
 religious societies in, 17, 21–22, 40
 social hierarchy, 4
 standing order, 3, 10, 24, 33, 34, 35, 36, 134
New Haven, Connecticut, 8, 64
New Lights, xv, xvi, 22, 25, 29, 32, 33, 38, 39, 40, 41, 44, 45, 46, 47, 58, 59, 61, 70, 74, 77, 79, 82, 97, 99, 104, 107, 113, 117, 121, 126, 127, 132, 134, 135, 137, 146, 148, 149, 150
 clericalism of some, 36–38, 46–47, 63, 147, 148–49
 Great Awakening, perspectives on, 29
 Old Lights, theological common ground with, 29–32
 pastoral activism of many, 38–40, 41–43, 46, 146, 147, 148, 149
New York, New York, 106, 110
Newburyport, Massachusetts, 108
Ninth ("West" or "Lynde Street") Congregational Church, Boston, 45, 90, 97, 116–23, 147, 152
 pastorate of Jonathan Mayhew, 118–21
 pastorate of William Hooper, 116–18
 records of, 122–23
Noll, Mark A., xi, 20, 22, 27, 28, 147, 148, 151

Northampton, Massachusetts, 27, 41, 81, 149
O'Brien, Susan, 28
Oakes, Urian, 3
Olbricht, Thomas H., 151
Old Lights, xv, xvi, 22, 25, 29, 32, 33, 35, 36, 38, 41, 44, 46, 58, 82, 99, 104, 113, 122, 124, 132, 146, 148, 150
 clericalism of, 34–35, 41, 146, 147
 Great Awakening, perspectives on, 29, 32–36
 New Lights, theological common ground with, 29–32
Onuf, Peter, 43, 149
ordination, 4, 9, 39, 40, 56, 83, 86, 95, 96, 101, 103, 105, 106, 109, 114, 119
ordination sermons, 9, 10, 39, 40, 46, 52, 73, 87, 92, 96, 101, 103, 105, 109, 110, 114
Packer, J. I., 23, 65
Paine, Robert Treat, 125
Palfrey, John G., 79, 80, 83, 84, 87
Park Street Congregational Church, Boston, 135, 152
Parkes, Henry Bamford, 149
Parkman, William, 97
Parrington, Vernon L., 1, 2
pastoral activism, x, xvi, 8, 9, 39, 42, 46, 48, 57, 61, 63, 75, 95, 110, 114, 115, 146, 147, 148, 150
pastoral ministry, xv, xvi, 2, 5, 7, 10, 22, 23, 25, 39, 41, 42, 46, 54, 56, 71, 73, 75, 89, 92, 94, 96, 105, 109, 114, 115, 122, 125, 135, 136, 148, 149, 150, 151
 Great Awakening and, xv–xvi, 25, 41–43, 44, 46–47, 63, 77, 99, 137, 146–47, 148–49
pastoral visitation, xv, 6, 7, 8, 10, 11, 12, 15, 16, 23, 38, 39, 45, 53, 73, 84, 85, 87, 93, 95, 96, 103, 104, 105, 110, 115, 122, 135, 136, 148, 149
pastors

distribution of books to parishioners, 10, 13, 16, 23, 50
isolation from parishioners, 5, 6
lifetime tenure, 47
preparation of sermons, 5, 6, 8
relations with other clergy, 4
relations with parishioners, 4, 5, 6, 7, 8, 24–25
religious societies for, 18
training manuals, 6, 7, 17, 18
Peckham, Howard H., 141
Pelagianism, 13
Pemberton, Ebenezer, Jr., xii, 102, 106–11, 150
   clericalism of, 109–10, 110
   evangelism of, 107–9
   George Whitefield and, 107
   on George Whitefield, 107
   pastoral visitation, neglect of, 110
   preaching of, 109, 110
   theology of, 107
Pemberton, Ebenezer, Sr., xii, 65, 77, 107, 150
   Cotton Mather and, 49
perseverance, 91
Peterson, Mark A., 21, 40, 64, 65, 66, 71, 72, 73, 75, 77, 127, 146
Pettit, Norman, 50
Pietists, Pietism, x, 1, 8, 20, 23–24, 72, 125
Plymouth, Massachusetts, 21, 126
Pope, Robert G., 64
Portsmouth, New Hampshire, 84
preaching, xi, xv, 2, 5, 8, 9, 17, 30, 34, 35, 37, 38, 39, 40, 47, 48, 52, 53, 57, 59, 60, 67, 71, 73, 79, 83, 84, 92, 94, 96, 105, 107, 109, 110, 112, 114, 116, 117, 121, 125, 126, 128, 131, 135, 136, 146, 148, 149, 150
   preparation for, 5, 6, 8, 34, 39, 53, 57, 96, 109, 115, 121, 136, 150
preparation for conversion, 3, 31–32, 50, 93, 96, 131–32, 133
Presbyterians, Presbyterianism, 4, 42, 44, 106, 107, 127, 148
primitivism, 151
Prince, Deborah, 73, 74
Prince, Thomas, 39, 40, 65, 71–75, 77, 79, 89, 108, 139, 140, 151
   Andrew Croswell and, 127, 145
   Charles Chauncy on, 73
   Cotton Mather and, 25, 71–72, 102
   covenant renewal, use of, 77
   evangelism of, 72
   Gilbert Tennent and, 58
   Great Awakening, support for, 74
   Jonathan Edwards and, 72
   Joseph Sewall and, 74–75
   journalism of, 39, 73
   pastoral activism of, 73–74, 92
   pastoral visitation, writings on, 73
   preaching of, 73
   religious societies, participation in, 18, 71, 102
   religious societies, use of, 74
   theology of, 72
   William Waldron and, 104
providence, 69, 86, 92, 93, 120
public lectures, 6, 40, 54, 121
pulpit exchange, 121, 136
Puritans, Puritanism, xi, xii, xv, xvi, 1, 3, 4, 5, 7, 8, 10, 12, 20, 22, 23, 24, 42, 45, 50, 64, 65, 80, 93, 130, 131, 134, 146, 147
Quakers, 13, 138
rationalism, xv, 86, 116, 117, 118, 151
reforming societies, 19, 20
Reforming Synod, 63
regeneration, 30, 31, 49, 50, 52, 59, 81, 101, 104, 113, 119, 120
religious societies, xv, 14, 17, 18, 19, 20, 21–22, 23, 38, 40, 41, 66–67, 85–86, 92, 102, 119, 148
   for pastors, 18
   for students, 17, 66, 71, 102
   for young people, 18, 40–41, 67, 74, 85, 92, 101
   Great Awakening and, 22, 40–41, 101
   heterodoxy and, 21, 22
   in early New England, 21–22, 40
Remer, Rosalind, 28, 52, 88, 124
repentance, 69, 73, 99, 112, 113, 129
revivals, xi, xii, 27, 28, 41, 54, 61, 63, 69, 73, 138, 147, 152

Robbins, Chandler, 56, 57, 58, 59, 60, 61, 94, 103, 125
Roeber, Anthony Gregg, 79, 82, 86, 88
Rogers, Daniel, 43
Rowland, Daniel, 148
ruling (lay) elders, 97
sacraments, 4, 14, 21, 45, 79, 135
Salem, Massachusetts, xi, 113
Salter, Richard, 96
sanctification, 12, 81, 92, 113, 116, 119, 120, 130, 131, 133
Savelle, Max, 29
Schmidt, Leigh Eric, 126, 127, 134, 136, 148
Schmotter, James W., 5, 6, 33, 146, 149
Scott, Donald, 5
Seacoast Revival, 54
Second ("Old North") Congregational Church, Boston, 3, 15, 18, 19, 24, 34, 45, 46, 52, 56–63, 85, 90, 91, 99, 112, 124, 125, 146, 147, 150, 152
   pastorate of Joshua Gee, 56–60
   pastorate of Samuel Checkley, Jr., 60–61
   pastorate of Samuel Mather, 58, 59
   records of, 16, 61–63
Second Baptist Church, Boston, 45
Seeman, Erik R., 6, 13, 19, 40, 41, 43, 53, 54, 77, 138
Selement, George, 7, 8, 42
Seventh ("New Brick") Congregational Church, Boston, 9, 34, 35, 90, 94, 102–11, 122, 147, 150
   pastorate of Ebenezer Pemberton, Jr., 106–11
   pastorate of Ellis Gray, 105–6
   pastorate of William Waldron, 102–4
   pastorate of William Welsteed, 104–5
   records of, 110
Sewall, Joseph, xii, 65–71, 71, 72, 73, 74, 77, 79, 89, 108, 140, 151
   Andrew Croswell and, 127, 145
   Cotton Mather and, 66, 102
   covenant renewal, use of, 77
   evangelism of, 68, 70–71
   Great Awakening, support for, 69–70
   on family devotions, 67
   on pastoral activism, 39
   on preparation for conversion, 32
   on revival, 69
   pastoral activism of, 71, 89, 92, 146
   preaching of, 68
   religious societies, participation in, 66–67, 71, 102
   religious societies, writings on, 66, 67
   theology of, 67–70
   Thomas Prince and, 74–75
   William Waldron and, 104
Sewall, Samuel, 66
Shepard, Thomas, 21
Shipton, Clifford K., 1, 47, 50, 51, 56, 57, 58, 59, 60, 61, 65, 66, 68, 70, 71, 72, 73, 74, 79, 86, 87, 91, 94, 95, 99, 102, 103, 104, 105, 106, 107, 110, 112, 113, 115, 116, 118, 119, 120, 121, 122, 124, 125, 126, 127, 136, 137
Shryock, Richard H., 2
Sibbes, Richard, 130
Sibley, John Langdon, 65
Silverman, Kenneth, 2, 3, 6, 8, 45, 72, 91, 94
Sixth ("New South") Congregational Church, Boston, 60, 75, 90, 97, 99–102, 147, 150, 152
   pastorate of Samuel Checkley, Sr., 99–101
   records of, 101–2
smallpox, 2, 24, 141, 144
   inoculation, 24, 143
Smith, Mark M., 153
social hierarchy, 5
soteriology, xv, 30, 32, 35, 77, 80, 83, 99, 104, 112, 147
Spellman, Peter W., 27
Spener, Philip Jakob, 20
Sperry, Willard L., 29
Sprague, William B., 47, 51, 56, 66, 68, 71, 74, 79, 86, 94, 95, 96, 97, 102, 103, 106, 112, 118, 124, 125
Stein, Stephen J., 41
Stiles, Ezra, 58

Index

Stoddard, Solomon, 24, 81
Stoeffler, F. Ernest, 23
Stone, Barton, 151
Stout, Harry S., 5, 8, 24, 26, 28, 30, 42, 43, 66, 80, 82, 107, 149
Sutton, Massachusetts, 41
Sweet, William Warren, 29
Tager, Jack, 143
Tennent, Gilbert, xv, 44, 48, 52, 58, 81, 147
Tenth ("Bennet Street") Congregational Church, Boston, 45, 59, 90, 124–25, 147, 150
   pastorate of Samuel Mather, 124–25
   records of, 125
Testimony and Advice of a Number of Laymen Respecting Religion, and the Teachers of It, Address'd to the Pastors of New-England, The, 36
Testimony and Advice of an Assembly of Pastors of Churches in New-England, The, 37, 58, 82, 104
Testimony of the Pastors of the Churches in the Province of the Massachusetts-Bay in New-England, The, 35, 36, 58
Thacher, Peter, 38, 39, 91, 94–95, 102
   evangelism of, 95
   ill health of, 95
   pastoral ministry of, 95
   preaching of, 94–95
   Samuel Willard and, 94
   theology of, 94
   William Cooper on, 94–95, 95
Third ("Old South") Congregational Church, Boston, 146
Third ("Old South") Congregational Church, Boston, 6, 18, 32, 40, 45, 63–78, 85, 89, 90, 106, 127, 147, 150, 151, 152
   pastorate of Ebenezer Pemberton, Sr., 65
   pastorate of Joseph Sewall, 65–71, 74–75
   pastorate of Thomas Prince, 71–75
   records of, 75–78
Toulouse, Teresa, 80

Tracy, Joseph, 27, 29, 40, 74, 82, 84, 93, 113, 125, 126, 127, 138, 147
Tracy, Patricia J., 2, 149
tribalism, 7, 8, 64
Trinitarians, Trinitarianism, 151, 152
Trinity, 35, 101, 121
Trinity Church, Boston, 118
Trinterud, Leonard J., 106
tuberculosis, 57
Turell, Ebenezer, 79, 81, 127
Unitarians, Unitarianism, xv, 29, 121, 147, 151
universal redemption, 124, 136
Universalists, 125, 136
Valeri, Mark, 127
Van de Wetering, John E., 19, 23, 144, 147
Van de Wetering, Maxine, 24
Van Dyken, Seymour, 65
Waldron, William, 9, 10, 102–4, 104, 105, 110, 122
   Cotton Mather and, 102–3
   Cotton Mather on, 102, 103
   early death of, 103
   pallbearers of, 104
   pastoral activism of, 103
   pastoral visitation, practice of, 103
   religious societies, participation in, 102
   theology of, 103
   William Cooper and, 103
   William Cooper on, 102, 103
Walker, Williston, 4, 52, 53, 63, 64
Walsh, James, 28, 77
Ward, W. R., xii, 20, 28
Warden, G. B., 141, 143
Ware, Henry, 58, 59
Webb, John, 91–94, 94, 95, 97, 99
   Andrew Eliot on, 93–94, 97
   Cotton Mather and, 25, 91
   Gilbert Tennent and, 58
   Great Awakening, support for, 92–93, 93–94
   ill health of, 94, 97
   on preparation for conversion, 93
   on revival, 92
   pastoral priorities of, 92

pastoral visitation, practice of, 93
political thought of, 91
theology of, 91
Weis, Frederick Lewis, 47, 56, 58, 60, 65, 79, 91, 99, 102, 112, 116, 124, 125
Wells, David F., 147
Wells, Robert V., 140
Welsteed, William, 35, 102, 104–5, 105, 107, 112
  clericalism of, 104–5
  Cotton Mather on, 105
  Great Awakening, neutrality toward, 104
  on revival, 104
  pastoral visitation, practice of, 104–5
Wendell, Barrett, 1, 2
Wesley, Samuel, 22
Westerkamp, Marilyn J., 21, 42, 107
Westminster Shorter Catechism, 12
Weymouth, Massachusetts, 94, 95
Wheelock, Eleazar, 74, 82, 113
White, Eugene E., 27, 51
Whitehill, Walter Muir, 47, 56, 64, 79, 91, 99, 102, 112, 124
Whitefield, George, x, xi, xv, 13, 29, 30, 32, 37, 44, 50, 58, 70, 74, 82, 93, 101, 104, 107, 108, 113, 121, 126, 127, 136, 137, 138, 146, 147, 148

Andrew Eliot on, 95
Thomas Foxcroft on, 50
Wilkie, Richard W., 143
Willard, Samuel, 6, 17, 18, 65
  covenant renewal, use of, 77
  pastoral priorities of, 6
  Peter Thacher and, 94
Williams, William, 7
Willingham, William F., 144
Wilson, John, 4, 20, 64
Wilson, Robert J., III, 119, 121, 122
Winship, Michael P., 5, 6, 22, 42
Winslow, Ola Elizabeth, 2, 5, 24, 26, 64, 68, 72, 73, 75, 79, 90, 141, 149
Wisner, Benjamin B., 64, 68, 70, 73, 74, 75
witchcraft, xi, 113
Woodbridge, John D., 27, 147
Worthley, Harold Field, 46, 97
Wrentham, Massachusetts, 41
Wright, Conrad, 26, 29, 35, 147, 151
Wright, David, 21
Yale College, 108
Youngs, J. William T., Jr., 5, 7, 8, 18, 24, 39, 53, 54, 66, 79, 97, 148, 150
Ziff, Larzer, 27
Zinzendorf, Nikolaus Ludwig von, Count, 17
Zuck, Lowell H., 23, 24

www.ingramcontent.com/pod-product-compliance
Lightning Source LLC
Chambersburg PA
CBHW062037220426
43662CB00010B/1534

A PEOPLE SO FAVORED OF GOD

§

Boston's
Congregational Churches
and Their Pastors,
1710–1760

George W. Harper

Forewords by
Richard F. Lovelace
and
Mark A. Noll

Second Edition

WIPF & STOCK · Eugene, Oregon

Wipf and Stock Publishers
199 W 8th Ave, Suite 3
Eugene, OR 97401

A People So Favored of God
Boston's Congregational Churches and Their Pastors, 1710-1760, Second Edition
By George W. Harper
Copyright © 2007 by George W. Harper
ISBN 13: 978-1-55635-729-9
ISBN 10: 1-55635-729-X
Publication date 11/28/2007
Previously published by University Press of America, 2004

First Edition Copyright © 2004 by University Press of America.